A TIME FOR EVERY PURPOSE

Life Stories of Foster Grandparents

Edith Sarah Stein

Cover Design: Bob Josen
Photography: Inge Reethof
Book Design: Cindy Parker

First published in 1994 by:
Knowledge, Ideas & Trends, Inc.
1131 Tolland Turnpike, Suite 175
Manchester, CT 06040

Library of Congress Cataloguing-in-Publication Data
A time for every purpose: life stories of foster grandpar
ents / by Edith Sarah Stein; photography Inge Reethof.
Includes bibliographical references.

CIP: 93-32167
ISBN 1-879198-11-8:
1. Foster grandparents - Massachusetts - Boston -
Biography
HV885. B7S74 1994
362.7'33'092 - dc20
{B}

10 9 8 7 6 5 4 3 2 1

First Edition
Printed in the United States of America

Table of Contents

Acknowledgements

Thirty life stories told by thirty individuals whose self-esteem and humility permitted them to invite me into their homes where together we explored the legends of their years. They are indeed the co-authors of this book. Without their trust and their ability to recall and recount the saga and sound of their lives, there would be no book. Any deficiency in the interviews is my responsibility alone.

Inge Reethof, the photographer, worked side-by-side with me, honoring each individual as she fulfilled her desire to reflect all that was possible. Her communication with the foster grandparents operated on many levels as she clicked her camera with inspiration and sensitivity.

Julio Pabon guided my efforts in finding translators and transcribers in the Hispanic community.

Monica Maxwell Mendozo spent long hours doing on-the-spot translations during the interviews with the grandparents of Hispanic descent.

Fiona O'Connor devoted many hours to transcribing the interviews of the Hispanic grandparents. She helped me understand the cultural backgrounds of those who came from the Caribbean Islands and included comments for my consideration in her notes to me.

Anita Wong of the Senior South Cove helped augment the interview with Kam Kew Lee by translating my questions and supplementing the responses even when spoken in English. She reviewed and edited the final transcription.

I am deeply indebted to my friends Ruth Jacobs, Susan Kooperstein, Shura Saul, and, particularly, Jan Solet for giving me the benefit of their own writing experience. Their support and editorial expertise helped me through difficulties I had never anticipated.

Many former colleagues and friends offered their insights on the significance of this book for their co-workers, patients, clients and students. Among that group were Anna Bissonette of The Home Medical Service of Boston University Medical School; Larry Brown, Center on Hunger, Poverty and Nutrition Policy, Tufts University; Tom Cottle, Psychologist; Elsie Frank, President, Massachusetts Association of Older Americans; Alice Freeman, Executive Member, Women's Service Club; Virginia Robinson, Elder Specialist, ABCD; Joseph Perkins, Corporate Retirement Manager at Polaroid; and Barbara Schram, Professor of Sociology, Northeastern University.

Many other women and men in the Aging Network and in the greater Boston colleges and universities with whom I have had long-lasting associations inspired me to undertake this writing. In our years together, we had initiated communication via workshops, theatre, creative writing and dance that challenged existing notions of growing older and expressed the spirit of young and old together. When I became director of the FGP, I discovered a most beautiful example of that spirit.

To Robert Coard, Executive Director of ABCD, valued friend, I extend a special thank-you for encouraging me to take many risks. It was never a frivolous offer for he stood by me always, giving dauntless help and sustenance. For his words written in the Preface to this book, I am forever grateful.

For financial assistance and encouragement to persevere, I thank those friends who contributed funds anonymously because they believed in this book. To ABCD, Families U.S.A. Foundation (formerly The Villers Foundation) and The Polaroid Foundation, I express my very special thanks for their generosity during the writing of this book.

To the circle of women in my women's group and to my family of daughters and sons, grandsons and granddaughters and to my sister I say you are all my well-spring of inspiration. Without you, my dreams would be unfulfilled and my work impaired. I wish particularly to thank my partner of almost thirty years, Lou, who sustained my determination to see this book through by his steadfast day-to-day belief in me and his patience with my demands for his editorial assessments. He enhances an already rich circle of support and love.

The understanding and sensitivity offered me by Rita McCullough, editor and friend, could only come from a rare person. Her letters to me touched exactly on the little bundle of anxiety I harbored within, relieving me of my own harsh judgments, and establishing a rapport that writers wish for but rarely experience.

Growing Old

And surely it is too often forgotten that the old can give as well as take.

Many of our arrangements cut the ancient lifeline between the old and the very young. There can be a rewarding relationship between the sevens and the seventy-fives. They are both closer to the world of mythology and magic than all the busier people between those ages.. After seven we start disinheriting ourselves, and after seventy, with any luck, we begin to unload a lot of the damned rubbish that has been weighing us down for fifty-odd years.

J.B. Priestley
New Statesman, July 1966

The system is carryin' everything so fast the kids, everybody, just got caught up in this mood. Look like if they could get their minds settled down to earth, their mind is way up there floatin', they not down to the nitty-gritty. Sometimes I just wish I could take the world and say, just STOP. Settle down for a while. Settle down enough to think! I tell my grandkids education ain't gonna be the thing; it's good and I'm glad to see you have it, but get down to common sense, motherwit! Motherwit, you get down and know what's really happenin'.

Susan Calloway
Foster Grandparent,
Jamaica Plain, Boston
NICE Day Care Center

Preface

(Written with pleasure for a colleague I have always admired.)

Creativity — that spark of the imagination that knows no boundaries — that pushing against the edge of what's possible — that exhilaration when an idea takes tangible form — is not the sole province of painters, sculptors, or poets. We see the creative process in many realms . . . and certainly in the best of human service programs. Edith Sarah Stein, Director of ABCD's Foster Grandparent Program (FGP) for 12 years, turned program management into an art. Under her orchestration the Program expanded beyond its prescribed form and offered new vistas for both grandparents and staff to explore. A model for what old and young could accomplish came alive as the foster grandparents themselves gained a reputation as "movers and shakers."

The type of concern that inspired the initiation of the FGP flourished in the 1960's when John Kennedy conceived the War on Poverty. Public officials combined their talents with the nation's poor to fashion programs that would end hunger and need and offer all Americans the opportunity to live with dignity.

They put their knowledge and faith in human involvement together in new and exciting ways. That was the time when ABCD and hundreds of other antipoverty, human service agencies were born, and many soon became the home for the FGP. It was an enticing program for the resources and the needs meshed so perfectly. Not only did those of low-income and over 60 receive a minimum salary for a twenty-hour week, but the children were endowed with a grandma or grandpa. They were nurturing each other, so to speak. In antipoverty circles, it became "a winner."

In local offices the director and staff drew contracts with the sites and interviewed applicants for placement. It is here that Edith showed her singular talent. When the grandparents were moved from the state schools and hospitals where they had first been placed, they were given every opportunity to relocate in their own neighborhoods and chose the type of site they wanted. Did they wish to be at a day care center, or a school, or a hospital? They were encouraged to participate in the full process.

Edith used to say — "Sure it takes longer, but it also lasts longer when you offer some power to those who are directly involved." She maintained that process so that future grandparents, those newly recruited, could examine all the choices and participate in site selections. "Grandparents and staff learn from each other," she would say, "but it is the grandparents who are in the front lines, directly with the children, and we, on staff, must listen and evaluate carefully."

As the Program grew, Edith initiated a new recruitment goal. She was determined to invite minority women and men into the fold. Flyers were prepared for church distribution, for community centers and for elder housing projects. Soon the myth that minority grandparents were always at home with their own was exploded. Slowly, the Irish and Jewish grandparents who had been the majority in the Program were sitting alongside Black and Hispanic women and men at the FGP monthly meetings. When the community sites were opened, it was possible for Spanish-speaking grandparents to select like children, and African-American grandparents could choose day care centers, schools and hospitals with children of varied backgrounds from our city.

Edith Sarah Stein came to us from ABCD's Allston-Brighton neighborhood center where, as Elder Specialist, she had organized a program in the local high school called "History Through Life Experience." Elders carefully surveyed their own lives and selected an event which illuminated a particular piece of both personal and social history. The group studied their presentations together and developed a new appreciation of what they had lived through. When they shared all this with the students, there was immediate response. The Boston School Committee applauded this intergenerational model and initiated an expansion of "School Volunteers for Boston" with similar programs for older volunteers.

An intuitive practitioner of the art of social change, Edith created an environment within the Program that attracted a great deal of public notice. Not only did the 60-70-80-year-olds offer their personal gems to the children, teachers, and nurses at their sites but they also created theatre pieces and a chorus featuring the music of many cultures. Edith offered a tradition of community activism, a fierce commitment to older people and all the oppressed and a personal ethos that inspired everyone to "be all that you can be." That combination of talents became a true inspiration at ABCD.

This book sheds light on the magical link between generations which helps us see what old people can do for our children in this difficult time. The grandparents have become invaluable to our children in public schools, day care centers, everywhere they have chosen to be with them. We dare not overlook that message.

Edith's sensitively edited interviews provide us with an intimate chronicle of the lives of people who, after day-to-day confrontation with life's challenges, joined together to pioneer day-to-day attention for all our children.

Robert M. Coard
Executive Director
Action for Boston Community Development

Introduction

The Foster Grandparent Program (FGP) was initiated back in 1965 under the Federal Economic Opportunity Act so that older people could earn a minimum wage and work part-time with children.

The notion of having old people work with children was almost revolutionary. The least controversial starting place appeared to be the state schools and hospitals where a FGP staff person could be on hand to support and guide the grandparents through each four-hour day. The children at these institutions were severely handicapped and needed sensitive one-to-one attention that the professional staff could not provide.

The grandparents responded with both caution and resolve. They took their individual children out for walks (usually pushing a carriage or wheelchair), fed them their noontime meals, talked with them, and, in some cases, even taught them to speak a few words. Those who had more difficulty adjusting to the tragedies they encountered were surprised to find that the tiniest evidence of progress in their child's response brought forth a sense of fulfillment.

The small remuneration, which later became a non-taxable stipend of $44 per week, motivated the grandparents also. However, the shared experience of poverty had little to do with income but rather with the ability to live within each day's hours, believing all the while in a better time. That display of hope bonded the two seemingly disparate groups. In the years to come, when the grandparents were ensconced in community settings, that bonding would emerge as "the magic effect" — the communication between young and old.

As these day-to-day relationships were developing in schools largely secluded from public notice, people of rare vision in Washington conceived The Older American Volunteer Programs under the aegis of ACTION in 1971. That agency which became the home of the FGP also initiated two other programs for elders plus the more well-known Peace Corp for those of all ages. Within a short time, the state schools and hospitals began to move those boys and girls under twenty-one to smaller facilities and group homes. The grandparents were expected to turn to children with totally different needs in community day care centers and public schools. The number of children remaining at the state schools would be minimal.

"The grandparents bring their life experiences to the children; the same kind of loving care and playfulness they shared with their own. They bring the patience and wisdom of years also," I told the teachers and principals at the community sites. "There is a natural affinity between old and young for, at both ends of the spectrum, the imperatives of the years between are gone," I added, "and that makes for the natural connection." And the foster grandparents moved on — even into hospitals with pediatric patients.

It was a time for reassessment. In the workplace, both men and women were being dismissed from their jobs simply because they had turned sixty-five, perpetuating the notion that the old folks were relatively useless. The big push against mandatory retirement and age discrimination had not yet begun.

It was no surprise that some of the grandparents were reluctant to leave the protected environment of the state settings. They were unaware of their own abilities and they feared rejection, even in their own communities. Would they be welcomed into intimate day care centers and busy public schools? How would they know what to do with children who were experiencing emotional distress? Could they help children who were "slow learners?" The staff of FGP helped with many workshops led by child care specialists and psychologists. The teachers and administrators of the sites helped with concrete examples. Most of all, the grandparents learned as they had during their lives; they listened, observed and added their natural inclinations.

When work on this book began, there were approximately 19,000 foster grandparents in our country. Some had chosen to remain within the state institutions, but the majority were in neighborhood settings including battered women's shelters and youth detention centers. The latter were facilities for adolescents from thirteen to eighteen, committed by the courts to the Department of Youth Services where they were evaluated for future placement. Such challenging assignments for foster grandparents indicated how innovative the program had become, how much the grandparents had learned and how much more they were willing and ready to do.

It was not long after I became director of the FGP Program at Action for Boston Community Development (ABCD) in Boston that I realized that these foster grandparents I had come to know were truly remarkable. They imparted a new dimension to day-to-day communications wherever they went. It wasn't just what they were doing with the children, startling in itself; it was also the effect they were having on the total environment. They bestowed love and trust in their work with the kids; they supported over-worked teachers as they helped the youngsters read and write; they were mothers and fathers to young aides and nurses; they were counselors to battered mothers and teen-age children; they were healers for those in hospital. It was as though a void had been filled, a void which grandma or grandpa might have filled some years ago.

Who were these women and men who had chosen to be pioneers and become foster grandparents? Where had their gifts of sensitivity and commitment originated? How had they managed to survive poverty and loss and enormous cultural changes and continue on? And why in their later years had they chosen to work with children? Many had searched for months, and sometimes years, to find what they wanted and could scarcely believe it when they could once again take a child into their lives.

When I left my post in 1987, I interviewed thirty of the Boston foster grandparents in their homes accompanied by Inge Reethof who photographed each person as we spoke. The backgrounds of the group selected included African-American, Chinese, English,

Hispanic, Irish, Italian, Jewish, Latvian, Portuguese and Scottish. They were sixty-four to ninety years old. Though some editing was necessary, all the words are theirs except those spoken in Chinese and Spanish where interpreters and translators inevitably lost some of the color of the original language.

The life stories highlight the vast historical and cultural differences in the group. The Hispanic men and women reveal the effects of corrupt political systems, fast-changing governments and the grinding poverty of the masses in the Dominican Republic, Barbados, Puerto Rico and Haiti.

The men adapted differently from the women who for the most part worked close to home and children. When they found their way north, either from the Caribbean or southern U.S., they determined to help their children achieve lives with more significant choices. Pearl Anty came north from South Carolina. She tells of her childhood picking cotton and learning from her mother how to make jam from the apples given by her "bossman." She says, "I don't know, I just enjoyed." She and her mother raised her two daughters together within that immediate and valued experience of every effort. And that same sensation accompanies Pearl Anty to the day care center now, fifty years later. "Sometimes the teacher would say, 'No, gramma is not going to help you, you have to learn to do for yourself.' And so I keep watchin' and finally I will help 'im. I don't know there's somethin' about it, I can't help it."

Today it is difficult to believe that public schools and day care centers were reluctant to accept foster grandparents. Within five years there were not enough foster grandparents to meet the community requests. Some of this change in attitude is due to the pioneering work done by the grandparents themselves and to the growth of a staunch Aging Network throughout the country.

But, in the late eighties in the U.S., the attitude toward old people was changing for the very best reason: more and more people were living longer. They were signalling the time for greater understanding of the changing life cycle. If at age fifty I know that I may live to ninety, perhaps I will go to school and become a lawyer or a musician or choose to emulate Grandma Moses. Or perhaps at sixty, I will want to become a foster grandparent.

Those who initiated the FGP could not anticipate all that was to evolve. They had no idea what these people who were not only money-poor but old were capable of doing. They did not know that "old people" could be in a time of exploration and self-expression nor had they experienced the magic connection that was to emerge between the two generations.

I did not interview any of the teachers, nurses or day care personnel. I felt it best to allow the life stories to stand alone. However, one day a teacher insisted on telling me how she felt about the foster grandparent who had been with her for ten years. Kam Kew Lee works at a school with many Chinese and Vietnamese children. When Inge Reethof and I arrived to take photos of her with the children, her teacher, Janet Shih told me, "She is so wonderful. It's so important to have a grandmother in the classroom. She's here all the time from 7:45 to 2:00. All the school day she works with the children. Whenever we need her, she comes with happiness, so willing to help. You don't have to tell her what to do, she sees it herself and does such a fine job. We have to learn from her. She never claims any credit. Many old people in this country are being wasted. It's so important to have older people with the children. They themselves don't realize how important they are. They are needed in our lives. They are not old-fashioned and unimportant. No. They are the most important to give us the sense of where we come from and so we know where we are going. Kam Kew Lee does all that."

Writing in the 1989 fall issue of Gray Panther Network, Marian Wright Edelman, Executive Director of the Children's Defense Fund tells us, "All groups of children are poorer today than they were at the beginning of the decade . . . By the year 2000, seven of ten pre-school children will have working mothers. The twenty-five million children who are living apart from their families in foster care, group homes, residential treatment centers and other such institutions will increase if we don't begin to make our political leaders hear that these very young children and teenagers with severe mental and emotional problems need help." We also know that twenty-three to thirty million Americans are functionally illiterate, and every year 750,000 high school students drop out.

In 1990, the Massachusetts Office for Children issued a report called "Massachusetts Childwatch '90." Here are some of the facts relating to Boston's estimated 136,000 children:

- One in four lives below the poverty level.
- One-fifth of white children, one-third of Black children and three-fourths of Hispanic children are poor.
- One in twenty were reported abused or neglected in 1989.
- One of every twenty teenagers will give birth annually.
- One out of three Boston school children who enter ninth grade will drop out before graduation.
- Youth newly placed in detention by the court increased forty-one percent from 1988 to 1990.

The picture in other large urban centers is very similar.

Without intention, foster grandparents have shown us what could evolve on a far larger scale. In these life stories, we discover the vigor of undaunted spirit, seasoned and mellowed by the years, that had never been realized before. Money-poor and soul-rich, they nurtured our children. And they continue and continue.

At the Day Care Centers

In the late eighties, there were twenty pre-school sites in the Boston neighborhoods where seventy-five foster grandparents worked and played with the children. Of the fourteen interviewed for this book, ten were at ten different centers, and four Spanish-speaking grandparents became "language specialists" for the children at three neighborhood sites. With the grandparents beside them, the Hispanic children blossomed in the easygoing communication even as they began to assimilate the second language they would come to speak. Their foster grandparents sanction a continuing pride in the language of their families.

Day care centers play an indispensable community role beyond the care of pre-school children. They are part of larger community schools addressing many community needs from elementary and pre-school classes to varied adult activities. In Children's Centers where youngsters live as well as learn, they meet the needs of children-in-crisis in the pre-school settings. The community function varies, but the teacher's role with the children and their parents is the most significant. Attention to the individual adjustment of each child, to mental and physical health education, and concern with after school problems fill each day's agenda. If funds are available, professional counselors augment the day care staff. The FGP contracts only with non-profit day care centers that receive public funds, usually from an Office for Children on the State level, and federal funds earmarked for preschool education. Many centers are ingenious in raising funds for special needs and essential equipment. Fees are assessed according to a sliding scale.

In large cities, pre-school centers welcome both the children and foster grandparents from the immediate neighborhood. In rural areas, the FGP must pay for the transportation services. In some cases, an applicant will come to the FGP office armed with the name of a center "right near my home where I would love to be." Some urban foster grandparents elect to take two and sometimes three city buses to get to a favored site.

"The magic connection" flows freely in pre-school settings. Since many grandparents come from far-away places, the sense of where they were in the scheme of things is not too different from what the children experience. Foster grandparents also encountered big-city life for the first time and quickly identified with the fear of being in a strange place.

Foster grandparents have a natural sensitivity to the culture they share with their day care children and their families. They are attuned to the traumas of change. They understand that it is more than a language difference; it is also the loss of immediacy, community, accompanied by the sudden expectation of staunch individuality. A social worker tries to substitute for family, friends, and neighbors. Foster grandparents become interpreters of whole systems.

Chapter 1
At the Day Care Centers

Pearl Anty

Pearl Anty

You know, now I work with those children, and I really enjoy them. I love 'em and I works with 'em and I enjoy it. The doctor keeps sayin', that's what keeps me young, and I believes that. I believes that's what I'm here for 'cause I like to help people, I like to do for people. Some people just sees 'em, but I loves 'em.

I believe children would have a chance if we start talkin' to them when they young. Bring them up, like in church and have a counsellor in church and things like that. But, you living all kinds of life and tryin' to bring up children, it ain't gonna work. It won't work.

I was born in 1923, in McCormick, South Carolina. My daddy used to work at a saw mill so we kids used to go to the saw mill and bring little planks and things to burn. I was about four when we did that. After my daddy passed, my grandfather came from Georgia and got us and carried us all to the country, my mother and us five kids. I was six then, but I was not the oldest. I had two older than me, just a year's difference from my sister's age and my oldest brother. And then my youngest brother almost four years after me and then another child. My father had heart trouble.

My grandfather came and just moved the furniture and everything — carried us to a farm about twenty miles on the other side of Anderson. He was my mother's father, and she said ever since she was born, that's all we did, work on a farm. Yeh, my mother, she raised all five of us, and she never married again. And she never went to jail to pick nobody up 'cause nobody go to jail 'cause they were scared of police. You know how children gets in trouble? Well, we, nobody get in trouble.

Well, we were out in the country most of our life, pickin' cotton an' pullin' cotton and pullin' corn an' cuttin' sweet cane. Everything we ate, we had on the farm. My grandmother would can,

4

and we would pick at the apple orchard and get peaches and help peel 'em. We all had tasks, and we all had to get water and not at a well; we had to go to a spring and get water. It wasn't that far, and we enjoyed it. My grandfather wanted every bucket filled up. We would help work the vegetable garden, and we all would have a little patch of our own, and we would raise things in our garden: onions, tomatoes, and a lot of cabbage.

My mother would be inside making our clothes, and we would be outside. Every Sunday she'd have us in church and sometimes we'd go in the wagon. There was somethin' about it - I just enjoyed. My grandfather would take in the wheat and take it to a mill, have it ground, and we would have flour. And we had cows and young calves, and we had plenty to eat.

We'd milk the cows. My brothers, they used to milk, and I used to churn and get my grandmother to let me make the bread. She let me do it, and I would clean my finger nails and wash my hands good and then I sifted the flour, and I sifted the meal. My grandmother said, "Put in the salt, baking powder, and soda," and then she said, "Now you goin' to do it yourself." I was about nine, and I said, "You better put it in 'cause I may put in too much." "It doesn't matter," she said, "They'll eat it anyway." She didn't come in the house, my grandmum. She stayed in the garden, and I cooked. Yeh, she showed me how to make jelly, she showed me how to make canned fruit and different things that we going to eat. We canned up a whole lot of food for the winter.

Well, we went to school, but not too much because it was too far. You had to walk ten miles to school, and sometimes it would be so cold, grandpa says, "too cold for ya all to get out there," and so we didn't go to school that much. We went to school in church, and they would close it down 'cause it was so cold until the ice was starin' up out the ground. And we didn't have clothes like chillun here, and we had snow there like we have it here.

We clean out the springs in October for the summer 'cause we had to use that soil for fertilizer. My uncle put fertilizer in the ground, and then they put the seed, the cotton seed, and we had to handle the cotton seed. My grandfather was pretty hep. "There's a big ole snake here," he said, just to tease me. He knows the snake had gone. I said, "I ain't drinking that water out of that spring." He would sit down and explain it to me, "Pearl," he said, "the snake ain't nobody's business, and a spring do not carry germs 'cause the water runs all the time."

I learned a lot about a farm, and we stayed until grandpa passed. I was ten then. After they gathered a crop, we went to Anderson. I went to school there up to the third grade. We didn't have a farm there. My mother did washing and cooking for folks, but she didn't live with them. We stayed in Anderson till I was thirteen.

Then we moved to Ware Shores where I joined the church, and I was singing in the choir. I used to get out in the fields and sing. I learned psalms in church. I stopped school in the third grade because my mother said I could make more to help her 'cause my oldest brother was just picking up odds and ends, cleaning up yards and cutting grass and things like that. I started doing housework then. When people come 'round wanting someone to pick cotton, well, mother would quit her job, and I would quit my job, and we would go and pick cotton until November. We came home every night — they'd drive us home. If the man like the way we picked cotton, he would give us apples, and my mother would make jelly. I would stay up late preparing the apples, and I would say, "Oh, boy, I know I can't get up in the morning." But I did. I made it. We would get up, get the apples, didn't want them to ruin on us, and make the jelly. That's how it was.

Mama was making about $6 a week, and I was making about $5, but we made it. And I thank the Lord. Yeh, we all pitch in, my older sister and I and my two brothers. They would pay the rent because my older sister, she stayed in school. We sent her to college, and we all pitched in. Even when we got married, we pitched in. I helped my husband to send his sister to college. I didn't care that I wasn't going. I enjoyed what I did. Now both my sisters are dead. My youngest brother is dead. I'm the only girl living and my oldest brother. That's it. Just the two of us. My brother had cancer of the throat, and both my sisters had heart trouble. I get check-ups almost every year, and so far I been fine.

When we moved to Ware Shores, that's where I got married. He run the restaurant for the company, a mill. They made material. Take the cotton and make material out of it. I was working in private homes and carried dinner to the mill to the people I was working for. I would go by the cafe and get me something to drink and then go back to work. My brother worked in the mill, too. He was there until he retired. I don't know what the people did there — the ones I worked for. I ran into nice people to work for. They was white. Some of the people at the mill was black and some white. Well, we know where we stand.

One night, we was coming back from Greenwood, my sister and I. We went to the movies, and we was coming back, and these sailors was white, and they said, "Don't sit in back there, move up here." Now we was happy, and I said, "No." The bus driver said, "Well, he's white so it's O.K." So they all passed the cup around and drank, but you see, I never drank 'cause I just could never drink. I couldn't smoke. I tried it, but I couldn't make nothin' of it. So we all mixed, and we talked until they got full, and then they went on to sleep, and they don't even know when we got off.

Everywhere I went, I really enjoyed people. I didn't visit them at their house or anything like that, but I sit on the porch, and I would talk to them. I enjoy being by myself. Some people say they get lonesome, but I don't 'cause I turns on the radio, and I got three radios, and I listen to ministers coming on. And sometimes I start singing. I don't sing in the choir, but sometimes they puts me on the program, and I sing solo. Yeh, I can sing without music. This psalm is called "Somewhere Around God's Throne"

I went to the place where I used to live
The graves they grown up and covered the door
Someone cross the street and said whom do you see

7

For no one, no one lives there anymore.

I went to the church where I used to go
The preacher was still there and he met me at the door
He said, I know who you are and I know who you are looking for
But they, they don't come here anymore.

They are somewhere around the throne of God,
They are somewhere around the throne of God.
I keep searching, searching, till I shall find them
They are somewhere around God's throne.

Well, I keep singing. I sit around and sing to myself. Yes I do.

The way it were with my husband, he was just nice to talk with,
and he would come down our house on Sunday or either I would
be in church and he would come back home with me. Him and
his sisters, we all used to run together. Then finally he asked me
to marry. I was surprised, yeh, and my mother said no. She tole
me, "No." She said she had heard people say something about
him, and she'd rather for me not. But I still saw him. I got
married, myself and him, no wedding or anything. My mother
tole me to go on get out of her house. She wasn't angry with me
'cause I used to go over and help her do her wash. She took in
washing, and I used to help her. What a lot of people tole me, that
she was afraid to lose me. I used to get all the white shirts and
iron them while she had take in washing. She thought I was going
to let her go, I guess, but I didn't. I still cling to her. We all lived
close by.

I wanted to have five children but I had only two and two
miscarriages. One of them live in the project nearby with her
family, and the other one live out in Randolph. I goes out there
and spends time with her, like on a holiday. I goes out and stay
with her. And I have three step sons, and they clings to me. You
see, my husband, after we separated, he start staying with this
woman, and he had three boys with her and so, after he passed,

the boys tole my daughter, they said, "Sister, let's stick together."
So they all stick together. I spent time with them when I went
back home, and they like me.

When my husband went off, I don't know, but it didn't bother
me. No. Long as I had my mother. I would just close the door and
go over to her house. I would send her money when I start
working. It didn't bother me one bit. I missed the children a lot,
but I couldn't take it no more, his running around like that. Well,
my husband had got to the place, he stay out all night. I tole him
the bible said, "Separate for a season," and so I'm gonna have to
leave ya. I can't put up with this. I tole him, "Listen, you go ahead
on with her and leave me alone and the children gonna be down
at my mother's." So I stayed down to my mother's, and then, on
the 4th of July, I left, and I got me a job and start working in a
private home.

My mother said, "That's the reason I didn't want you to marry
him." I told her, "That's alright. I'm still with you." And I stay
with her 'till she passed. He, my husband, he died. He had sugar,
and him and his brother had been drinking, and, when he came
home to this woman, he told her his stomach was hurting, and
she gave him a shot of insulin and it killed him. He's not
supposed to be drinking. She thought the shot would ease him,
but it killed him. He was young. He was in his fifties then. I don't
recall how long I was with him. It was so long ago, I can't keep up
with it.

I left my children with my mother, and I kept sending her money.
I would wire her the money every end of the week. I didn't come
home that much, trying to do extra work. Sometimes I would help
serving parties and things like that so I'd have more money to
send her. So later, when I start working at the hospital, I was
making more. One day I'd taken sick. I had pain near my kidney,
and I told the nurse that I had to go home. She said, "Pearlie, I'm
not gonna let you go home." "I'll get alright." She said no and
takes me down to the emergency ward and call the doctor. He
start to touch me, and I said, "Don't touch me on my side, my

9

appendix is swollen up." "Get her ready for the operating room," he said.

After he had taken them out, he said, "Pearlie, I didn't want to frighten you but it was fixin' to bust." That was on a Friday, and then Sunday my mother came up, and it was snowing and sleet, and the ground was freezing. I said, "Mama, why you come here in this bad weather?" She said, "I didn't know how bad you were." "The preacher gave me this money," I said, "And I want you to take it, and, soon as I pick up my check, I'll send you more." I got up out the bed that Saturday and walked around.

This friend of mine, she came up to Boston, and I said, if you find a job for me, let me know. But I was saying it for a joke. Then she kept calling me, and so I said, I guess I'm gonna have to go. I worked for some nice people in Brookline, and I like it, and so I called mama and tells her, I staying 'cause I'm making more money. So when Jesse and Betty had finished school, I sent Jesse the money, and then I sent mama and Betty a ticket. And my sister sent for her two children, and we got 'em all up here. My mama always lived with me. She was nice, a Christian lady, and she was kind, and we got along nicely. The kids, they all liked her.

I kept working in private homes, and then I got a job at Massachusetts General Hospital. They called to Anderson to get my references, and they told them that they wanted me back in Anderson. "Well, we got her here in Boston." And she said, "O.K. 'cause she's a good worker, but don't make her angry or she'll walk out." I had worked at Anderson Hospital for four years. They was putting more work on us, and I ask the head man was he gonna pay us any more. He said no. I was serving food in the dietary department, and he wanted us to work like for breakfast in the morning and serve lunch and have about two hours off and come back and serve supper. So, we girls were talking about it, and I said, "O.K. I do the talking, but if any of you back off, I'm gonna beat ya." Yeh, I told them. So we all went to his office that morning after breakfast, and I ask him, we would like to have

10

more money 'cause that's working like double shifts. He said, "I don't see where I can pay it." I said, "I don't see where I can work it, 'cause I quit my husband, and I can quit your job." He said, "Do you all agree with her?" I looked around at them and they all agreed. So we walked out. So I got a job working in private homes. I got a job the same day. They got us all jobs, and I worked in private homes till I came up here to Boston.

I like working in the hospital. I worked in the children's department serving the food, and my younger daughter worked there with me. I worked there for twenty years, and I wasn't late nary a day. And I found out about the foster grandparent program after I left there. My niece talked me a notion of going into the program. She said, "You come down to where I work at," and she carried me to the office, and I signed up and they sent me to Massachusetts General, to the children's floor. But I didn't work there but two weeks and I taken sick. I was operated for gall stones.

That was when I couldn't get back to the program. My sister passed, and six months later my mother passed. Hard, yeh, that what it was. I had to stay home with her. The doctor says to me, "It's a miracle she don't have no bed sores, who wait on her?" I does. "With your bad back?" "I put her over in the bath tub. I pull my shoes off and get in the bath tub and let her put her arms here, and I pick her up and let her stand up, and then I get out and I take her out. That's how I did it." One night, I gave her a bath and put her on a clean gown, an' she said she was going to Eva to thank 'em for everything. Well, Eva was dead. "I'll thank them for you." I just went along with it. She got to the place where for two months she didn't eat a bit — she stopped eating and then she passed.

That's something we all have to do — we all have to do it. The way I figure it, one day it will be done. The only thing, I just wanna be ready. I just keep trying to live right and do things in the right way, try to treat people right because if I treat them bad I may not have a chance to get back to this person and say I'm sorry. That's why, when I'm going along, I tries to do it right the first time.

11

Now I work with those children at the day care center, and I really enjoy them. I love them, and I works with them, and I enjoy it. The doctor keeps saying, that's what keeps me young, and I believes that. I believes that's what I am here for 'cause I like to do for people. Some people just sees them but I loves them. The other day, a boy was up here in the store. He wanted a loaf of bread, but he didn't have enough money so, after I got what I had to I gave him a dollar. He smiled and said thanks, thank you. He just kept thanking me. Well, I don't know, I just love them. I believe children would have a chance if we start talking to them when they young. Bring them up, like in church and have a counsellor in church and things like that. But, you living all kinds of life and trying to bring up children, it ain't gonna work. It won't work.

I work with children who are two, three and four. When they get five, we transfer them to another class. We goes out for a walk, me and the two teachers takes them sightseeing. We walks up to Centre Street, and they say they want pizza and we buy them pizza, and we buy them milk and then take them back. When a new child come in, we want them to come in late 'cause she don't take to ya, she close to her mother, and she don't want her mother to get out of her sight. She stay only one half day, and tomorrow she'll be there all day. I get a chance to be with her. I get some puzzles, and we start playing with puzzles or play dough, and I put out something and say, "How you like this?" And she'll start, and that's how I get to her. We get acquainted.

And there's Manuel. He beckons to me, and the teacher says, "No, grandma is not going to help you." So I keep watching, and finally I will help him. I can't help it. She says that they need to learn it themselves, like put the shoes on and pull the clothes off, but some of them, they don't want to do it and when the teacher says, gramma ain't gonna help, I keep on until finally I just helps them. Sometimes they jealous, they don't want you to hug one. I have to hug all of them.

12

Sometimes we would set down and read books from the library room and they do have bible stories, and we talks to them and tells them how to treat one another. When they hit one another, we say, "Well, you have to talk to them yourself and tell them you're sorry." We teach them like that. And we say, "Your hand is not to go on nobody's body." I believe by we talking to them, they learns. It don't matter where they see me at, in the street, they gonna say, "Hi Grandma." When we goes on trips, I gets all the children in the bus, and I straps them in and then I gets to know those on other floors, and it seems they all loves me. I don't know, it just seems that way. Yeh, and I give them a smile all the time. The doctor told me not to lift them so I sit down on the chair and hold them around like that (gesturing with arms). They wonderful. To me taking care of children, it's a gift. You see, I don't know how anybody else thinks, but to me it is because you give children love, they love you, and they won't forget it.

When I come home, I set around and read. This is my mother's bible. I got a bigger one, and I have a small one that I can carry around with me. I don't know if everything I need to know is in here, but it's a lot, and I enjoy reading it. It does teach you how to be kind to everybody, how to treat people, things like that. Well, you see, I treat people like I wish to be treated. That's the way my mother always told us.

Madeline Butcher

Madeline Butcher

I started in '80, and there it is. A purpose. I always wanted to be a teacher so there it is, all wrapped up into one bundle, a lot of children, teachers! There's the answer right there. And, lots of people say, "Why is it? You raised your children, so why?" That's not it. This is what I always wanted. It's something like when you eat, you're not satisfied you say, I want my dessert! The rewards I get? A lot of kisses and hugs and love.

I always thought of a grandmother as one who sat in a rocking chair with a white apron on holding one or another of all her grandchildren. I was one of ten children, and my aunts and uncles lived very near so there was always a little one around. I was born in Downington, Pennsylvania in 1907, and at the age of six I went to live with one of my aunts and uncles in Germantown. They spoiled me rotten. I received my education in Germantown, completing two years of high school. I saw my parents vacation time, holidays and sometimes weekends. I was the only child with my aunt and uncle so I got all the petting I wanted, and they could afford to give me anything under the sun I needed.

I went to work when I was about twelve, taking care of peoples' children while I was still in school. Later, I got a job full time taking care of children, and I learned how to cook some and do real housework. I became a homemaker. I didn't want to go to school because I already met the man I was to marry. When I got out of school, I stayed in the house I worked at so then I had more freedom. I was sort of held down a little bit so when I got out ... I went to a party on a Sunday afternoon, and he saw me and asked me to marry him. I said, "You must be crazy. I don't know anything about you." Anyway I partied around a good little while, got sick and tired of it. The people I was with were going on vacation so I said to Charlie, "I'll give you my answer when I come back." I had plenty of time to think while I was gone, and I said, "Well, I don't think this is the life I want or need." He kept writing, writing the whole time I was there.

16

Well, all the adults in my life had taught me so much about boys. Boys is poison, I was scared of them to tell you the truth. You know back then. It was "keep your dress tail down if you wanted a man to respect you, so you wouldn't look like a little cherry with a stem stuck in it!" So you were a body by the road. I did want to marry a man, not be fooling around with Tom, Dick, Harry and so time presented itself. But we didn't marry right away. I went back to work, and then he took me to Chester to meet his family.

When we married, I thought the honeymoon was supposed to go on forever and ever and ever. We lived way out, far from where I was used to. Carry my own water, build the fire in the stove, yes, in our own little place. It had been his, and he had everything in there. The first thing he brought home was neck bones. I had never heard tell of neck bones before, collard greens, the same, and corn bread meal. I said, "What do you want me to do with that?" He said, "I want them for my dinner when I come home." I said, "Well, you must be kidding, I'm going back home." He said, "You can either have that ready when I come home or else you can go back home!" And I thought and thought. I was too ashamed to go back home. I knew how to wash the stuff so I washed it and made the fire so I had them done. "Well," he said, "They're not like they're supposed to taste but you did try."

But I did leave and go home once, and I had to get the bus about six o'clock downtown. He followed me, but he left me alone, and I went home. My aunt was surprised to see me so late at night — strange time for a visit. She said, "What's your problem?" I said, "Nothing." I asked her could I stay overnight? "Sure," she said, "you're not going out of here tonight." Then the next morning I told her I had left. She said, " Who told you to marry him?" "Nobody," I said. She said, "Then you going back." My uncle, he's the one who really spoiled me, "Don't make her go back." "Oh yes, she's going back," my aunt said. "Did you have an argument?" "No," I said, and I told her what I had to do there and all, and she said, "You going on back." I stayed with him till he died. All right, I found out I had to do it, I went on an' done it.

17

Well, I had an awful lot of miscarriages, but I had my two boys, twins, with him. They were five years old when their father died. We were only married nine years after going through all of that hassle. He died of lumbar pneumonia. Sick about three days, and he died. It was a good marriage, and he was a good provider.

What happened is that he took me to Chester to his family to learn to cook the way he was used to, and I would go there every Sunday. And, finally, the work in Doylestown got so bad, we moved to Chester and lived with them. There, I really got into pots and pans, but it was beautiful. It was a beautiful nine short years. Beautiful! And I had a hard time there for a while. I don't know, I don't think I'm over it yet really. I went to my doctor, and he said, "You're too young a woman really to be alone with just two children." I said, "I made up my mind I would never remarry." "You're silly. Why not?" I always thought when you married that first time that was it. "This is not your doing," he said. "This was death. Didn't the minister say until death?" "Yes." "So what's your argument?" I didn't really want to marry again, no, because I was still in love with him, Charlie.

I told Mr. Butcher point blank, I said, "Mr. Butcher, listen, I'm gonna tell ya the truth. I will marry you, I will do my wife's part, but there's no love there, there's no love." He had his own home, and all I had to do was walk out of the house my husband had bought and walk into his and sit down. I told my doctor, "But I don't love the man. I only love but one time, I mean deep. This is infatuation when you think you love a person." I was forever throwing it up to Mr. Butcher that he wasn't like Charlie, and I just had to check myself a lot. But he was a very good man, very good to the children. Wonderful. Still, that love was down there in the grave with Charlie.

Now this is what my children approached me with when I told them I was going to marry Mr. Butcher. They was only five years old, and they said, "Daddy was big and strong when they put him in that hole. He's gonna be big and strong enough to get up out of there and what are we gonna do with Mr. Butcher?" "Your daddy will never be back," I said. They still didn't believe it until they got a little older. They didn't like him at first, but after they grew older, they realized that that was where it was at, and they liked him. Their own father never put a hand on them, and Mr. Butcher never did either - it was always up to me. All the discipline.

There is only one thing I would have liked to change in my life. That's for my first husband to have lived longer. He has a brother now, going into his nineties. Why did my husband have to go at forty-six? We were just getting settled, just bought a house, and he had a good job at Sun Ship. Very good. Things were going well. Very well. I would have liked to live those lost years with my first husband.

I had one child with Mr. Butcher. I could have had more, but I didn't want any more. Well, Mr. Butcher was much older than I anyway, but he was a good husband. We were married twenty years. I never wanted to get married again. No. I never wanted to get married to start off with. I wanted to be an old maid. This aunt that raised me, playing music, going to high school, playing for school, for church, I was always into something. Didn't have time to think about boys. I really wanted to do all those things. I wanted to be a school teacher — always wanted to be a teacher, that's why I love the kids so. I could have done anything I wanted to do. It's my fault, I got married, fell in love with the man. See how your mind does, plays tricks on you. He was very nice, nice looking, what I thought I always wanted.

But my life has been good. I have no complaints. I had a couple of very sick spells, but I got around those, you know. All my tests from Harvard Medical Center show everything is fine. I turned eighty in March of this year. I like to cook, but my kids won't let me do it anymore. I do get tired I've noticed lately. That's the only thing. But after getting over there with the children — that bunch of kids. The last bunch I had, I got so attached to those kids sometimes I find myself sitting down crying, I miss them so. A funny thing to say, but of all the kids that I have dealt with. They, this class, they got next to me.

I'm getting older. Getting older and getting senile, that's what my granddaughter says. (laughter) I have always gotten on to the kids but this last bunch, I don't know what it was about those children. They were all so willing to learn, and whatever I told them to do, they would do it. I have a bunch coming in there now. I think it was last week, I tried to teach them the days of the week. I taught from Monday to Saturday. I come right back and ask them the day. "Today is Monday and tomorrow will be Tuesday," and I ask them, "What's tomorrow?" "Saturday" (laughter) Well, they done very well this morning. I asked them what day is today? "Thursday" What's the month? "September" What's the date? "The seventeenth" What did you have for breakfast? "I don't know." I said, you sure are smart! You know what happens when you know your lessons? Happens every Friday? Always get lollipops! I love every last one of them. One little girl was sitting down on this table this morning, and she was sneezing and I said, "You have a cold?" "Yeh," and she smiled the sweetest smile. I said, now here it goes again. You know it goes right there (pointing to heart). It starts right up again.

Maybe it's because I'm easygoing. I've never been really pressured. Not in my whole life. Now my kids, after my first husband died and I married Mr. Butcher, I had life easy, didn't have to work. It was my own doing that I went to work, but the reason I did is I didn't want Mr. Butcher to feel as though he had the whole load on his shoulders. I was taking in peoples' children. They were leaving them there, and they would go off, and I raised the whole gang of them at home. One day I said, "You know something, such and such a person hasn't come and gotten his baby yet and what we gonna do with it?" And Mr. Butcher would say, "Oh, Madeline, don't worry about it. We'll feed them. We'll keep them." I said, this is too much pressure on this man. I'm gonna get myself a job. So I went to school at night, and I became a licensed pratical nurse, and I got a job working at night.

After he died, we hadn't finished paying for the house and a lot of bills, you know. Got two jobs. Too much work and had a heart attack. I was still cooking for the church; work at night, come home every Sunday morning, into the kitchen and cook great big banquets and things like that. I had a banquet for five hundred one time, did all the cooking myself, rolls and all. So really. Now I have enough to live comfortably so there's no pressure. But I'm changing. Yes I am. My daughter-in-law says to me, "Look ma, nobody's going to do anything like you!" She has sort of calmed me down on that. I find myself thinking, doesn't taste right, but, if I can't get in the kitchen and do it myself, I better be satisfied.

Well, you know, I always wanted a lot of children. I did. I come from a big family, naturally. But it wasn't in the making. So these children, I have them five days a week and then when they leave for good, they get next to me. They've all been over here. I've had all fifteen of 'em over here one time. I tell ya, I'm crazy about them. Indeed I am! The staff over there at the center, I call them the big ones. Can't do more for one than I do for the other. They're just like the little ones. But I think myself that to be eighty years old and have the activity in my limbs, eyesight is good, little problem with my hearing which I'm going to get all squared away, my health is good, no new cancer cells arriving. Remember, I told you, I'm not going to get to my seventy-fifth birthday? Now I've made it for five more years. I lost one of my twins when he was twenty-seven, and now the other one is sick. I keep calling to see what they say. He's got sugar and has to be careful. But I really count my blessings about my own health — I guess I gotta keep going for all the kids, those little ones and my own too.

One son has one daughter — my granddaughter, and she's something. My other son had two little girls by his second wife and two boys by the first, but they both live with their mothers. But I get the kids sometimes and have them all here, treat them. That's it! That used to worry me, but worry is one of the worst things that can happen to anybody. That'll take you away from here quicker than anything else.

When I stop to think, I say to myself, well, I must be here for some purpose. It's these kids, I guess, these children. You think little children don't have problems? You'd be surprised! I had a little boy one time, he came in, it was last winter and I said, "What is your problem?" He wouldn't do his work. Shirley, one of the teachers, called him, and he said "Nothing." You know me, I don't move unless something moves me. "Come on with me, I want to talk to you," I said. "What's the matter? Something is the matter." He said, "My brother was doing nasty things to me, and my mother had to take me to the hospital." "Where is your brother now?" "They sent him away," he said. "Well, don't you worry about it. You forget about it and come back tomorrow morning. Go home and have a good night's sleep, and I'll see you in the morning. You come with the idea that you are going to do your work and grow up to be a nice big man." Shirley said, "How did you get it out of him?" "Simple," I said, "Everybody was busy, and we just talked." I've had two or three of them to do that. That's why I figure I'm here for a purpose. I can get more out of those children than anybody can. Say, it's a gift, say what you want, it's just there, and I cannot speak until it's given to me to speak. I help the staff there too — give them my opinion if they ask. Sometimes I just have a feeling about something, and it turns out to be just the right thing. That happens a lot.

But I'm here for a purpose. Must be. How much longer I'm gonna be here I wouldn't know that but the Lord above. Why did I have to leave Pennsylvania and come up here? Move to Boston? Well, that woman, when I saw her going in and out, in and out, where is she going every morning? I went down early the next morning. "Where are you going so early every morning?" "I'm going to work." And she told me. I said, "Do you think I could get on over there?" She said, "Yes." That was it! It was right to Children's World where I am now, within walking distance of my house. I started in '80 and there it is, a purpose. I always wanted to be a teacher so there it is. All wrapped up into one bundle. A lot of children. Teachers! There's the answer right there. And lots of people say, "Why is it? You raised your children so why?" That's not it. This is what I always wanted. It's something like when you eat, if you're not satisfied you say, I want my dessert! The rewards I get? A lot of kisses and hugs and love."

After that, there is the the other life. There is the other life if you live right. Many people question me about that. "What do you mean about living right?" Treat your neighbor right. Don't take life that you can't give. I do not believe in abortion, I do not believe in homosexuality. I'm not a religious fanatic, but I think when I used to take those children down in PA the mother would say, "I'll be back, Mrs. Butcher, tomorrow." Tomorrow never came. I have raised children in my house who are mothers, and I'm their grandmother. I think if I had turned those children away that would have been a strike against me, but I couldn't do it anyway. I don't believe in stealing. What you don't have, do without. Do without. Treat everybody right. We cannot help what we are, we cannot help who is our parents, but you don't look at it that way. There is only one God, one heaven, one hell. If you're not going' in one and if you land in the other, you will burn and burn and burn. But, if you're fortunate to make it into the other, you will have eternal life. That's the way I feel about myself.

I don't believe in gossip. I have too much to do, too many things to think about. Thinking what can I tell my kids tomorrow, what can I do to interest them tomorrow when the teachers are busy? I think that's the way everybody should feel. It's not like that, of course, but that's not up to me. There is a book, and every deed that's being done by your body, it is being recorded. When you stand to the final judgment, the wheat and the chaff in the day of harvest. He's gonna do it, don't worry. Who sends the sunshine, who sends the rain, who does that? You see what's happened? I'm not saying for sure that I am going to heaven, but there's nothing I have done that I know is gonna keep me out. I got two marriage licenses, a driver's license and a nurse's license — all well prepared.

One day, Harry, from the Day Care, called when I was sick to ask when I was coming back. I said, "As soon as the doctor discharges me, I'll be back." He said, "Because they need you." I've gotten such good reports. Children's mothers have called, teachers, so it must be. It's for them to say what they think of me, but the way they treat me, the way they act, you know. My own kids think it's wonderful that I'm not stuck up here in the house, but they knew that I would be doing something because it's been that way. But you know what I do think? I think foster grandparents are more important than a doctor or a nurse. You're at work — suppose some child was to knock on that door, tears streaming down his face, cold, hadn't had any breakfast, what would you think? All right, we have had the situation where the parents brought the child and shove them in the door, not take time to get up and see if they're in. So, here's the grandmother. You go to that child, their poor little hands are cold, tears in their eyes, the nose needs cleaning, sometimes their face needs washing. So you take the child, take the coat off, take them in the backroom, wipe their little face, take their hand and hold them in her hands and warm them up, pet them up, give them a good hug and warmth and says, "How do you feel?" "I feel fine." That's all they need. Bump on the head? "Gramma, I got a bump on my head. Kiss it." "How's it feel?" "All right." They go play. So there's where the important part of the foster grandmother. It's such a good feeling when children can come and say, "Gramma, Gramma."

Once an interviewer from the Boston Globe writing an article said to one little girl, "What does Grandma Madeline mean to you, in your own words?" "She's very special. Grandma Madeline is very, very special." I have one little boy there, Ralph, talk and talk. "Ralph, you know what I'm gonna do with you one day?" "What?" "I think I'll put a 'For Sale' sign on you and put you out on the front steps, you talk so much." Now he went upstairs and told everybody that he wasn't ever going to leave. That's why I had to stay away after the graduation so Ralph could leave. I look at some of the people in this building, young people, no use of their legs. Lots of tragedy. And I count my blessings. I walk to school, and the doctor says that's good. The kids have to do their little dances and exercises, and I get right on with them and do the exercises. I have a great time. Those kids over there is what keeps me going. They are what keeps me going. Yep, I love them. That's why grandparents are so important. It's the love.

Susan Calloway

Susan Calloway

You know, I still say that the Lord has spared me for a special reason, for the young people, not only in my family. This young generation need people to encourage them; to talk to 'em and try to love 'em and show 'em that somebody love 'em. True, true, that's the way I feel. So much is happenin' out there with 'em, and they need somebody to touch 'em. Sometimes, if you just pet 'em and give 'em a hug and a squeeze, hold their little hand when they go to sleep, they know that you care. They feel it. They can really tell whether you mean it or you just puttin' on airs.

I was born in 1914 on a farm near Columbus, Georgia. I think about it so much. I am so thankful for the family we grew up in. See the thing about it, they owned their own home because my mother's father bought this land when she was only about three or four. He bought about two acres on the outskirts of the city, and nobody could be up close to 'em, so they had plenty o' land where they could plant gardens and patches and vegetables and raise cows if they wanted to. They had a milk cow, pigs. They raised hogs for their own meat, and so that's the way it was.

And so my mother grew up. There was seven of them, and I remember my grandmother. She passed when I was about fifteen, but my grandfather passed before I was born. My grandfather, my mother's father, was born in slavery in Virginia on a slave plantation, and he remembered being auctioned off and cryin' and his mother, she had her apron up wipin' her eyes. So this man from Georgia bought him, a Mr. Harris. He owned a big plantation in Georgia. That was the last he saw of his mother, and he was wavin' at her when they was drivin' away in the wagon. When the slaves was freed, he was about twenty-one, and he remembered his mother's name, Stuart, and he went back to Virginia lookin' for his mother. But his mother was dead. He found some cousins who know about it, and they took him to the grave where she was buried. He went back to Georgia. He went back in the Stuart name.

So he was Sam Stuart, and he married my grandmother. My grandfather was part Cherokee Indian so that's where the Indian blood came into this family. So, he could build houses, and he built the one that we lived in hisself. But he built a cellar, and they didn't know what a basement cellar was. People used to come from near and far. They wanted to see the cellar. You know what they kept down there? They kept all the potatoes and vegetables, and they had one room for the preserves and one for the vegetables, and, in the summertime, you could go down in there, and it'd be cool. And my mother say he was a good provider. He would buy whole cases of cheese and everything. See, he could put it down there, and it would be cool and fresh when they wanted something. It was a wonderful life. It was wonderful. My sisters and brothers and I, we don't have anything to complain about because we were blessed. We didn't realize it then, but, after we grew older, we see that we were. You don't know anything else when you're a child.

There was ten of us, and I was the oldest and, you know, the big responsibility, it fell on me, but it came easy. The only thing I didn't learn how to do was milk a cow good. But working in the garden, you know, it came so easy. After I grew up, I had to start cooking and baking. I just fell into it. I was just born into it. There's about a year and nine months between my sisters and brothers so, you know, even during the depression, we never saw a hungry day.

My father, he was a meat cutter. He worked in a big market in town. We raised all these vegetables and everything. During the depression, they didn't have much money so they would pay him off in meat. He would take the meat and share all the neighbors, the whole little town. We would have to get up early 'cause, when we'd go to school, we'd go way over a mile or two and see Miss so and so or Uncle so and so and take them their meat so that they would have something for their family. They not really our family. Some of them was, but they get called that when they gets older, uncle or aunt, you know? You had to give them that respect, and it was close like a family. But, anyway, about half the town was related to us on my mother's side or my father's because they came from big families.

It was just so much love, you know, where we didn't have much money. But it was just so much love. I talk to my children and grandchildren about my sisters and brothers. You know, if one had money and they bought a candy bar, we wouldn't eat it unless everyone had a piece. We shared whatever we had with each other. My parents showed us how, and, after we came to Boston, a lot of people that came from down there, they would tell us, "You know, during the depression, your mother and father kept us from starving to death." And so that's the way it was, until I tried to bring my kids and raise them up that way. Some of them care and some don't.

It was a town about two thousand people that would include white and black. Yeh, it was mixed, and there were some of the white who were very, very nice. Some of my best friends were (laughter). I'm telling you because at that time, the depression, I quit school to help my mother and father. I was about sixteen. I started cooking at a hotel, and then after that I went to private families, working for white people, yeh, nursing and cooking. I was cooking three meals a day. Had one day off every week. And, you know what they don't understand today, two and a half dollars a week! And that was good money because some people was out working every day, and they was making one dollar seventy five cents. But they was nice, some of the white people, I mean.

Our house had four bedrooms, a dining room, kitchen and a long hallway and a front porch, back porch, and plenty of yard. Then, we had an extra room built on to the house. We called it the little house, and they kept it for company or people who would come in sometime and didn't have anywhere to stay. He would take them in until they found somewhere to live.

My grandfather was a well-digger too. The money he made at that time, you could get an acre of land for less than $25. So he bought the land. They call that side of town the MacDonald Woods. These very rich white people, they owned it. Acres and acres, and they sold it to a lot of black people. Yeh, it was like field and timber, and he used the timber for his carpentry. It was rich land, and it's very rich land yet. He cleared the ground himself. My mother had to do the plowing for her father. She would plow the land so they could plant the vegetables, the corn and everything. When we come along, it was ready for us to get out there and seed it and everything. My father, he had a good hand for growing things. He was raised on a farm too, and he knew just how to do. And the chickens he raised! We had to gather the eggs everyday.

It's there yet, the house. It's still in the family because it's their property, and it has to be handed to someone. It can never be sold. One of my brother's sons is there now. The house we were raised in, they tore it down and built another one, my brother and his wife. Both of them has passed recently so that house was vacant. It's new and all furnished, and if any of the family want to go down on vacation, they keeping it there for a summer home. I went down last summer, but I told them I have to come down when it's cold. Since I been up here, I can't take the heat like I used to. Look like it's hotter. It has a pump, the pump we used to pump water. They keeps that in the yard as a souvenir. When we go down, some of us, we walk there and put our hands on that pump and say, "Oh, Lord, how many days I used to pump that water." We had no running water and an outhouse. So now they have it fixed up so nice with pine trees and a lawn that's mowed. It's just like a park. Yet it just look like where we grew up with the plum trees and blackberry bushes, fig trees, peach trees and all so we could make preserves. My mother she learn us all that. Do everything. Always working.

Well, you know we had a pretty good school. They called it the Randolph County Training School, and we had Professor Henderson. He was very, very good. He done taught my mother. He was black and he was a professor, yeh. They rebuilt a new school from the time of my mother, and we had a very good training. Because in them days you could get the rat-tan if you didn't do the right thing. They go to the twelfth grade, and they had good teachers. They would get them out of Atlanta or Macon, and they was all black, and there was no white children. But they had some teachers there, when they finish with you, you was gonna know something. You wasn't walking away from there dumb. That's for sure. I got through the ninth grade and promoted to the tenth before I had to quit. After I came to Boston, I went to night school, after my kids was getting older and some of them had graduated. At that time, they was having school down in the South End. I went at night. I went at the day. I would go from ten in the morning till about two or three in the afternoon. I kept going until I complete the 10th grade. You know, get your brain power back in shape. Even the teachers, some of them would say, "Ms. Calloway, you sure can read fast!" You know one thing, you just don't let yourself go. If you're not in school, read papers, read books — that's what keeps me going. Newspapers, some books. You know what's going on.

We had two aunts here who came to Boston way back in the twenties. When my two sisters graduated from high school, they came up and lived with them. Then one sister got engaged, and my mother and father came up to the wedding, and they liked it so well my father stayed and got a job and start working for the Star Brush Company. All of us were grown up by then. My youngest brother was about sixteen. They brought him up and put him in school here.

Roxbury was a very nice community when we first came — I came in 1948. You know, there were a lot of things going on. Don't seem like the same place now. You could walk anywhere and nobody bother you. The parks, you could go anytime; the church, the drugstore, and it was a lot of mixture. Even though the streets was separated, no one bothered anyone. So, no wonder they all liked it.

Before I went to Boston, I lived in Orlando, Florida for a few years. Two friends of mine were down there working, and so I went down, and I got a job working with some rich white people in Pine Creek. All the lakes and the beautiful homes, but I didn't live in. My mother had come with me, and we had a room in town and went out there every morning, back and forth. I was one of the cooks. It was a great experience there. I worked six days and one day off. I made about $20 a week. That was good in 1940. And that's where I got married.

He was working for the company that made the fertilizer for the orange trees. I worked for the people who owned that company. I knew his family, but I never had met him. Mr. Holland, the big boss, used to have some of the guys who worked for him pick up some of the help, and so I met him like that. After the war broke out, he was being drafted, but he didn't want to leave me in Florida while he go in the service. He'd rather me be back in Georgia. So I went home. My mother, she had gone back before.

He had a medical problem; he taken sick with ulcers in his stomach, and he stayed in the service about a year and a half, and then he got discharged, you know. So we had a couple of kids born there in Georgia. Then I left him and come to Boston. That's what happened. I quit him! And I came up to Boston where my mother and father were. He was acting up, and I said I can't go through this, so I left him. I was up here about three months when he came up. We went back together then. He started working, and we stayed here about one year. My mother had gone back to Georgia because she loved that place down there, and she had said, "I'm not making this my home." Then my father had a heart attack and wanted to go back home, and we knew he couldn't travel by himself so we took him back. Then you travel on the train. Wasn't thinking about no aeroplane. We went back with the kids and stayed until '48. My father passed, like in June '48, and we came back up here — all of us but my mother. She stayed one more year and then she came.

Meanwhile, I'm having kids all the time, yeh, I'm telling you. I been here ever since. I just went back two or three times on vacation. My marriage got a little better, yeh. Better, and then it got worse and when it got worse, I stayed and stayed and stayed. I just felt it was no use.

My father, he was the type, anytime any of his friends mistreat their wives or anything, he would cut her loose from them because he said,"If you don't want the woman, you don't beat them, you don't knock on them, and you don't mistreat them. You can't raise them. They grown, you know. Take them back home to their mother." So he was the type, he didn't want to see the woman put down and mistreated. My sisters and brothers, we talk about him now; you know, he just look at us. We know he meant what he said. He never really had to discipline us in the hard way. He never screamed and hollered. Whatever he had to tell us, he'd sit down and talk to us just as calm. My brothers, he used to tell them that if you ever get married, I never want to hear tell that you're hitting your wife or mistreating your wife. You can talk to them in a nice way. They all say they appreciate him. They can see now where he was coming from. My mother never had to tell him when any food in the house was out. He made it his business to look in. Where is the flour, the sugar, the Crisco, the grease, everything. He checked himself, and he was the one did all the shopping. She never had to worry about that. He was a good provider. We used to tell other people that God is blessing us because our father was so good to other people.

But my husband, no. He had a good job when he was here. He worked for Bethlehem Steel, helping build ships in Quincy. He was a pipefitter and made time with the women when he got paid. He got to the place when he got paid, he wouldn't come to the house and buy no food. He wouldn't do anything. Like he got paid on Friday, and he wouldn't come to the house till Monday. The whole weekend would be gone by and no food. My aunt and my mother, they had to help feed my kids many a day. That went on and on, and I just couldn't take it. One of the city missionaries, this white woman, she's a good friend of mine now, Gail, she somehow heard about the family, and she came to my house and put in for us. They would send this company that had milkmen come to the house two and three times a week with milk and other food, and they just start feeding my kids. They used to send the kids to camp and everything. If it hadn't been for the City Missionary Society . . . . My kids was growing up to eleven and twelve when they first start helping me, and I was pregnant with Gail. I named her after this woman because she was so fine. After that he would jump on the family, the kids, myself so I knew I was gonna have to leave him.

My oldest son, Junior, he was twelve, and his father come in, and he done throw his money away with his friends, and he come in and take it out on me and the kids for no reason. These people who gave the kids toys and things, he would come in and stomp them and break them up and throw them out the window, and, if other people done give me food and it be done cooked, he wouldn't let them eat. He would eat what he wanted and throw the other out the window. So, then, I would have to slip some of the kids to my mother or somewhere and get something for them to eat.

Well, one morning I was making up my son's bed, and I never allowed them to have a knife or nothing at no time, and I found a knife under his pillow. When he come from school, I said, "Junior, what is you doing with a knife under your pillow?" He said, "Ma, Daddy has jumped on you three times and start to beat you for no reason at all so I had made my mind up if he jumped and hit you again, I was gonna get up and kill him in his sleep."

And so that's what really made me. I went to court again. I had been there several times with the missionary, and the judge moved him out. They told him he had to move, give him so long to get out of the house. And the judge, at that time it was nine kids at home, and the judge told him he had to pay $15 a week for support, and that's when he got mad and left Boston! He went to New Jersey, and I never saw him again. He left Boston. He left that job to keep from paying that $15 a week. For the nine kids, $15 a week!

And the kids knew how mean he was. I never talked against him.

So you know what the kids used to tell me? They'd say, "Ma, if anything ever happened to daddy, I don't want to go to his funeral." Because he was so cruel to them. It wasn't just to me, but that he would beat them until blood was running out of them sometimes. I would have to rub them with vaseline and everything. If he get mad, he would just sit there and pout and, then he would jump up and knock one down. And if you said, don't hit them, they didn't do anything, then he would just get on all of them.

So when he got killed in New Jersey, he got hit by a car in '69 crossing the street, drunk, they sent his body from there down to Georgia where his mother and sisters was living. We drove down to the funeral and buried him down there. I had said I wasn't going but .... They said, they couldn't understand me. I used to say, you can't do that. You can't say that because he's your father, you know. And right today, some of my daughters have went through almost that, and they left theirs in no time. They tell me now, "Ma, you're not telling me a thing because I'm not going through what you went through; I can work for myself and take care of myself, and I'm not gonna take it off no man. So you can forget that." If I be trying to tell them to think it over and trying to work it out, they say, "No, no, no, we ain't like you. We went through hell, and we're not gonna go through that again."

Well, I say, suit yourself because I know what it's like. There ain't nothing like peace of mind. I can go to bed now and wake up and if I don't have ten cents I say, I'm happy I got peace, girl! I know what it was like to live in misery so long. They used to hate to see him come home, and he didn't want them to have no friends. I couldn't even go visit my mother, my father, my sisters or brothers. He didn't want me to go out the house. I would have to stay in the house weekend, day in and day out. Yet it was hard for me to throw him out. It went on so long because he always would cry and say he was gonna do better. "I'm not gonna do it any more. I'm gonna change." And I wanted to believe it.

Gail, my youngest, was about one year old when I finally got him out. I start doing day work for people. The oldest one would take

34

care of the smallest ones. Then the people from the missionary, they wanted me to go to the summer camps. I would go there and cook at camps and take the kids with me.

So it was, I lived in Mission Hill, and, when my mother had the operation, I transferred to this building and got a two-bedroom on the second floor. I moved here so I could take care of her, be with her. My mother passed in '80, and, after a while, I moved up here, and that's when I went into the foster grandparents — right after my mother passed. Yvonne, my daughter, she had heard about it. I told her, I'll see about it and I was glad I did 'cause I was getting so bored sitting in the house all day 'cause I'm not a street person. If I got to go to the street, I'm going to take care of some business out there for a reason, not just to walk the streets, you know. (laughter) So when that come up, I said, that will give me a chance to get up in the morning and look forward to doing something. And I was so happy to be with the kids, 'cause they make me feel good, 'cause I'm used to kids you know.

I started right in 1980, at NICE Day Care. I see some of the kids now, they'd growed up. Every time they see me in the street, they always say, "Gramma Susan, hi." They run to me and hug me, and I say you all growing up so fast you make me feel like old antique furniture. But I'm gonna hang in there. Sometimes the kids, they talk to me and I say, yeh. I have a rocking chair in my bedroom, but I don't sit in it and rock. They say, "What do you do with it?" I put my clothes on it when I taken them off; that's what I do with it. One of the little boys, Alex, now he's done growed up, he's in the second or third grade, and he come by to see us. When he come in that neighborhood, he runs upstairs, "Gramma Susan, I come by to see you."

If I could change what went down I wouldn't get married so early. I probably would've waited. When I hear the ladies or men talk about it, I say, there's plenty of time. When they say, "I'm not ready, wait till I get thirty." I say thirty-five or forty, that's time enough and you really know what you want. You know, you don't have that many children. I'm telling you, in them days, there was no such thing as birth control. You can forget that. Getting pregnant was like always. Like always. My mother really had twelve children; she raised ten to be grown.

But, maybe my life the way it was, brought me to where I am now. You know, I think this is one of the happiest times of my life. I often have said to the Lord, I hope my last days will be my best days, and I feel that these are some of my best days. You know, my kids is all grown, and they O.K. after all of that, and I'm able to be with other peoples' kids that I know need me, and I need them and I feel good, and I feel happy, and I don't feel tired! When I come in, the first thing I do, wash up, get myself together and cook my dinner. Then, I relax and read the papers and listen to the radio. I go to exercise class every morning at seven o'clock in this building. Then, on Tuesdays, we have a ceramics class, and, on Friday, I volunteer as a librarian until about 11:30, until time to go to the day care. The busier I keep, the better I feel. They voted me in now, and I'm President of the Task Force in this building. That's a big responsibility. We try to get trips for them, and we try to get them to come down to the community room. The more I stir, the better I feel.

And this hip, it has a plastic hip bone and a pin, but I don't let it stop me. I don't dwell on it. When you dwell on your problems, your mind can make your body sick. I still say that the Lord has spared me for a special reason — for the young people. This young generation need people to encourage them, to talk to them and try to love them and show them that somebody love them. That's the way I feel. You know sometimes the devil will try to burden you — put things on you. He'll be saying now you praying, you trying to live right, trying to reach out and do and look at so and so, they're such and such a thing. When that come to me, I just hold my head up high and just have faith in God 'cause I know it's gonna work out. His will must be done, and I believe that it's his will for me to be here to try to encourage and help this young generation.

People don't care no more. So much is happening out there with them, and they need somebody to touch them. At the day care, if you just pet them and give them a hug and a squeeze, hold their little hand when they go to sleep, they know that you care. They feel it. They can really tell whether you mean it or you just putting on airs.

I tell my own grandchildren. I sit down and talk to them. I say, "You'd better straighten your lives up and do the right thing and care about other people besides yourself. You all know that young people are filling up the cemeteries, ain't giving us old people a chance. We won't have no where to be buried! (laughter) Them sneakers you got, I could dress my whole ten kids with that money when you all was growing up. I don't care how fancy you get out there and dress, I'm telling you that don't make you nobody. Because you got on everything from top to bottom, all glitter, that don't make the person."

Well, the times are different, and I know it. Yeh, I know the world changes. I guess it's the system. People are the same, but the system is carrying it so fast, they just get caught up in this mood. Their mind is way up there floating. They not down to the nitty-gritty of the thing. Looks like if you could just tell the world to stop for a while and think, that's what I wish. I tell them grandkids, "Now, that education ain't gonna be the thing. It's good, and I'm glad to see you have it, but get down with the common sense. Think about what the world is like. Motherwit is what they really need — motherwit. It means common sense! You ain't flying up there. You get down and know what's really happening — think about what the world is like, and slow it all down."

You know, when I was growing up, I think those was great, wonderful years. I can't call back then, but now I think these are the most wonderful years. I understand more about life now, what it means to live, let live and how to love and care for somebody else and reach out. I am so grateful that I am spared to be here, and I'm so happy, and, you know, I really saying this from the heart. I so thankful to the Lord for meeting you all 'cause if I hadn't come in to the foster grandparents program, I wouldn't have all the children. That helped make my life; it enriched my life. Makes me feel good, I'm telling you.

And, when the time come to leave this world, I know I will be ready. Sometime I feel tired of so much that's going on. I just feel like if I go home to be with the Lord where there is peace and quiet ... That's why I try to reach out and do something for other people as I move along this way. I know my living would not have been in vain. I feel like the Lord is giving me some of my last days as my best. So I say, "I thank the Lord, 'cause it could have been worse!"

Agnes Conti

Agnes Conti

I get so attached to these kids. I even try not to, but this little boy, Johnny, he had a mother who couldn't hear or speak and a father who spoke, but it was hard to understand him. The first day he came to the day care, he was holdin' on to his father's leg, and he was cryin'and cryin'. Then, in the middle of his tears, he saw me, and he said, "Gramma," and he sat on my lap for three days. He even ate sitting on my lap. After the third day, he decided to sit at the table with the other children. He liked me so much, he owned me. I loved him so much that when he left, I didn't know what to do.

I was born in 1905, in Boston right next to the Paul Revere House in the North End, but I lived all my childhood in Plymouth. I didn't come back up here until my first year of high school. There were seven in my family, four boys and three girls. I have one sister who is nine years older than myself, and all the rest of us are only one year apart. When my older sister was getting married, my mother was getting her dowry ready, and, suddenly she collapsed. My mother was only thirty-eight. She got a shock, paralyzed on the whole right side, and she couldn't talk. I was only thirteen years old, and I had to take care of the whole family. I don't know how I graduated high school. They used to call me "the girl who never smiled." My mother lived to be forty-two, but she had to be taken care of all that time. While she was sick, we came back to Boston. I like life better today than when I was younger.

After I graduated high school, I couldn't go to work; my father wouldn't let me. He wanted me to be his devoted slave. I had to prepare the clothes for all my brothers and sister and have dinner ready when my father came home from work. Later on, he had a shock, too, and he was sick for seventeen years, handicapped and not tidy. My husband and I, we had to take care of him.

I really didn't want to get married, but you know in those days everybody thought you had to get married. If you didn't, they would say, "What's wrong with her?" My husband had a store in the North End where he sold pianolas and victrolas. On my first date, my father saw me getting ready, he said, "Where do you think you're going? Going some place?" I said, "No," and stayed put. The next time he wanted to see me, he just came to the house, and from that time on, he was always talking to my father. That's the way it was those in days, yeh. My father was very strict. I got married 'cause, I don't know, I was twenty-nine, and everybody thinks you're going to marry so . . . I really didn't know him that well 'cause it was always the three of us. My father held the reigns of government till he died. My poor husband took it.

My two daughters said, "You didn't have to do what he told you to do." But, in those days, we respected our parents and did what we were told. I wanted to be a nurse. First my father said I could go, but, when it came time for me to leave, he said, "No." Even when I was married, I did for my father first, always. But I did want to have children, and I had three. My son died at twenty-eight. They didn't know what was wrong. It was terrible.

After my father died, my husband went to California because we were going to move there, and, while he was gone, I got a job at the Windsor Button Shop. I never worked outside the house, and I thought it was great to work. He came back, and he said, "You're leaving." I said, "I'm not." Finally. I was a salesgirl and I loved it. I never got fat, and I could eat and eat. Well, I'll tell you, he made me leave. My father never let me work so he learned it from him. I was back home again.

When my husband died, I went into a state of shock. He had a cerebral hemorrhage and died in one day. I used to hang around the house in pajamas, an old robe, and do nothing. My daughters were very good to me. My younger daughter postponed her marriage two years because she wanted to help me. I wasn't old enough for social security, and I couldn't get anything as a widow at that time. But what really saved me was the lady at Windsor

Button Shop. She called and said, "Come back. Come back. Just try." And I did. I worked there for four years.

It was 1966 when I saw an ad in the paper for foster grandparents needed in Wrentham State School. I didn't want to work full-time any more. I went in and applied, and they took me. I wanted to go there and be with the children. Maybe because I had to take care of children so much at home. I'm used to doing that. I must like it. I'm in the program twenty years. Now I'm at Little Folks Day Care right here in East Boston. I've been here eleven years. You know, when the children at Wrentham saw our bus arrive each day, they used to jump for joy. They used to laugh and be so happy to see us. Some of the grandparents got kinda scared when we first went there, but then everybody got comfortable. It was a nice bunch there, and we did good work with the kids.

One time, my daughter and I and my granddaughter went to the circus, and there I hear, "Gramma, Gramma, Gramma." There were a lot of kids from Wrentham (State School). They remembered me. When I was there, we used to meet with the doctors so they could tell us what had happened to the children and what they were trying to do for them. I thought I was gonna be a doctor myself almost. All kinds of weather, I went, even when we were not expected.

Now I do the same at Little Folks. We're gonna have Hallowe'en now. Those teachers do everything. Everything. Even cook. They're all young girls, and I get very close to them. I get along good with young people, better than with old ones. You know, in the summer time, we are out in the yard playing all the time. In the morning, we all have breakfast, and then off we go to the play area with the slides. In the winter, every single day they have curriculum — babies — they have to learn to do things. The teachers cut the pumpkin, and the kids put the eyes on. You should see! The way they do it, that's the way we leave it. They put the mouth here and the eyes there — it's such fun. Now we're making witches and bats — all so beautiful. The older children help set the tables for lunch. I help the little ones wash up, and I even used to change diapers on the very little ones. I knew I didn't have to, but the teachers were so nice. In my room, the children are fifteen months to two years nine months. They all call me "Gramma."

One day, I'm walking up the street, and this little black child calls out, "Gramma" and everybody's looking — I laugh and call out, "Hi." I've got so many grandchildren now, some of them in high school, and I meet them on the street. They still call me by name. They remember because I used to be with the older children in the kindergarten class. One day, I had gone to a movie with my daughter, and we stopped at MacDonald's, very unusual for my daughter, but it was late. When we got there, I looked at the carousel and who should be there but Johnny. I said to the lady with him, "I'm his Gramma." She said, "You are, I thought I was." She had come all the way from California to see him. I wanted to see him and suddenly, there he was.

When I was visiting my sister at Youville Hospital, she said to everyone, "This is my sister, and she works as a foster grandparent." I think she's proud of me in a way. I think I'm proud of myself, too. Remember that Recognition Party when I got the award for being in the program so long? I wasn't prepared to speak, and I was shivering up there, but I said, "My life wouldn't have any purpose if I didn't attend Little Folks Day Care Center every day. I love it, I love it, I love it." It doesn't even seem long, the twenty years. As long as I can walk, I'm going. I don't know how much longer but I'm going. My daughter wants me to move to Revere near her, "in case something happens" she says. But I say, "If something happens, it's gonna happen, and I don't care — so what?" My other daughter wants me to go to Hawaii, and you know where I'm going? No place. You know, I've been living in this house since I was a young girl. My father bought it and left it to me "with love and affection" for all the years I cared for him. The cemetery will be my new home, the next move I make. I don't have any fear of dying. I believe there is life after death and the time comes, it comes. Why should I worry? I'm happier now than ever. Here I am in my eighties, and I know I have no fear of dying. There is life after death. In death, life is changed not ended. I am thankful that this time of my life is the best.

* * *

Agnes lives in her beautiful house in East Boston with bedrooms upstairs all lovely and cared for. We stayed for tea she had prepared with all sorts of pastries. She takes care of everything around her with a kind of attention that speaks of concern and tenderness. Her history sits there in that house where she won the right to be herself.

Sister Leopold D'Arcy

Sister Leopold D'Arcy

And now that I'm eighty, it brings me closer to God. That time is shorter. I appreciate Him for giving me good health and all the blessings of life, and I am ready to do whatever He wants the rest of my life, and that makes me happy, it really does. I have always liked being with people and especially with children. It's their innocence and their helplessness that gets to me, you know.

I was born in County Clare in Ireland in 1907, and lived there for about five years, and then my parents moved to Dublin. I lived in Dublin until I was sixteen, and I went to parochial school — The Sisters of Charity. I had a brother. We were the two oldest, and we were together most of the time. Three more babies came after, but I really grew up with my brother. When I left, the others were still young children. I always wanted to be a Sister, but my mother was against it. She didn't want me to enter the convent; she didn't say why. I think she didn't think I would stay, and leaving the convent in those days in Ireland was considered a disgrace to the family. My dad gave me his permission. Otherwise, I wouldn't be accepted. Finally, my mother said to me, "If you go, don't you ever come back to me."

I was so scared, I didn't know what to do. So one night before I went to bed, I prayed and asked God if He really wanted me to be a Sister. That same night, I saw Him in my dreams. He was carrying the heavy cross, and He wore the crown of thorns on His head. I entered soon after that in 1927. I was twenty years old. I have been happy in the religious life even though it has its sorrows as well as its joys.

I had a first cousin who sent me some money to go to the States, and I had an uncle there, and so I made my home with him when I came out. But before I left I told my aunt of my plans, and she helped me too. She had only one daughter, and so I remained with them for two years. I went to school part-time and I worked part-time, and I almost completed high school before I left. After

I got to my uncle's house in the States, I made plans to go down to Alabama. I had everything ready when my uncle said, "Alabama is too far away. You can go up to the Sisters in Chestnut Hill — the Franciscan Order." My uncle knew them, and he took me up there. I was happy about that, and so I entered right after I finished high school. I was so happy to go in the convent. I really didn't realize enough, but I guess God helped me. I prayed a lot. I was so worried, but it really worked out good. I had a lot of fear though on account of my mother, but prayer helped me through. My uncle used to come up to see me. That was a blessing from God because I don't think I could ever have managed if I had been down in Alabama. Yes, when I think of it now, it was an answer to prayer. I was there at the Franciscan order for almost three years making my novitiate.

A lot of my school friends entered the convent. The missionary sisters would come around to the schools looking for girls who wanted to be nuns. Well, I did want to stay in Ireland, but the only way I could have entered the religious life was to go far away. I was worried about my mother. I felt if I left, it would be easier for her. The hardest thing was when my mother didn't want me to go. She did write to me some years later, and I went back after twenty-five years. That's when we were allowed to visit our parents, after twenty-five years. She was happy to see me, but she still wanted me to stay at home.

I never really wanted to live out in the outside world. It's hard, and it's even worse now. And I felt that I had a calling. I love my family very much. My brother came here and got married in this county. He had four children, but he died when he was sixty. So I have a sister-in-law, and she takes me to her place, you know, at Christmas and Easter. She lives in Arlington so that's really a home for me here.

My first mission was in Minnesota in a Catholic School. I began there when I was twenty-four, and I had a first grade for a little while. There was a boarding school there and we had little children, and so I took care of the little ones. I lived in Minnesota about thirty-six years, and I always took care of the little children. We took little babies in like when the mother died and the father had no one to take care of them. It was an Academy. People who traveled left their children there, too. They would stay for the school year, and then go home every summer, every holiday. Other Sisters changed around, but they left me there all those years. I really wanted to work with older people, that was the truth, but they gave me the little children. When I was transferred they sent me to the Italian Home here in Roslindale, and I worked there for about twenty years with the little ones. I worked with all little children from three to seven. But, by this time, I was used to children, and I loved it. I still love them. I came to love them, you know.

So, when I had to retire, I decided to become a foster grandparent, and it's really great. What would I ever do with my day? Now I have the children again. God has been good to me. Being a religious is my greatest joy. I am happy, I appreciate my vocation, and I appreciate what God has done for me, brought me through the years, taken care of me.

Now that I'm eighty, it brings me closer to God. That time is shorter. I appreciate Him for giving me good health and all the blessings of life. I am ready to do whatever He wants.

I have always liked being with people and especially with children. It's their innocence and their helplessness that gets to me, you know. At Nazareth, I play with the little children, and we sing together, and we play games, and I talk to them and tell them stories. If they are upset or angry, I hold them. When they have a fuss with somebody, we go and make up, and I teach them how to do that. I feed them, and I hold them and comfort them and clean them, and I give them a lot of love. Some of them are distant in the beginning, but then they make friends, yes, little by little. They're bashful at first. Right now, we have a few tiny little boys about a year old, and they're scared of everything and everybody. They just want their daddies or mummies. They just need to be treated gently and with understanding, and, you don't realize, but you really have to come into their place where they are.

It has been a very rewarding life for me. It has given me courage to go along. I see a lot of children. They need so much help. And I am in a situation to help, and that gives me a lot of pleasure. You know, in the olden days we lived such a quiet life. We never mixed up with people. We always stayed with the Sisters. We were never allowed outside alone. We used to sit around the table, a big table, and we'd talk and sew about an hour at night. We lived by the bell, had to go to bed at a certain time, the lights were out at a certain time, get up a certain time and talk only in that one room for that one hour. We were never allowed to get our picture taken, and we could only write four times a year. We were supposed to be praying all the time, all day. That was the rule.

Now times have changed. But, then, we lived in the same building as the children, and we used to take them out a little ways, but we couldn't take them too far. We couldn't take them in town or anything like that except when we were on buses and all together. It was hard when I was young, but you get used to it. Yes, you get used to it. The minute you were through with the children, you had to be quiet. Now, we can talk anywhere and anytime. So when I came to the Italian Home, it was all different and I like it. Yes, I like it better now.

* * *

I interviewed Sister Leopold in a house she shared with three other Sisters in the West Roxbury section of Boston. Toward the end of the interview, one of the Sisters came home from the school where she teaches to meet us and listen in on the interview. She prepared tea, and we all sat down to enjoy the refreshments together. About a year later, Sister Leopold went back to Ireland and wrote to us. She had elected to work with young mothers and their children in Dublin.

It was a lovely little house on a quiet street where Sister Leopold was going about her business in a totally free manner. She took

49

the street car to meetings of the Foster Grandparent Program; she did shopping and visiting as though she had done it all her life. She had suffered for almost twenty-five years thinking that her mother was lost to her forever. And yet, her calling was so powerful, she was able to give of herself tirelessly for over fifty-five years. She was eighty years old when the interview took place.

In 1987, she left for Dublin. She wrote to us that she will be working in the area of Balgaddy where there was a great deal of unemployment and poverty. She chose to make that change so that she could be close to her family. She spent time with her sister which was a great joy to her. So at age eighty-one, she moves on to continue her work with children in the country of her birth — after being away for sixty years. Sister Leopold exudes an other-worldliness which, after knowing her, you realize comes from her deep faith. It actually shines in her eyes.

Thelma Dunning

Thelma Dunning

I didn't have good sense. I was taught that the man is the head of the house and the woman can't do nothin' without the man. If you don't have a man in your life, you can't do nothin'. I'm gettin' it out of my head but it's kinda late. There are children at the school that need love. They need love real bad, and that's all they need. When they get like they're livid, I say, come here and give me a big hug right now. I say, NOW! (laughter) RIGHT NOW! The teacher doesn't have time for all these little extras. But for workin' with the children, I don't know what I would've done 'cause I don't think I would have bounced back as quick.

I was born in 1924 in this house, in the room upstairs, in the very bed that I sleep in now. I have the furniture I had when I was a little girl. We always had plenty to eat. My father was an engineer and my mother, she was a housewife. I had two sisters and one brother. My oldest sister died of cancer at forty-seven, and the younger sister just retired from teaching school. My brother turned out to be an engineer, too, but a different type. In his older years, he developed an industry in Hawaii. I don't know what kind of industry. You know men never tell women things. They don't.

One thing I remember. When I was young, I had a china doll. It was wonderful. Every Saturday I had to take the berry butter and put it all over the doll and take another cloth and polish it. Prettiest thing you ever saw. And I had a straw carriage with a window on the side and a bakelite handle. Oh, I used to love that. I did not have a baby sister for seven-and-a-half years. Every day I used to run in and say, "Oh mother, you're gettin' heavy." I'd put my arms around her and say, "Oh, mother, my hands won't meet."

My father came in one day and said, "Go in and tell mother how beautiful the baby is." "The baby is not beautiful, and I won't have a sister." I said it again and again. He took me by the hand

and dragged me in there. I looked at my sister, and I looked at my mother. I couldn't understand it. My sister, she was peaches and cream, and the visiting nurse said to my mother, "Don't put the baby in the sun, Mrs. Littleton. You don't want her to get tan." My mother laughed till she cried. "Come here, honey, let me tell you something. You see, when a baby is born it looks peaches and cream and they're always gonna be tan, don't you know that?" My mother was part American Indian, Irish and Black, whatever they want to call it. She talked to me in parables. I didn't know. I didn't know I was her favorite child.

Mother used to make cakes, and I used to put walnut frosting on the top. One day, I sat on a little box and ate all the walnuts one at a time. My older sister, she'd say, "I know who did it, I know who did it. You always doing things." I used to have so much fun when I was little. Devilish. I can teach children things.

When I went to the junior high school, Mrs. Jones, my teacher, wanted to know what does your father do for a living. Robert Williams and I, (the two of us Black kids) she asked us. Robert said his father was a porter on the railroad. She came to me. "My father is an engineer." The teacher said, "You mean your father is a janitor." I said, "No. My father is an engineer." I wasn't answering her back or nothing. Just couldn't understand why the teacher didn't understand what I said. I always felt so good because my dad would go to his job, all this machinery down in the power house on Commercial Street — not there any more. He made the steam for the Metropolitan Boston Transit Authority (MBTA). I'd go there with him and see all these meters and things. They used the water from the ocean to make the steam. Well, the teacher was upset with me. She said, "You're an intelligent little girl, but you shouldn't embroider like that." "My father is an engineer," I said. "Call him and ask him." What did I know?

They gave me a test when I was three and a half, and I started school. Then, after third grade, they wanted to put me into the fifth. I got all upset. I cried to my mother, "I won't have no friends if I don't keep up, and then they're gonna keep me back. I don't wanna go in the fifth grade." My father took me back to school and told them. They said I belonged in the fifth grade. You know, after that I used to draw pictures of Snow White. I'd do my English, my math, do everything I had to do, and then I'd draw pictures. I didn't try no more, and I didn't go to college. I went to the High School of Practical Arts.

But it was my mother taught me to sew. When she sewed, I used to sit on the other side of the treadle and watch her. She wouldn't say, "Do this or that." She'd say "You just watch and you'll learn." And I did. In those days, the boys had to take woodwork, and the girls had to take sewing or cooking, and I didn't want either one. It bored me. Then my dad said, "College?" I said, "I'll be bored to tears. I'm bored with slow moving people, and college is intricately this and read that, and I would be tooth and nail with the professors. I would always have trouble. I don't wanna go to school." Then I began to sew; I made hats and I made bags and I made wedding dresses. Oh, I had so much fun. Yeh, but I didn't marry good.

Listen to me. My dad went to college, but my mother did not go. Where my people come from, south, if you're not married by the time you're nineteen, you're an old maid. When I turned seventeen, oh my gosh, where are the fellas? I ran away from the first man, and I said to my mother, "You don't have to give me any money. I'll get a job." I took a job down in Hull, being an in-housekeeper.

This guy who was after me, he got around her. I was on the sand in my hours off, and I saw this shadow and there he was standing. My mother told him where I was. I ran away from him all the time. Then I said to myself, "I might as well get married." I made the wedding dress. He told her her sweet potato pie was good and her apple pie was good and she was a nice person, you know, foolishness. But, if it was left to me, I'd have gone to Europe or Alaska, gone anywhere, 'cause I enjoyed doing what I did. I liked to draw, paint, sketch; I liked to sew, to cook. I loved to dig in the yard, ride a bike, go play tennis. What did I need with a man? But I know why she got upset.

One day, I was about fourteen, I said, "Mother, can you have children without having a husband?" I'll never forget that time. She looked at me and the words that came out of my mouth were, "What is it that you're afraid I'm gonna do; what is it that you did when you were a little girl that you're afraid I'm gonna do?" And that time my mother spanked me. But I used to talk to my mother. I think my mother was unhappy. She was ill and in constant pain from cancer. I used to say to my father, "Mother is not well. There's something wrong with her." "Oh, she's fine, she looks wonderful" She was unhappy about something, and I don't know what it was. Mother never talked to me about it.

I used to say to her when we locked horns in conversation, "You know I didn't ask to be born." And she slapped me on the mouth, and I looked at her. Wouldn't say nothing else. But I loved my mother. She taught me everything I know. She taught me how to bake bread and pies, how to clean the house. I can paper walls, roll a ceiling, lay a floor, build a chicken coop. My mother taught me, not my father. I couldn't talk to my father about anything, and I would have talked to him if he'd let me.

My mother had some beautiful green Irish wool, and she told me I couldn't touch her fabric bag unless I asked. Well, every time I asked, she said I wasn't old enough. One day, she and my father went off, and I ran upstairs like a bandit, got the fabric, and made a suit. Then I took a little straw hat and put the green around it. When they got back, I put the suit on and came downstairs. My mother said, "Oh, that's beautiful, but didn't I tell you not to go into the room, into the fabric?" And she spanked me. Then the neighbor next door came over for tea, and she told me, "Puddin,' go put your suit on so you can show it to Mrs. Brown." I thought, I'm gonna lose my mind. I used to go upstairs, and I would eat anything I could find. I was fat between fourteen and sixteen, and then I got skinny and I stayed thin until now.

I liked my mother, and I used to talk to her then. I'd say, "When I have girls, I'm gonna talk to them. They won't have to come and find me." I always loved children. I took all the children in the street, bring them home, feed them. I love children. People say, "That child's impossible, can't do nothing with him." I would say, "Give him to me." Children know. They know; they feel the vibes. I'd say, "You're beautiful. You don't like people today, I don't blame ya. Some days I like people, some days I just hate them. But don't cry honey because it makes your face look awful." Then I'd jump around like popcorn. Laugh, laugh.

My marriage was terrible. I'll tell you how it happened. I used to visit all the neighborhood ladies, play the piano for preserves. I'll play the piano if you give me some preserves, not one minute before. The little lady around the corner, she used to wear those high button shoes you put on with a little hook, and she would give me preserved plums. Wonderful. After church, I used to go around and play for her. One day, in walked her son. It's winter time, the man had on white shoes, grey white-striped flannel pants. I said to myself, he doesn't know how to dress. I can't stand him. Let me get out of here. And his mother said, "I want to introduce you to my son." I wanted to scream, "I don't want to meet him." That's how I met the children's father. The mother says, "He can walk you home." I said, "I can find my own way." My mother taught me and the old times taught me, be polite to older women and men and so she told him to take me home, and he never stopped coming to this door. Walk, walk, walk, walk.

The only thing good out of it, I've got two healthy children, a boy and a girl, very good looking and very intelligent. And they're not knocked-kneed, bow-legged, and I can look at them with pleasure. In other words, God knows I can't stand ugly so he sent me these two children.

I married him. What do I know. You might as well get married, he's around here all the time, you know? He gave me a diamond, and his mother said, she's laughing, "It's my son's birthday and you're getting the present." My mother said, "He's getting my daughter." I thought I'd die. I wanted to crawl in a hole. I made a wedding dress, the veil, the whole bit. Come down the stairs, my sister played the piano, married right here in this room. An old fashioned piano was over here, a Tiffany lamp over there, an old fashioned rug, leather chairs, and then he went in the service! He wasn't drafted. He just was not ready to be married. He wasn't ready to go and work and come home and do things. He went to Germany and then to Paris and other parts of France. When he came back, they quarantined him. They said, he needed to be de-flied. They kept him there. I don't know what was wrong with him, but I stayed clear of him. It's terrible to talk about. He messed up my life, and I'm not concerned with what he did with his.

I started sewing: I got back into it. I always could support myself. Then I met another man, my other children's father. I didn't know where he came from. I met him in my sister's house. I didn't have good sense. I was taught that the man is the head of the house, and the woman can't do nothing without the man. If you don't have a man in your life, you can't do nothing. I'm getting it out of my head, but it's kinda late. It's ridiculous. It's ridiculous, but that's what I was taught, and it's very hard to re-learn something that you've been taught. I mean, the only thing you can't do without the man is have a baby, and now they're working on that. Now I have two and two, two boys and two girls. I've got healthy children, and I have grandchildren. I had to put him out. He was terrible.

It's the devil's station with a man. I married the third time. I needed to have my head examined. I made a lace wedding dress, lace for the maid-of-honor, lace for everybody. And I married sombody I knew for twenty years! A woman said to me, "Ha, ha, I could've told you. You want a monster on your hands, marry a friend." He turned into a person I didn't know. That's when I went down. I was terrible, married in '82. But I've got the rest of my life to live, and I will LIVE it! I don't need nobody around here, nobody, just children and grandchildren, I'll be fine. I was so devasted. I said, "God, just help me get out of this hole, I will never get in that hole again."

He had a big old Cadillac, and I said to him there are some people who never should have a big car, especially if you can't call it an automobile. The doctor told me I was gonna go down. My complete body was in pain. He gave me novocaine. Then he said, "You have to get away from that man. He's gonna kill you." And I did. I put him out. That was 1985, and I was bad, bad. I didn't go anywhere. I'd sit and talk and make flowers of crepe paper. I couldn't talk about it. I just kept beating my head with a stick. Why did I, what did I, why? Why? And, if you look at the person, you'd say, "Such a nice person."

Then, one day I sat down and thought what my options were; what can I do? I didn't feel like sewing. I had flowers all over the place, and that wasn't enough, so I got out and went to the Brighton Center for Seniors, and they said, "I got something for you." I went to the doctor to get my physical and said, "Just tell me am I healthy; all right to work with children?" Everybody said it would work, and I didn't believe it 'cause it wasn't coming off fast enough. And then the first week that I went, I met a little Spanish boy. "Gunty," "Gunty"— you could hear him all over the school. When my grandchildren were babies they couldn't say, "Gramma" so I taught them to say Gunty. So when I went to school, the children said, "What we gonna call ya?" "My children and my grandbabies call me Gunty, so you call me Gunty." This little boy went home to his mother: "Gunty this and Gunty that." The mother come to school looking for me. I said, "I'm Gunty." "You're Gunty?" "I am and we're friends." "My son talks his head off when he comes off the bus. He doesn't go to sleep, yappity, yappity, yap, yap." Because of that she dropped off her little girl who screamed for one half hour, just screaming. I went to her and said, "Sylvie, I never saw anybody cry with no tears. How do you do that?" Huh, huh, huh, gasping for breath. Then she wanted to wear my earrings. So now they're all walking around with my junk. And I notice that as the children improve, I improve.

There are children at the school that need love. They need love real bad, and that's all they need. When they get like they're livid I say, "Come here and give me a big hug right now. I said, NOW!

58

(laughter) RIGHT NOW!" Sometimes I get the teacher upset. I say, "You want this child to function, don't you?" She doesn't have time for all these little extras, you know. I hear the child crying a long time, and nobody is bothering. I say, "I want to go over and see what the little fella is doing." She says, "Help yourself." Wonderful, that's all I want. The green light.

Sometimes I find the children have had a rotten time at home. One little boy said to his teacher, "I don't like you, I don't like you at all, I hate you." "You hate the teacher? What if the teacher hated you what would you do?" And he stopped saying it. It's just a little bit. How much time does it take? Two minutes, five minutes? But for working with the children, I don't know what I would've done 'cause I don't think I would have bounced back as quick.

I stopped going to the church here, and I went in town to Trinity. It's a beautiful building, beautiful music, beautiful service. And I listen to the organ recital right after, and I come out feeling wonderful. I know what it is now; self-esteem. I don't know my worth. So now I teach little children, "You're worth something. Gunty knows." I think my dad made my mother feel little, and my mother in turn made me feel little. There's a song "You Are My Sunshine." My mother went out and bought a little portable box, and she bought this record and give it to me. I listened to the words, and I said, "My mother is saying that she loves me. She's saying I'm the one that makes her smile. All these other people in her life and I'm the only one. I don't know if I can do that." People say, "You're an artist, Gunty." And I know that. I thank God that I can go upstairs, take a piece of fabric, cut it, stitch it, put it on my back and go through that door.

Crawling out of the quick sand back onto the sound ground has been a hard job. And I need the children; I'm gonna need them for the rest of my life. I don't know any other route. One of the foster grandparents said to me, "Why do you wear those clothes?" "For the children: who else? There are no men around I want. But the children. They help me to think."

My own children, they know I love children. "Mother did you go to school today?" "Of course I went." Years ago, I wanted to teach teenagers to sew and cook and all that stuff. It's funny how things work out. My kids are happy that I'm there, I can tell you that. Now I'm with the young children, and I think they're the best. They speak the truth more than other people. "How do I look?" "You look awful." "Do you like this?" "No, it doesn't look right." "What do you say that for?" "Because." (laughter) You know, for the longest time I said that all the things that I know to do, I did them for people so I could raise my children. But, now, I think that all the things that I learned to do I need to give back in some format. That's what I think. No matter on what level, every day that I go to school, I teach one of those children something, something that I have learned. I've taught the children to gather their emotions. That's what my mother used to say, "Gather your emotions." Little girl crying, crying, "Sweetheart, don't cry today. Cry tomorrow." And they listen. They listen. The tears that are running all down stop, and I say, "Isn't that nice?" Teaching. Teaching. I think it's marvelous. My mother taught me. She taught me. I can't thank her enough. She died when she was fifty-eight. Young. But all the living of life that I know, I learned from my mother.

She came from Ohio, and I did know her mother, and one day I'm gonna get on a train or a plane, and I'm gonna find out more. Nobody seems to know. My grandmother, she looked like those Indians in the back woods. Her cheeks were so far up, her eyes so far into her head. I used to look when I met her, stare, 'cause I never saw nobody look like that, alive. I only saw it in books. I used to get upset with something someone would do, and she would say, "Honey, don't you worry about it. You might be the last somebody who'd give him a glass of water." She lived in Dorchester, not too far from us. She was beautiful; reddish, rusty complexion, and she had dark eyes. I'd never seen anybody with cheeks like hers. She lived that old, maybe more than one hundred, nobody knew. When I had my second daughter, she came to be with me. She told me she was coming, and I said, "You don't need to be doing this." I didn't tell her, you're too old. She came, and she's washing the diapers on the scrub board. I had a fit 'cause I had a washing machine. She wouldn't use it. "I don't know nothing about no newfangled things. They don't clean nothing." And that was it. I want to find out more about her. Someday.

If there's an after-life, Lord, let me be an eagle so I can soar above all the chaos and come down just to feed. Watch, down, get it, gone. And I don't have to worry about getting up there because I believe God has a plan, and I don't have to be concerned with that. I have enough to do to live each day the best I can — twenty-four hours, work, sleep, get up. That's the truth. And I don't worry about dying; I'm not afraid to die.

I don't think there's anything else unless you'd like a cup of tea.

* * *

The house in which Thelma Dunning lives exudes history. She seems a part of all that transpired there. The dog, the cat and the plants — even the piano and the Tiffany lamp were all there. And her mother's picture was prominently displayed. The school in which "Gunty" works is a community school with pre-school programs in the Allston section of Boston.

Virginia Hurley

Virginia Hurley

My Billy was in Vietnam, but he came home safe, thank God. Oh, it's all so political all that stuff — the bullets and the nuclear weapons — they're makin' money out of it, that's all it is. And our children are canon fodder. That's how I feel.

Some o' the stories of what those children had to live with — lives so sad — and yet they're so beautiful to look at. And there's more and more of it, isn't there? In our day, kids weren't off to nursery school. I feel that even though we might have gone to bed hungry, if you were loved, it wasn't awful.

I was born in February of 1918 in Randolph, and we lived there, I don't know exactly how long. My mother was born in Canada and my father here. It's all very vague about my childhood. Then we moved to South Boston. I remember the third grade, parochial school. My problem was I was left-handed. The nuns really wanted me right-handed, and I got a wack on the hand for that. I couldn't help it. They don't do that now, and they don't put hands on children. Unheard of! My father worked on yachts as a steward, cook, on rich people's yachts. He'd be out on long trips, and we'd be home with champagne and caviar. Excuse me! Yah, he'd come home acting like that after X amount of months, really. It wasn't altogether wonderful. Then we moved to Weymouth. I had an older sister, Marie, who just died about a month ago, and I had an older brother who is gone now, too. Now, I have my own family.

I started high school in Weymouth, and then the house broke up. My father wasn't feeling very well, and my mother was not doing well either. We won't go into those details — I'd rather not. But I went to live with my aunt. She had a daughter my age. It was nice living there. A father who had his own business, and it was lovely. They were doing a service, having me. They had their own family, after all. Then my sister took me in with her. She was ten years older than me and married in '29, and that's the depression. He had his mother, his two brothers, and then they took me in. He was the only one that was working. I loved high school and graduated in 1936. I got a job two years later.

Funny how I got the job because there were no jobs. I had met this Billy Hurley when we were at a dance in Neponset, and he was the most wonderful dancer. We stopped to have a coke or something, and a girl standing there said she worked in personnel in Gillette's. So I said, "Oh, I need a job so badly." She said, "Come down tomorrow." I went down, and I had a job. Moldy, dirty and greasy, but I didn't mind. It was a job - $13 a week. I don't remember how long I worked there.

One day, Billy Hurley and I are riding on the street car — no one had a car then — and he opened up a little box, and he said, "Let's get married.". On the street car! It was April, 1942. I said, "That's a good idea." So we got this nice little apartment, and then in September, he was drafted. Suddenly, he was gone, and I had to break up the house, put everything in storage, go back with my sister. Her husband was older and wasn't drafted.

When I went to visit Bill, I had to get out of the train at three in the morning and go across town to get the train to his little town. I was so scared, but, when I got there, he had a little Christmas tree in this little room there in Texas. A lady in the building said, "If you want to stay here, I can find you a job in the Electric Power Co." It was Christmas, 1942. I couldn't stay down there with him. I was too babyish, too juvenile, but he was only in the service for a little over a year. He had asthma bad so they put him out. He had his own bookbinder business, but he gave it all up and went to work at the John Hancock Insurance Co.

We got an apartment on the third floor, and every Friday, the landlady insisted I scrub both back and front stairs. I was so afraid of her. And then I had five kids there! I had five kids up in that top floor apartment. One day a friend of mine said, "Wannie, (that's what they called me) I hear there's a house for sale." The father came flying up, and that was it. He bought it. We borrowed

$500 from my sister for the down payment, and we've had this house ever since. It's amazing. It is a nice house. Well, they all went to St. Peter's, all the children. I did work after I got married in Gillette's, but then I got pregnant. It was tough because I had to work nights, and that wasn't too good. So it really didn't last very long. I didn't work outside the house when they were small. Susan in '44 and then Billy wasn't until '49, and then they were right down. I went to the doctor when I was pregnant with the last, and, when he told me, "Mrs. Hurley, the more the merrier." I was upset. There was no such thing as birth control — who ever did even think of that? I don't know anybody who ever did in those days. Never. We were brought up and trained — another baby is a gift. We never had any money.

Susan always worked from the seventh grade. Then, she went into the propagation of the faith; it has to do with missionaries, like going out over the world and making more Catholics, converting all the natives and whatever. She worked at that for a long time but in the office. Then she went into the stock market, and she worked there and got married. When you think back about things it all comes up in a rush and you wonder how you ever did it. I had three girls and two boys. Billy went to Amherst, University of Massachusetts. What a beautiful school. And then he went to Vietnam. Every night I put my head down, I could see the enemy coming after him. He walked the perimeter with a dog, a guard dog. They put a sleeve on an arm, and they train the dog to bite that sleeve. Well, this dog wasn't feeling very well, and he bit Billy while they were training him, and the teeth went right through the bone and everything. So they took him out of that job. They put him in a night club, and he served drinks to the officers the rest of the war. He came home safe, thank God. Oh, it's all so political all that stuff — the bullets and the nuclear weapons., They're making money out of it, that's all it is. And our children are canon fodder. That's how I feel.

He's O.K. Billy. He works at the stock market, and he has three and another baby on the way. Everything is good with them. All my kids live in Milton now. It's nice down there. I wish I could afford it. Big bucks. My God! I have a boy who's in real estate now. He's not doing good now, not at all. And my other daughter is a systems analyst, something to do with computers. And her husband is a comptroller in a huge furniture store. I say over and over, I never had a policeman at the door. They went up that park, and they played baseball and football, and it was a good life really. A good man makes a huge difference. And the foster grandparent program really rounded it out.

I don't do much in my church because the fact is that you don't trot out at night. If you have a car and you drive, you can, but . . . I went to a couple of mothers' clubs. I'm really ashamed, but I never got into any of it. My husband was very friendly. He was a swell guy. He was too good. He would never say no; too good to believe. Bill made $30 a week at the Hancock. He was a paper cutter, in charge of all the paper they used in the offices, and he was the boss binder. He made $35 later and a little later a bit more. He worked hard yet we never would've had this house if my sister didn't loan us the money. Imagine what this would be now! A two-family house?

I miss Bill. I miss him plenty, all the time. He died in '74 in the Carney Hospital. He had heart trouble, bad. I had gone to a mass for a nephew who died so young and left 8 kids, and I told Bill I'd be back after the mass. When I got back, he was gone. After that, I took a job as a lunch mother. I stayed in the room with the children while they ate their lunch so the teacher could have a break. I worked from ten to two, and I don't remember for how long. But I do remember going to Tremont Street and seeing this big sign "Foster Grandparents." I said, I think I'll investigate that. I can't remember who saw me, but Paul met me at the South Boston Day Care Center, and he said, "They really need you." He said that, and then I felt so good, and then I fell in love with all of them.

In the morning, I sit with them while they're learning their shapes and their colors, and, then lunch time, I set the table, and they all sit down to have their lunch, and I help them. Then, they go to the bathroom and onto the mats, and I would rub their backs to help them go to sleep. I loved it. I loved it. And I wasn't very good for discipline — wasn't very good. I never, never had a problem.

Some of the stories of what those children had to live with — lives so sad — and yet they're so beautiful to look at. And there's more and more of it, isn't there? In our day, kids weren't off to nursery school. You were home with your mother. I feel that even though we might have gone to bed hungry, if you were loved, it wasn't awful. You know the little dream I have sometime. I dream of this house as a nursery school. Wouldn't that be something? Put little bathrooms in, get little tables, chairs. I have three teachers, my daughters, and one's a registered nurse, so we could all run it. It might come to pass, who knows? If the stock market goes down the drain, Putnam won't be there. If they ever heard me, they'd kill me on the spot. Though who can tell; my kids might go for the idea. In my dreams that happens anyway.

And, you know, one time, there was a party at some hotel, The Foster Grandparent Recognition Party, and the guest speaker, I can't remember his name, sat next to me, and we talked about little things. And the thing he told me really shook me up — that the foster grandparents save the government lots of money. He did. He said that. But it isn't the money that gets us into the program. It does something for us. Isn't it true that when you're with children you feel like another person, loving them and protecting them? When I take care of my own grandchildren, it's like that too.

The children — all the time — that's the reason for my being here. That's my only contribution. So far so good. I think my kids are proud of my work with the children at the day care. You know how it is, everyone has their own life. You do your own thing, if you're smart, or else you're in the rocking chair. I am lucky I can do my thing. He's been good to me, God. I'm getting very weepy.

I'm not too happy about getting older. The thing I think is that I am a solitary person, and I'm not interacting that much. I do the thing with my grandchild, and I do the foster grandparent time with joy when I can, but I'm not so social to interact or feel about people. I like to read. I've been that way all my life, actually. I don't want to live as long a time as my sister did. Her daughter put her in a nursing home after the fire that destroyed their home, and that was the end of my sister's real life. And I wouldn't like that. It's that, when you stop being busy, that's no good. I've kept busy, but not enough. I've been totally around my family and very few friends. My neighbors say, why don't you run in? I don't want to, really. I have taken trips with my daughter. We've gone to Ireland, England, Paris and California. I always travel with Mary, the one who lives here, upstairs.

I'm not a foster grandparent right now. I want to go back as soon as my daughter has another arrangement. If she gets pregnant, that would be great, and then I could go back. It's called South Boston Neighborhood House now, and that's where I want to be.

Funny, my Mary has met a man who is a coroner. He was discussing violence - all that he encounters all the time, and Mary came home and she said, "I told him what you said one time, that we're all like flowers and we grow and we go back to the earth." That's how I feel. And now the leaves are going back to the earth, and then everything is perpetuated into eternity. I've surely done the best I could. I'm poor, and I would like some more money but, I'm only kidding. I'm grateful for my life.

Helen McGee

Helen McGee

I enjoy giving love, and it's easy. I think I was put here for that purpose — mostly to take care of my sister. And now helpin' these little children. I just love it when little Frankie says, you gotta give me another hug and another kiss.

I was born in Dorchester. My father and mother both came from Ireland in 1913, shortly after they were married. I was born in 1917 and my sister in 1915. We had a nice and happy life. We had our own home in Dorchester, a two-family home that my father actually built.

Then things changed. My father died when I was fourteen. He took sick on Friday with pneumonia, and he was gone on Monday. My mother was terrible. At the same time, my sister was showing signs of unsteadiness in her walk . She was really smart and graduated high school in three years and then took a course in law because her marks were so great. It turned out to be Frederick's Ataxia which is similar to multiple sclerosis, like a creeping paralysis.

Our life suddenly turned around the opposite way. In those days, there was no welfare, nothing. My mother was left without anything — barely enough to pay the funeral bill. But we managed. My mother got a little job at the Boston School Committee. I left high school in my third year because I felt she needed help. It was against her will. That was about 1935. I did get a job in a factory. With my sister, it was just a matter of going from one doctor to another, one hospital to another. She just kept getting worse, and then we had to get a paraplegic walker so she could wheel herself around. I worked for a while, but I did go back to South Boston High School and got my diploma when I was in my late twenties. I thought I'd feel foolish at the graduation, but I didn't.

Those days were hard. I never married. I had chances but I took

72

care of Marguerite. Some people say my mother tied me down, but that was wrong. Wrong. She'd say to me, "This is my life, it's not yours." Then I went to work at Bay State Bindery. I worked out in the plant at first, but eventually I became the assistant to the boss. I hated the place when I went there. I said to my friend Mary, "I'm not going to stay in this place." Twenty-five years later, I left. It was a small place, and it grew and grew, but I got too involved with Buddy, my boss, and his whole family. I would think, "What would Buddy do without me?" I liked working with him.

Marguerite kept getting worse, of course. One morning, I heard my mother up real early, and she was throwing up. She said, "Oh, I just don't feel good." Then she said, "Helen, I think you'd better stay home from work." That was not her. She'd never been sick a day in her life. That was Thursday. I called the doctor, and she said, "Perhaps she'll need a gall bladder operation." Friday she died. A coronary. I thought, what am I going to do? I thought and thought, "What am I going to do? What am I going to do? How am I going to work?" She took care of my sister and went to her little cleaning job at the School Committee at 5 o'clock, and she was home at nine. My mother was 68, and overnight she was gone. Marguerite was 34, and she couldn't walk or even use her hands much. During the mass, when it came time to stand, she put her two hands on the front of the bench and stood up. I couldn't believe anything, my sister standing holding on and my mother there in the casket. All I could think of was, "How am I going to work and leave her alone?"

My mother was buried on Monday, and the following Sunday, Marguerite was having a terrible cough. I figured she caught cold. My neighbor, Mrs. Foley, came by. When she came in Marguerite said, "I can hear her, Helen, but I don't see her." Mrs. Foley went right to the phone and called her son, Joe, who is a neurologist, and he came right down. We had always been together as little kids, the three of us, Joe, Marquerite and me. He brought me out in the kitchen and said, "Helen, I've got to get her to the hospital because her heart is bad. Bad." I'm not one to cry but I told Joe, I knew mama wouldn't go and leave her here with me. He put his arms around me and hugged me.

They didn't expect her to live that night. She was five months at Boston City. She came through that, and her sight returned, but they said I couldn't take her home. Joe got her into the Youville Hospital. This was 1949, and nothing was easy, very little help, and I had practically nothing but the little money mama put aside for her. I had to give all that and the rent on the other apartment and pay $7.50 a week, and I still had to pay the mortgage, the water bill, the taxes. In those days, that was a lot of money. She was there for thirteen years, and I never missed a Sunday except when I was on a vacation.

But, suddenly, I'm all alone. It was a shock. All of a sudden there was nobody. And that's how Marguerite was when we were told she had to go that chronic hospital. The day we took her over in the ambulance, my heart was broken, but I couldn't give in or I'd be licked. My friends took me away up to Canada, and, when I came back, I was able to say, "Marguerite who could take care of you at home?" "I don't need anyone to take care of me," she said, and went on and on. Finally, I had to say, "Look Marguerite, I'm not your mother. I'm just your sister, and I can only do so much. Whose gonna take care of me if I get sick?" She said, as I was leaving, "Well, you don't have to go away mad." So I got outside, and I broke up, cried and cried. I cried from Youville down to Harvard Square. Two days later, I get this note from her, the handwriting all shaky. I was afraid to open it. I was afraid that she didn't want to see me any more. I should have kept it because it was the most beautiful note, saying that she realized that this was her life. She said it was the first time in many years that she was able to get to services because they wheeled her to the chapel. "It isn't the chapel or the statue, but what it represents," she wrote.

Then Joe Foley told her that I could take her home for her birthday. Everybody was against me doing it, but we did it. All the kids in the street were waiting and everybody helped. We carried her up the stairs and all the kids shouting, "Marggie's home. Here's Marggie!" It was great, but, when it came time to go back, she took a heart attack on the elevator in the hospital. But she came out of it O.K. We took her home again at Christmas. But she never, never once said I don't want to go back.

She had several heart attacks after that, but the boys (my cousins) got older, and they got a car so everything was Marggie. My cousins, Tommy and Eddie, they've been better to me than if they were my brothers. My mother had twelve in her family, but many of them stayed in Ireland. Actually, the boys were children of my mother's cousin who lived with her when she came from Ireland. So we could take Marggie home for a week or for day trips. She got so used to the hospital, then, that I used to call it the jolly-jingle place. I never went there empty handed and we shared with the other patients. Then, suddenly, it all began to happen. One thing after another: blindness, infections and clots of blood in the brain. I went every night. Soon she was in a coma. It was strange because her eyes had been closed the whole time, but, at the end, she opened her eyes as wide as could be. I let them do an autopsy because I knew she would want that. It was a strange disease, but if there's just one little thing which would help some poor soul along the line ... But I don't know if they ever really came up with anything. She was forty-six when she died, and she had had it most of her life. Life. A lot of my life was lost with all this going back and forth, going back and forth.

I stayed on at the bindery, and, one day just after Christmas, I seemed to be upset over everything. I decided that I'd better go to the doctor, and I never got home. I was walking around with lumbar pneumonia. Things had got really bad at work. I didn't want to go back there with the new bosses and all. One day I could've jumped out the window I was so upset, and this is after twenty-five years. A friend told me to go over to City Hospital because everybody at Southie (South Boston) works at City. "Ask for Marguerite Mahoney," she said, and I did. She was wonderful. Mary, my old friend, went with me, and she told me they'd rather the older ones, and it was true. They were so happy to see us. I became a ward clerk in pediatrics, and, poor Mary, she got stuck in office supplies with math and all, but she got to love it.

I was only on the unit about fourteen months when the assistant director of nursing said, "Our budget has allowed me to have a secretary if you'd like to come and work for me." I did and I just loved it. I had my own little office. She was a great administrator. In fact, I spent the weekend with her a week ago. I used to make the rounds for her, after a while, to see if some babies needed special nurses. And I did the payroll and the vacation schedules. There were one hundred in our department. They were a great bunch of girls. I was fifty-five when I went to work there. I really enjoyed it and worked there until I was sixty-two. That was when I got a lot of attacks of bronchitis, and I was running out of sick time. If I retired, I'd have social security and the city pension. Not a whole lot. I thought it over, and then I told them that I'd be leaving.

After the shock of it, they were happy for me. I had a beautiful retirement party down on the waterfront. Everybody I ever worked with was there. My boss gave a talk and they gave me $400. I was overwhelmed. On my last day, my boss took me to dinner. She wouldn't take the keys from me. I was lonesome when I locked the door, I really was.

I had just got to know Mary Elliot (not my old friend, Mary) the past few months at the hospital. She said to me one day, "Don't say anything, but I'm retiring in July. "And so am I," I confided. The time goes by, and it's getting on to the fall, and I said to Mary, "What are we gonna do?" "Well, there was an article by Sister Julie in the Southie paper saying that she was gonna give a talk on the role of the Older American in the world today. Let's go and see what she has to offer." Out we went. She said there were jobs at ABCD. I said, "Let's do it." We had an interview, and they sent us to the Foster Grandparent office. Paul was there. He told us about two openings in Southie. We both ended up going to Laboure Day Care Center.

It was 1979 when I started, and it's been really a joy. When I was laid up last year, in the mornings, I'd get depressed — maybe I'll never walk again, never get to the kids again. We have one little toddler — the only thing he could say was Nana. Now they got a speech therapist, and he says, "Give me hug, Nana." And little Frankie, he's just a darling little kid. He's in protective custody. "Did you fall off the bed, Frankie?" "No," he says, "my mummy, she goes like this to me." So we watch him for marks so we can report it. There is a father, and they fight. I take care of the babies, the ones who are just starting to walk. I say, "Come on, Katie, let's dance," and she's going like this and like that. And then exercise — shoulder up and shoulder down. Little Sara, with red hair, she laughs and smiles. I say, "You got a silly little face," and she laughs. Every day, we take them over the park. They have the slides and everything, so it's great.

It's a joy, it really is. The teachers and the kids all call me Nana. We could use another foster grandparent there. They're short of teachers, too. They don't get a decent salary. Mary Elliot is with the pre-kindergarten. She teaches them numbers and colors. Today, I'm teaching my kids, where is your nose and where are your eyes? When I was sick, the kids made cards for me. It's so nice. Most of the kids that Mary has now, I've had. When they're two and nine months, they move to the next class, and they go up to age six. Then they go straight to first grade. It's wonderful. And I just love it when little Frankie says, "You gotta give me another hug and another kiss." I thought, that poor kid, he doesn't get any of that at home, that's for sure.

I enjoy giving love, and it's easy. I think I was put here for that purpose sometimes — mostly to take care of my sister. My mother had a lot of heartache, and God decided to take her home and leave my sister with me. And, now, helping these little children. I visit the sick at the hospitals. It just became a part of my life to do all this. In my religion, I'm an extraordinary minister, and I'm also an lector, giving out the readings at mass.

I like a good time, too. I have lots of friends, and I love having company, friends over for dinner. Mama used to invite soldiers over for dinner during the war. It was always people coming over. My feelings of life haven't changed. I feel the same as I did when I was forty. I have the same personality, I think. You know I've had eight trips to Ireland. I've been to Cuba, Hawaii, Florida several times, Nassau, Bermuda four times. My cousins that I speak about, the six of us, it's intergenerational, the group. I'm the oldest of the bunch now. Only one couple in the group. The boys never married. They took care of their own mother and then their aunt and then they helped me with Marguerite. If it wasn't for them, I never could have done all that. It's a family heritage we have — taking care of people. We often talk about that. But all our trips were so good. We were a great bunch.

My cousin in Ireland has a commercial farm where they raised pigs and cows, too. We always visit them. Of course, the first time, I saw my mother's house. There were twelve of them, and she used to say there was a bed in the kitchen. So, when I got there for the first time, sure enough, the bed in the kitchen, half the size of this couch, and most of my mother's family are big tall ones. Oh, my God! No accommodations, not even an outhouse. They had to go out in the fields. Of course, it's all changed now. But they survived. It was pure survival. But they used to prepare such good food and cover it over with a white table cloth until we set it all out in the bedroom. It was something. Then we all had to have a drink of Irish whiskey. I'd love to get back. Possibly next year we'll go again. I've had wonderful times there.

I got this place after I sold my mother's house. I love it. It's smaller, but it's good for me. Every once in a while our rent goes up, and it's tough when you have a small social security, but I have my electricity and heat so it's O.K. Now the rent is thirty percent of our income. There's so little for taking care of people, like the nursing profession. A lot of them are leaving to become real estate brokers to make money. It's scary. I feel bad for the young people today. They can't buy a house, and they have to pay five hundred or six hundred dollars a month for rent. It's a vicious circle. I just hope for the future we'll be in Laboure for years to come. I want to keep up our heritage, taking care of people - helping the kids, that's what I'm here for — it must be. I've had my troubles, but I've had a good life.

Esme Rajapakse

Esme Rajapakse

I was born in Sri Lanka where my grandparents had migrated during the 19th century. Many Portuguese and Dutch lived there. The Singhalese had a very high caste system and in some ways that affected us.

I am sixty-eight now, and I feel young. Being with the children, you feel young, much more young that is true. See, if I were home I would have been so sick. This is keeping me healthy.

My grandparents came to Sri Lanka from Portugal when they were young. You know, like the Mayflower came here. Well, there were ships that went from Portugal. I guess they came looking for spices, too. So, they came as seamen originally, and then many stayed, and they married. Some intermarried with the Singhalese. After the Second World War, Sri Lanka got its independence from Britain. (It had been known as Ceylon.) The Singhalese wanted their language to be taught in all the schools so that is why most of our people and the Dutch migrated to Australia. They wanted to keep the English language. Some of my family migrated at that time, too.

I had a very good, very good childhood. The family was small and we were all close. My father worked for the railway doing clerical work. I was born in 1919, and I went to Methodist College from the age of four. You start at kindergarten, like baby class, not like here, and go to the senior year, just one school all the way. I left when I was about fifteen. We didn't go to work. No women, no girls went to work. It was after the Second World War that the ladies went out to work. When I left school, I stayed at home and did the housework. In fact, my sister used to do all the housework and I used to go and play. That's true. Go and play with all the boys. A real tom-boy. We could have gone to higher education, but my parents couldn't afford it. There was no public school. My parents had to pay, and I had two older sisters and a younger brother. Of course, being girls, we could be in the house.

They had to spend the money on the boy so he could get a higher education and get a good job. Jobs are not necessary for the women, you see.

My parents were very strict with us; we couldn't go out after six. Saturday, we do all the work for Sunday. Then on Sunday, we were taken to church and Sunday school. So we were kept carefully watched. We didn't even have a radio in the house. My mother wanted a radio, but my father said, "No, the children will be disturbed and won't do their lessons." So strict he was. But anyway, he was fortunate to see all four children married. I met a man, he was a friend, but they didn't allow me to marry him. They said, he comes from a very wealthy family and not our nationality. He was Singhalese, and we were Portuguese. So, since this man came from the very high caste, they were afraid that, if I got married to him, I might not be treated right. They thought my sisters and brother might be jealous. When my second sister got married to a Rajapakse, I married the other brother who my family knew because he worked with my father in the railway office. They made that agreement. I could have said no, but it wouldn't have been too good. My marriage was a very happy one, I must say, even though I didn't expect it to be. He was very good for all the twenty-three years, until 1964.

We lived in a house we put up on government land that was provided for those who worked in railway department, electrical department, etc. We got one half acre of land and built a house to our plan. Last year, when I visited Sri Lanka, I said I must have a look. The man who bought it from me renovated it because he was a man of money. I felt so sorry when I walked down that street. Everything was changed. There was a person seated outside, and he said, "Looking for anybody?" I told him who I was, and he said come in. All different.

In 1964, one day we were having a big celebration for my birthday, and suddenly my husband got ill. He said he couldn't breathe. I managed to get a car to take us to the hospital, and, by the time we got there, he had passed out. It was a bad heart attack, and he didn't recover. He was fifty-four. He had been worrying about our son who was fifteen then but what they call "a backward child." He had to be fed and bathed. My husband was so fond of the child. That's why I said, you know, God knew what was best, taking him away, not me. What could the father do if God took me? He'd have to give up his job and sit with the child. We didn't have these institutions like here where they can take care of children. We had nothing. Nothing.

I struggled for one whole year, and, after that, I went to a home where they took old people. I paid a man who was in a wheel chair to look after him and feed him and all that. Well, I put my little boy in the home, and I got a job in the YWCA as a secretary. My education was enough for that. In fact, I was in charge of the hostel, like a matron. Many of the girls who worked in the shops and offices came from the countryside, and they had to have places to live, and they had to be looked after. Most of them worked doing shorthand and typing. Some were telephone operators. So, I used to be in charge of them, giving them their food and checking them out in the morning and back in for dinner. I was able to pay for my son's upkeep and for my house. I even had servants. That's the way it was there. The wages were low, and everybody had servants. Now, it's not the same. Those people have gone to the middle east, and they are getting more money there.

At the YWCA, I met a professor who was doing research in anthropology. She had three children, and, when she was going back to the U.S., she wanted to take her cook along. But that cook could not get the correct papers. She advertised in the newspaper, and, one day, when I walked into the office, the secretary said, "Oh, Rajapakse, I'm sure you would like to take this job." I told her I don't know now. My child is in the home, and I have my house, but I'll let her know. She wanted someone to go to the States with her and sign up to take care of her three children for five years. I asked my sister if she would take care of the child, and she said yes. Yes. I went and interviewed with her, and I got the recommendation from the YWCA.

She finally picked me out of thousands of applicants. She arranged to leave in September of '67 and I to follow in October. She bought me a ticket. I arrived at her house in Billerica, a nice old house but no proper heating. When they moved to Brookline, later on, after a couple of years, I told her I don't think I'll come with you. She had many friends who she would invite to the house for "Ceylon" food. I had to cook and then sit with them and show them how to eat with fingers. Now, really, the staple food of Ceylon is curry and rice, but we have courses where we use the fork and knife. She liked to show all the things about our eating, and I had to cook for all of them. She said, "I can't accept your notice." I went to the immigration office and asked if I have signed a contract with this lady to work for five years. He said, "No, you came as a permanent resident. You came today, you can leave tomorrow, but you can't vote because you are not an American citizen." Mrs. S. got very mad when I told her. I really couldn't get on with her. She put everything on me, and I felt there was no discipline, no order to anything. I just couldn't take it. I gave up my vacation money to pay her back for the fare, and I got an apartment for myself. My friends helped me with a folding bed and a chair. Then I got a job at Deaconess Hospital in the Dietary Department. You know what I went through here. I came only with two shillings, six pence because she bought my ticket, and that's all I had. My husband's pension was there for the child. We couldn't bring that money here anyway.

I stayed at the Deaconess only four or five months. I was going to school, at that time, to learn computer work, and I asked them whether they had any work like that. They said no. You know the people here had a very poor impression of us, the Singhalese or the Indians who came from India. They think we don't know anything, that we don't know English. One supervisor asked me, "Are you going to learn English?" "No," I said, "I graduated in English, you see, and I must tell you that we speak better English than some of the Americans here." Anyway I went to Beth Israel Hospital after that, and I was very happy until I left. It was like family there. I started in Dietary. When I retired, I was in the

Central Processing Department.

After five years, I sponsored my brother and sister and their families. At that time, you didn't have to pay so much down so I bought a house for them to use. Then, they could pay the mortgage when they started to work, and I could buy another house for myself. I knew they were suffering there. They had to stand in lines to get food. The country had bad problems. I lined up jobs for them at Beth Israel. I bought the necessary furniture, and they arrived. Then my brother's wife had a heart attack, and he went to Australia. After that, my sister left with her husband, and I was alone again. I married a Chinese Jamaican, and I went with him to Hong Kong and then to Sri Lanka to show him my country. When we got back we got divorced.

He was not my type, definitely. He married me because he thought I had all this property, and his whole idea was to get all that. Well, anyway, it was very lucky that I didn't sell the property or anything before I divorced him. My property was here in Boston. He lived in Lynn, and he said, "Oh, all these Black people." I said, well, you know who your mother was so what are you talking about. One fine day, when he went to work, I took all my things out, and I left. At least, I had a home to go to. He didn't contest the divorce because he knew it wouldn't work. I went out peacefully.

I sold one house and lost all the money on the other so now I have nothing, only my pension and my social security and the little bit I get from the program. After my baby died in 1970, my husband's pension could not be used for anything else. I do cakes once in a while to sell for parties, but since my eye operation I can't do anything.

At the day care, I work with toddlers. Some of these things are new to me in my old age, but I'm learning. Bringing up children was quite different in my country see; we used to discipline them a lot and baby them, too. Here the children are in charge. The teachers are of the modern world, but I sometimes feel that

I've got to open my mouth and say something. And, here, they allow me to say it. Then, sometimes they say, "That is right, that's right," and they say to the children, "Listen to grandma. Listen to what she is saying."

For example; today a little boy, he's only just two, a little Chinese boy, his parents go to work, and who knows when they get up, maybe five o'clock, so by 9:30, he's tired. We should give all the children a half hour sleep, you know, so they can rest a little. This little boy, anywhere he can keep his head, he's going to keep his head down. "Tired," I told the teacher. Then, she took him and put some cold water on his wrists. Then again, the little boy came back to me and put his head on my lap. He needs to rest. He's only a baby, really. I bring them to the gym room and do games with the children. I sing with them and let them be quiet if they want. Here everyone is nice, the director and the teachers. I help out, I'm telling you. I go at seven o'clock, and I help out with the breakfast. I like to fix some things for the children. I give out supplies for the day — all the things we're going to work with before the children come in. Then, if I need a day off, I can take it. When the kids come, I'm all ready.

Last week, I was invited to the Commission on Affairs of the Elderly to a meeting so I went early and fixed breakfast and all, and then I went. Now, when the kids come into the classroom, we have play dough and all the other things, finger paints. We do that with the children. We change diapers a lot, too, and now we are trying to train them. Then, we have infants in the other room, the babies. I work everywhere. I like it. I can't sit in one place. I have to be on the move. The thing is, they are wonderful here. They take the little ones for a couple of hours into the new class day so they feel all right when they have to go to a new classroom. They do the same when a child is new to the center. I've been a foster grandparent about three years now. First, I was at Jackson Mann Community School and now here at the day care, Roxbury Tenants of Harvard, right across the street from my house.

When I was at home, you see, with my child, he was always in a wheel chair or pram. I had children at home from the neighboring houses, like a day care. I always said, when I get married and have a child and Christmas comes, I'll be so happy to take the child shopping, but, unfortunately, I couldn't do that. I used to take the neighboring children and go there. Now I do it with these kids. I think I love being with these kids because I didn't have but the one child, and I wanted more all the time. Perhaps God put me here to be with children and the elderly because I share myself with them. I'm not sure if I am here for that purpose. I don't know about life after death when people ask me. I do think, if there is something after, who knows? God has sent us here for a purpose, maybe to help anybody in need and have that nice friendly relationship. What you do is what you feel inside, and maybe that is given to us.

I am sixty-eight now, and I feel young. Being with the children, you feel young. The other thing is, at this age, if I was in my country, I would look so old and feeble because they say, when you are fifty or fifty-five, they think they are so old, and they won't do anything. They sort of sit and rot. See, if I were home, I would have been so sick. This is keeping me healthy. I'm kept active.

I don't have any regret. I enjoyed my life from childhood, but, if I had a choice, I would have come to this country alone. But I enjoyed my life from childhood, and I was a happy-go-lucky person, no worries. Now I am like that again. I belong to the Merry Makers group that get together on Mondays and chat and chat and have cake and tea and all that. They organize trips, and when I get a chance, I go. So those are my friends, and I have my older Beth Israel Hospital friends who visit me and call me on the phone. It's a good time for me, this time of my life.

Jetta Sommer

Jetta Sommer

*When I was a kid, I don't remember a meal on the table. We ate
very good in the summertime because there was all kinds of land,
and all the kids had gardens. But, in the winter, we had only
potatoes and onions. None of us would eat if we thought the
other was hungry. Everybody scrounged.We baked potatoes outside in the woods and we grew up, and we had a good time.*

I was born Jetta Rosenwald on October 28th, 1911. Today is my
birthday. I'm seventy-six years old. My mother told me that the
minute a baby was born someone would rush over with a chicken
because they wanted to be your godmother or godfather. Jetta
Schultz was my godmother, and so she and me and now my
granddaughter have the same name. I was born in Boston on
Highland Street which is now Roxbury. My family were refugees
from Latvia. Around 1905 when the men were being rounded up
for the Russian army, they left and sent for the women later. They
all came to Boston, and then they moved to Roslindale when I
was about two years old. I grew up there with my three brothers,
Charlie, Johnny and Bobby. My parents bought a house. I don't
know how they bought it because they had no money. Then, my
father died in Boston City Hospital of what was diagnosed as
kidney trouble in those days. I was nine years old, and he was
buried on my birthday.

Things were very bad. I don't ever remember a meal on the table.
We ate very good in the summertime because there was all kinds
of land, and all the kids had gardens, but, in the winter, we had
only potatoes and onions. None of us would eat if we thought the
other was hungry. They called me their homely sister but don't
let anyone else dare say it. My mother did housework. She
wouldn't eat lunch at the families where she cleaned, but they let
her bring home soup and stuff. Very, very good. When my father
died, she had only three dollars to bury him. She was too proud
to take money from the church. You know how poor people were
in those days, and there was no assistance. He died during the flu

epidemic. Everybody died. The bodies were all over the street. There was a poor Portuguese family in back of us, I'll never forget it. They lost their mother, and the poor father, he couldn't handle it after that. I don't know what happened to them. Everybody scrounged. We baked potatoes outside in the woods, and we grew up, and we had a good time.

I graduated from Jamaica Plain High. My mother, she worked until she was about forty or forty-five. Then she said, "Now the kids can take care of me." She retired! And we did. We always took care of my mother. While we were still at home, everybody worked, and you turned in all your money. Mother let you have a nickel a day for a coke. In the sixth grade, they said they were going to give me a double promotion to go to Latin School. My mother said, "Oh no! She's going to quit after grammar school." But I couldn't. I wasn't old enough. Even after high school, I took a couple of courses at Harvard. I got a kick going over there in the summer and taking English.

I always wanted to do bookkeeping and accounting, but when I graduated in 1928, that was just before the crash. They were jumping out of windows, the banks were all closed, and I couldn't beg, borrow or get a job of any kind. People were standing in lines outside the banks trying to get some money out.

Well, I got a job at Rayburn Country Club waiting on tables. It was nice. You lived there, and you didn't make any tips, but they gave you a Christmas present. I didn't stay there long. When things settled down with the market, I realized I was spoiled rotten with waiting on tables. It fascinated me. So I waited on tables. My brothers had all moved to Detroit as die-makers since wages here were bad. They married, had kids, changed partners, more kids, but always home for reunions and their mother! They had her fly everywhere, and she loved it.

I got married in 1938, and my Barbara was born in '39. My husband was very, very charming. He was my high school sweetheart. He wasn't in a hurry to marry me, but then, later on, I heard through the grapevine that he had to marry me because he was afraid somebody else would. Oh yea, that was nice. The Sommers were supposedly in the social register at one time. They were furriers. They were French and German and came to America to settle in Argentina or somewhere in South America. But the boy was born in New York. They came to Boston and opened a fur business. But I had to go to work right away because my husband, he was a play-boy. All the business that my mother-in-law transacted behind closed doors he took care of because he was the oldest son. He looked after his family. I really didn't count. It's funny, that's how life is. And, oh, I had a lot of chances in-between but see, that's what happens when people start going together so young. I think those early associations are bad and, then, when I realized what a sap I was .... He used to go to the bar rooms every night, and I found out that if I walked down the street, heads would pop out of doors and windows. He was paying all the bums off with a glass of beer to give him details of all my activity. Yea, I always said, if you're such a big shot, why don't you drink in the Ritz Carlton with the boys. No. He used to drink in the slimy places where they would all "salaam" and get up. All these things I realized later.

But my daughter had the most marvelous childhood — as much as he neglected me — here's a man-about-town. He used to wheel the baby in the baby carriage to show the boys on the corner. He spent every minute he could with that child. He'd take her and all the kids on the corner to Nantasket Beach in the truck. The kids would come home in tatters, with their teeth knocked out and everything else. But they had a marvelous time. So she had a wonderful, wonderful life.

And then, of course, I divorced him. It was kind of a nasty divorce. It was sometime in 1950, and, would you believe, he got cancer and died six months later. I screwed myself and lost everything. See, divorce is not always the answer. He left me nothing. We didn't even have our own home because he had to make sure his brothers and sisters went to college. He never left anything for Barbara, either. When she found out, she sued the uncle and got a couple of thousand to put on the house she bought later. If I had stayed married, I would have moved into the business.

He was always on the phone talking to this one and that one. One day, a Mr. Jefferson from Jordan Marsh called and said they were looking for a salesgirl. My husband had had a few drinks in him and he was talking, talking. I'm saying, "How about me? How about me? How about me?" Then finally I hear him say, how about my wife? And so I got an interview. I went into Jordan Marsh and started in the fur business. The first coat I sold I had a woman, she must have been a nice lady but she was a bitch. She bought a mouton coat that was very popular at that time for her daughter. And, here, all the brass is sitting there on the couch watching. It was my turn. You know, the beads of perspiration were this big going down my back. I said to myself, "They're not going to love you." So I sold the coat and fit it and put the pins in for the hooks and all the ladies there just watching. They were much older than me. Not one single person would speak to me. So I had nothing to do but sell coats.

Well, I sold so many coats that I was tops in about one month. Mr. Jefferson was so mad, and the president of Jordan's came down and said, "Here's a girl that don't know anything about the business and here in thirty days . . ." They had a big to-do about it. Well, after that, we became steadfast friends when they realized I wasn't after their jobs. And we had wonderful times. Jordan Marsh, at that time, was a store where people only had $300 for a coat, but, if we ever sold a coat for $9,000, he'd give this older lady $150 and he'd say, "Take all the wild asses out to dinner." And we'd go to Purcell's every time we sold a "piece-de-resistance." So I learned the fur business by listening to people talk about animals. Now I like the job at the day care because of the guinea pigs. I can't ever take a day off because of the animals, and now I wouldn't wear fur for anything.

In the meantime, I went through another trauma. Three quarters of the class in Roslindale High was pregnant, and my daughter was amongst them. That was the thing, then, but she got married. They had battles and fights. Terrible. I supported the kids for years, four of them, until Micky straightened out. But I'm so happy that they're not divorced. If I hadn't helped and raised all the kids ... There was no food, no clothes, and I saw to it that they had the best I possibly could. So the big mistake and the only thing I feel bad about is that I went back into waitress work, Durgin Park and Anthony's Pier Four. I was a cocktail waitress for years. I couldn't believe the money we made. As for tips! All the gangsters used to wait for me. They threw tens and twenties like there was no tomorrow. But I ruined myself by that. Had I known that your social security is based on the last years of your earnings, I would have gone back into the stores, as much as I detested them. You know, I had the chances. I opened the department at Bonwit Tellers in 1947 and used to work between here and New York. I had my mother home to baby sit. She was happy. She moved right in with me. I had her until she died. I continued to live in Roslindale, and Micky and Barbara lived with me before they got the house in Stoughton. I worked every place in the city. I worked at Crawford Hollidge, R. H. Stearns, and when the work was seasonal, like nothing doing until after Thanksgiving, I got a job during the summer. I worked Dini's, Nick's. I worked waitressing in summer and furs in winter. I wanted the fast buck, and waitressing was the way to make it.

Barbara had four children, and I have 11 great grandchildren all from the one daughter. All four of the grands got married. We also ran into a little drug problem. It's hard raising kids today. They all live in Stoughton and Easton. They're marvelous. If they had their way, I'd cook Saturdays and Sundays. But this house is too small for everybody. Five little dynamite balls arrive here sometimes, and, when they leave, the house is in tatters. I'd almost sit down and cry. Pages out of the books and everything else, and the cat would be hiding so she wouldn't be tortured. When the kids come now, the cat sits in her box and makes sure that no one steals any of her toys.

Barbara comes to see me every Saturday and Sunday. I say,

"Barbara you don't have to come every week." She says, "Ma, I've got to get away." The twins and Jetta, my grand-daughter, live with her. Her house is always full. One of her daughters, Susan, comes over to get two eggs so that she could make french toast the next morning. She's the thrifty one. Mike has been retired since he's twenty-five. He had the habit of falling off rubbish trucks and suing so he's got a disability. He's not Italian for nothing. But now Barbara does exactly as she pleases. She goes to bingo every night, and she and I go to the horse track. She'd bet on a cockroach if you let her. If Micky objects a little bit, she turns on the tears and gets her way. He does the cooking and housekeeping and pays all the bills with his disability, and he does roofing and stuff. If it were up to Barbara, it would be "pay it next week." But she became manager at King's Department Store and was there for fifteen years. The years roll by. The house in Stoughton that they bought for $11,000 is paid, and, now, it goes for $95,000, an old barracks. I turned in so much while I was in the fur business, but those were the early years. But now I get some SSI, and I get some food stamps, and I'm doing fine.

I worked with Ann Darcy. That's how I got into the foster grandparents. I worked with her in Warmouth's. God, what a place that was. I'll tell you, waitress work was fun — so many wonderful, wonderful people. Then, Ann worked as a foster grandparent at Massachusetts General Hospital, and she wanted me to go there with her. Oh, but that's not my cup 'o tea. I couldn't sleep all night. It's enough I worry about feeding the guinea pigs. She was a hell-raiser. Not one of us ever went to bed before four o'clock in the morning. When they say life begins at forty, you ain't kiddin.' I had more fun from forty on to sixty than I did in my whole life. You don't give a damn about anything. Every night, a bunch of us would meet. There was a dim light down in Chinatown where they used to serve drinks till you ran out of money. No matter when we went, everybody was down there till four in the morning. The man only closed when our money ran out.

When the kids were finally settled down, I got a car, and I took a furnished room here on Joy street. I had nothing of mine in it but a toothbrush, and I lived there for quite a while. Well, finally, when I needed a place to live, who the heck got it for me but Katie, my long-time neighbor, who always thought I could do nothing right. She said, "I think there's going to be a vacancy here," and, you know, she set me all up for it here. It was in '75. I had no furniture, of course, except one bureau. Everything came from the rubbish. I got all set up for no money.

These have been happy years. When I first came here to Beacon Hill, if you walked down to the corner with a pocket book, you got belted in the stomach, and your bag was gone. Now it's all gone condo. There's very little riff-raff around. There's a rooming house next door, but the new manager can handle them, and I cook for them. Oh, I send them over spaghetti and everything else because I think they eat sandwiches. And Tony, the manager, is a good guy to know. He's kept that place straight. Dope peddlers from across the street yell out sometimes, but they don't dare go near the place. Oh, my cat — she's Nosey Rosey. I just love her as you can tell.

I've been at the Day Care since 1986. I play with the kids. They rip me apart. They ask me how my babies are. Kids and animals love me. I can't say any more. We have play-time from 9:30 to 10:30, and I never had a toy in my life. So I'm in my glory. I don't know if it's me or the kids. They have such wonderful things — a whole new crop of toys almost every season. And we play, and we have fun. I never have to reprimand them. They fight to sit beside me on the floor when we have circle time. If there's any extra goodies, I share, and I give them my dessert. Tuesday and Thursday we live it up. We have Chinese food. Sometimes it's frozen chicken cutlets from S.S. Pierce's that are delicious. I buy a box of them for nine dollars and pass them out to my neighbors. They do marvelous things with the kids. They went swimming over at the Josiah Quincy School, right nearby in the same area. They do all the big day trips — and they go to Woolworth's and the Boston Common. That's something else. The times I dread is when we take them on the street cars. I couldn't stand it. I'm afraid they'll dash off the car or something. A few times we took the street car, the starter would get out and count the heads for us. But I always made sure that I went on those trips because I figured they needed me so badly, an extra hand for the kids to hold on to. The trips to the Common and to the stores are something else. We march into the Woolworth's, take the elevator, and they go mad just seeing everything. And a few times we were down at the Aquarium, and I was showing them how to walk home faster. But no, they insist on taking the street car. Most of the kids are Chinese.

The minute they have a little bit of a temperature or something wrong, they call the parents and check and so I saw Adam's father. Very, very charming man. Adam is brilliant. It's funny. Adam, such an American name, and there are Kims and Susies and Celias. They are adorable. I could eat them all up. I had a lot of them who never talked until I went there. They were never away from home. They opened up after a while and hung on to me. I was the only one who could get anything out of them. I didn't do anything — just let everything take its course. Play with them.

I'm going to stay there as long as possible. I love it. They say, "Oh, Jetta, you do so much for us." I say, "What did I do? It's just wonderful being here." If someone's sick, I stay behind with the child until the parent shows up. The Chinese teachers are a little bit too strict, but they mean business. The kids come to me for a respite. You'd be surprised how the Chinese cram them. For a while, I had to go two days to the other class to fill in for a grandparent who was out sick. I marvelled at Mrs. Chin. Those kids have to eat everything off their plate before they drink their milk. They give everybody so much food, I couldn't believe it. There are thirteen kids in my class and about the same in the others. Now there's a new grandmother, a Chinese woman, so every class had a grandparent. I go to rummage sales all the time, and I bring stuff in with me, beautiful silks and bunches of sweaters. There are a lot of poor Chinese so I bring in whatever I can. And, then, there are a few kids all dolled up, of course. But many of them come in with shoes falling apart. So you know, there's not too much money around.

Yes, I think there was a purpose for my life. I think about that many times. "Do things in a little way" it says outside that window. I must do a lot of good. I got some coupons today, and, inside, there was a brand new $10 bill, no name. I know it was Mary, my neighbor. It's all for my birthday. Tony takes care of me. Everybody sweeps the street for me, and so everybody likes me I think. I've spread a lot of sunshine in my own little way, I think. I'm sure that I attained some good. Just the fact that my grandchildren love me so and my daughter and I have such a close association. My kids gave me a trip to Atlantic City. They all chipped in for it, and they said, "Don't worry. If you lose, we'll give you another." When they have it, they're depositing money, and they buy me things all the time.

Now, had my daughter been with me in Atlantic City, I'da had the time of my life 'cause we like to gamble, we like to eat, and we would have seen all the shows. The resorts are building a new Taj Mahal. They even had the nerve to get on the bus when we were leaving and thank us. They said, "We'll take very good care of your money, and you can come and visit any time that you want." They know what they're doing.

You know, the kids sing a song, "Agramina, Agramina, she had two teeth, one went north and one went south." I always think of that when things are too crazy. Two years ago, I fell at Luigi's. Nothing really bad. But later on I found that I had broken a tooth so my dentist fixed it, and it cost about $400. I kept saying I need a bill. His secretary has been with him seventeen years, and I guess she likes me because I can't get a bill from her. I can't go back and complain about my agramina tooth because they won't give me a bill. That's the story of my life. But money is only to spend. If the kids are broke, I give them whatever they want. Only Susie, little greedy balls, she comes over, "Gramma I think I'll take your VCR seeing you're not using it." But it belonged to my grandson Charlie so that's the only time I've said no.

I have a friend, an old associate, I've known him thirty-two years. A Jewish boy. Very, very crummy. He sometimes buys me a half pint of V.O. because I like it before I go to bed. The V.O. ration has been cut off for three days because he knew I got a bottle for my birthday. Little petty things but they bother me. He sits here and smokes, and, the minute he has his three or four beers, he wants to go home to plug his radio in. No matter where I lived, he always lived only two or three doors away. And I have to make him eat so I cook. He doesn't have one single soul left in this world but me so I can't be harsh.

He's about five years younger than me, and he's thinks he's so handsome but I'd hate to see him without any clothes on. He's so thin, and he's got no teeth in him, but he's got plenty of money. He sits there, and he drinks his beers, and he goes to the bathroom, and he washes his hands, and he combs his hair for fifteen minutes. Then another beer, and the same thing again. By that time, I'm ready to throw him out. He was in show business, and I think he was married years ago and had a little girl, but it was too much responsibility for him. He never could take it. Somebody adopted the girl right away. Anything that costs him money, he can't deal with. People are funny. He'll bring me two bananas 'cause I've got to have my potassium. He'll bring two sweet potatoes and two onions. Now, I'll say, "If you're going to go to the Star Market, buy the sale items." So he's lugging cans of tomatoes, and, of course, he'll never eat them so I give them all away. He's so afraid I'll put a little pork into something, but, when he goes to a Chinese restaurant, he lays his ears back on the pork. Weird. Even if you have to fight and bicker a little bit, at least it's company. It's a check point Charlie for both of us.

Just two years ago, when I was at Brandy Peat's, Luigi's sent for me because I was fast. I would go in there at eleven and at three we were out. We'd set up and wash the tables and get ourselves set for the big rush. And, then, we'd go, we'd go — we had to serve the line fast because we didn't want to lose it. It was the most marvelous job. I loved working there because the hours were short, the money good, it's in your pocket and you don't have to declare it. They'd all leave you fifty or seventy-five cents. We made so much money we were afraid to count it, like about $125 a piece. Brandy Peat's was marvelous, too, but it's changed. That's a Bullfinch Building, and they're all landmarks that are being kept. Thank goodness. Boston is changed. R. H. Whites is gone, Stearns, the furriers, I.J. Fox, and all the old stores. The big shows at the Met — it's all gone. And there used to be a Scott's Furrier on Winter Street that had live models in the window all the time, too. It was beautiful.

Every year life gets better and better even though I forget things sometimes. One day one of the teachers said to me, "You can't remember the name of the little boy who gave us all the trouble last year?" I said, "Claudia, sometimes I don't even remember my own name." I don't worry about anything any more. Course the bones get a little bit stiffer, I'm walking a little bit slower and all, but it's good. It hasn't affected me like some people say. It's very important for me to get out of this house, and the foster grandparent is the answer. I'd be going to the race track or something else. Then I'd be in a real jam. It gets me out of the house. I feed three hundred pigeons in the morning, and I go to the Granary Cemetery, and I feed all the squirrels. They eat right out of my hand. I have a full day, talk to the neighbors, feed the birds, and, then, by the time I shuffle to the day care and then go to get my free bread, my days are very full. I buy everything for everybody with coupons at the Star Market. I'm never lonely.

* * *

Jetta Sommer lives a stone's throw from the Massachusetts State House, in a high rent area called Beacon Hill. Her apartment is tiny and filled to overflowing with signs of her brave life.

The Foreign Language Specialists

Elisa Ayala

Elisa Ayala

My life is like a novel. I couldn't really think when my children were young. I took in laundry, ironed; I would take it to the river, wash it, hang it to dry, iron it, and I would run and take it back to town and get more. I didn't get any help from anyone.

It's nice at the day care center. I find the love of many grand-children I don't have near me. Some of the children speak Spanish. When they arrive, they shout, "Grandma! Grandma!" with that love.

I was born in Sabana Grande in a small country area in Puerto Rico in 1923. There were ten of us, four boys and six girls. We lived on a farm where my father grew corn, rice, pigeon peas, and sugar cane. My mother raised pigs, chickens, cows, many cows, and she also milked the cows. We went to school, but we didn't go for long because papa just didn't want us to. Old fashioned people didn't . . . so I only went to the third grade. But I know how to read, write, add, and subtract. I haven't forgotten anything. If I need to speak English, I do it. Even my brothers didn't go to school any more than I did.

When I was young, very young, I helped on the farm. My father planted the seeds, and I pulled the weeds. Then, later, I planted and I harvested. Since my mother had to wash the clothes in the river, I would carry the clothes for her, and I worked in the kitchen. I learned to sew, and I learned to cook. When I got married, I lived in an even worse situation than my parents did. My husband only had day work. I had eight children, but I made them all finish school.

One day, all my family got food poisoning, all except my father and me. My mother and my sister almost died. My mother was sick for two months, and that was when I learned to cook. I was eight years old. I continued to work in the kitchen and on the farm until I got married. When I got married, my father didn't want anybody who was married living there. We had to leave. My father was compadre with his parents. (Compadrazco is the relationship between the parents and godparents of a child. It is an honor to be asked to be the godparent of someone's child, and the fact that you are then a comadre or compadre of the child's parents, is symbolic of a close and enduring relationship. You are then "co-parents.") But he did not want any of his children in the house after marriage.

I didn't want to get married. But I was so innocent, and my parents were so strict. The boy liked me. He was always after me, but I never paid any attention. Oh, it's an ugly story. One day, we went to a wake. I was with my father. Well, he saw us talking, and he called me over and said that since he saw us flirting when was he going to come to the house? The boy said he was coming to see me on Sunday. My father said, if he didn't come over, he would break his back. When he got there, my mother said, when a boy comes over, it is for some reason. No one ever came over just for a visit. Well, he liked me. He would keep coming over to visit. My father kept asking when we were going to get married, when was Emeterio going to let him know. That kept up for a year and three months. When he visited, my mother would sit in the doorway of the kitchen, my father would lie down in a hammock in the middle of the living room. They would put a stool in another doorway for Emeterio and another one in the doorway of the bedroom for me. We never had a private conversation. I lived with him for twenty-six years because my mother told me that, when a woman gets married to a man, only God can separate them. I spent a life of hell with him.

My parents should have asked me if I loved him, if I wanted to get married, but they never did. I had to do what they said. My husband was a carpenter. He drank and smoked a lot. That is what killed him. Always, every day, he would beat me. I would cry, but he was drunk so what could I do? It would get so bad I couldn't open my eyes. I went to a lawyer, and he said , "Why don't you get a divorce?" I was so skinny. By then, my children were all grown up. I had eight children. But, if I told Emeterio I wanted a divorce, he would kill me. When he did find out, he came looking for me at home, but I hid under a pile of bedclothes.

I worked in another house as a maid to buy clothes for the kids. It wasn't much, but it helped. So I kept trying to arrange the divorce. One day, I went to the lawyer and told him all about my situation. He said he would do it. When the lawyer showed Emeterio the notice, he took a machete and ran to the house and said that he had come to kill me. When I heard him at the door, I told my children to say I wasn't home from work yet. Then I hid. He left for the town to find the lawyer and to kill him. He made a big scene at the lawyer's office so they called the police. Well, at that point, one of his brothers arrived and took him home. Then, his family said that if I wanted a divorce he should do it. My parents knew the life he was giving me, but they didn't do anything. They never tried to help. My youngest child was eight, the oldest eighteen or twenty at that time, and I was divorced about three years later in 1966, after twenty-six years of being hit, slapped and beaten. He hit the children, too, but, when they got older, they started confronting him. What happened to me was so terrible, the brutality and the ignorance of my husband and my father. I kept on going and doing what I had to do.

Later, my children all got married and went on. I never got married, but I was with a young man who was very good. But it seems I wanted to make him pay for what the other had done to me. I started making him jealous. Finally, he left and went to New Jersey about the same time that I came to Boston . When I first arrived, I worked in other peoples' houses for a while. I left my youngest daughter in Puerto Rico in school studying social work. I had to send her money and clothes. All the others are here in the U.S. One daughter died after childbirth in Puerto Rico. The others came here in the seventies. The oldest went to work in a hospital laundry, and a year later she was married. Now she lives with her husband and two children in Florida. One son is an electrician. He is also in Florida and has a "mujer," and they have two sons. The others are nearby.

After I was here for about three years, Emeterio came here. He was here once in 1970, and then he came again wanting to get married. I said, I'm not crazy yet. Later, back in Puerto Rico, he got sick. My younger daughter took care of him, and, when she came here, she brought her father with her. She got married, and he lived with her. But then she couldn't take it because he was still drinking so I found him an apartment nearby, and he died there. They found him dead in his place. His mother is still alive. She is more than one hundred. I visit her when I go to Puerto Rico. When Emeterio died, I went there, and they were good to me. We took him there and had a wake.

Now, one of my daughters is sick. She has cancer of the bladder. They treated her, and she got better, but then she got something else. Serious. I'm really worried about her. She is thirty-eight, the same age as the other one when she died. But I have faith in God. She is right here in Jamaica Plain. She is a teacher, and she's the one who studied social work. She has a wonderful husband, a Puerto Rican, and two beautiful children. I hope, I pray she will be all right.

I think of my other daughter who died. I used to send her fifty dollars a week for medicine. Her husband didn't like to work. I went to get her, and I said, "This time I will bring her back either cured or dead." I didn't know what she had. I brought her back dead. Then, he took the child away from me. Now, I'm going to Florida because my daughter is bringing my granddaughter. She's nine years old now, and we're counting on her. When she gets older and realizes how we have acted towards her, maybe she'll look for us. Maybe in May, I can send for her again, and she can stay until July. Her father is calmed down now.

I pray to God not to take another child of mine. My youngest son was in the National Guard. Now he works for the Metropolitan Boston Transit Authority (MBTA). He sees me crying because of what's happening to my other daughter, and he says, "Don't worry. You'll bury two or three more, and you'll still be here. You have to be strong, have courage, because as the youngest, I would prefer to send all my brothers and sisters before you." You have to understand him. He loves them all, and helps them all. He has a woman and three children. She is a very good mother. My children are all very close.

I live alone, and I get Social Security Implement(SSI) from when I got sick from a nervous illness when my daughter died. I didn't want my husband's social security. I pay only $155 for rent here, and I get $454, and so it's O.K. I go to the day care, and I get my mind off things there.

It's nice there. I find the love of many grandchildren I don't have near me. Some of the children speak Spanish. They are only four-year olds. Some are even younger. When they arrive, they shout "Grandma! Grandma!" with that love. They jump on me and throw their arms around me. They kiss me. There is one Latina who is two years old. I help her with the coloring. There's one little girl, Teeni, they call her, she has stolen my heart. She's two also. She lives near here. In my room at the day care, there are nineteen or twenty children. They are so good, so beautiful, so lovely. I love them all.

I'm sixty-four now, and I'm tired of living. I don't know. There are friends who want me to go to parties, dancing, but I don't like that. I stay here sewing, knitting. I'm doing this (shows a table-cloth). I take care of my plants. I moved here four years ago, in '83, and I like it, but I'm scared of the elevators so I'm thinking of moving downstairs. Sometimes the elevators go crazy, and I have high blood pressure. Once, I got stuck, and I almost died. I yelled and yelled, I kicked and I wet my pants. When I do my shopping, my son comes, or my daughter or my grandchildren. The guards help me sometimes. They have guards here because there was a problem with drugs, robberies. Now it's better. If I have a dollar, I don't tell anyone.

I think God has sent me here for many things. He likes me to help people who need it, and the children who give me so much pleasure. When I was raising my children, I didn't even have enough time to tell them a story or sit down to play with them. My time went to getting the firewood, washing in the river, bringing water from the well, feeding the pigs - all the work. All of them came to my bed when their father wasn't there. When they heard him get home, they would all run to their beds like little mice and pretend to be asleep. My life is like a novel. I didn't really think in those days. I just worked, worked, worked. "That's why we love and adore you because you were a mother who struggled for us and gave us understanding," That's what my two sons say to me.

I never tried to get my daughters to sacrifice themselves to a man like some mothers do. I never had to go to court or a police station. I think I got my strength from my heart. And when you have children, you have to struggle for them. And they all call me. When my daughter-in-law had a gall bladder operation, she called me, and I went to take care of four children for two weeks; six, five, three and a newborn. The daughter who lives in Jamaica Plain is the closest to me, but all my children, they call, I call them. They can't come over too much because they work. My son, who works for the MBTA, will be coming over later tonight. They are all good kids.

The ones in Florida call — one on Saturday, the other on Sunday. The one in Buffalo calls me every two weeks, and the one in Puorto Rico calls me every fifteen or twenty days, I do have love around me, that's true. If the one in Buffalo calls and says, "I need you," no problem. I don't speak English, but I'll find someone to get me a ticket, and the next day I'll be there. If I need cash at night or on the weekend, I call my daughter. She has a bank card, and she gets it for me. I can pay all my bills for cable and everything. I bought a set of pans for $1400 which I still have in its box. I pay $57.37 a month for that. They will go to the first granddaughter to get married.

I'm not like some people who are all upset, who say, "Oh, I'm getting older." Getting older is a natural thing. As for my grand-children, if they want to get married, they should. If they don't, they shouldn't. The way life is today, they should do what they get pleasure from. I remember my life too well. I lived with that man, and, if he said, "This is the way it is," that was it. If I said no, he would have kicked me in the face. When my daughters told me they were in love, I would try to find out about the boyfriend. When they told me they were going to get married, I never asked anyone when. I always said, "Think about it carefully. Once you've put your foot in it, it's hard to take it out."

When I think of everything that has happened to me, I think of how nice it is to die. When you die, all your problems are over. You rest in peace. Everything is over. How nice! I'll tell you something. I'm a Catholic, I'm not a believer of anything else but, you know something, when my daughter died, I was sick with my leg. It's a rather long story but . . . One day, my granddaughter and her cousin were playing on the floor with their dolls. I stood up and accidently stepped on one. When I turned, the doll's hand hit me here on my leg. Nothing happened but later, I felt pain. It started to burn and then it swelled up and I got two blisters. They took me to the hospital, and the doctor prescribed some dressing and told my son to take me to a psychiatrist. I said I was there for my foot and that I wasn't crazy and my foot wasn't crazy either. But that doctor was right. They took me to an Argentinian psychiatrist. He worked and worked with me, and my leg got better. I went to him with my anger and my tears because I spent days crying. It was only two months since my daughter died. It's been four years now, and I go every month or two months. The idea of not going to him, I would die.

I believe that even when you die, you still hear. Because once I said to my daughter, the one who died, if it's true that you loved me, look at my leg and try to make it better. If it doesn't get better, I'll lose it. And stop calling me on the phone. At that time I thought she was calling me. Then, I got better. My sweet moments are when my son can get the time to come to see me. Then I hear the door, and it's him. What joy! Even if he just stays for a little while. Or, when my daughter calls and says, "Cook me dinner on Sunday." Then, she comes, and I fix things she doesn't know

110

how to make. She comes with her husband and her children. For me, that is happiness. My daughter's house, my daughter-in-law's house, I'll go there and cook and stay for a month. When I leave, they cry.

At the day care, I have sweet moments too — the children, they give me so much. Sometimes I cook a Thanksgiving dinner for the whole center. I bring it from home all ready to eat. I feel they are my second family. The children are so beautiful and so good.

Angela Celestino

Angela Celestino

Well, I'm so old what other plan can I have except to prepare for death, be in harmony with God. When I die, God will take me to heaven to live next to Him and the angels. That is the promise that Christ made.

I was born in 1903, in the southern part of Santo Domingo where my parents were born. In those days, women worked only in the house. My father was a shoemaker. I had one sister from my mother, but she died before I was born. When I was about eight, my mother died of cancer, and my father got married and had more children.

The lady my father married finished raising me. Later, my father and step-mother went to Port-au-Prince in Haiti with me when I was twelve. That is where I learned to speak French. There were political problems in Haiti so my father got involved and moved us there. My father was not a shoemaker then. I'm not sure, but I think he worked in the police department. The people loved the new president very much, but a year later the palace was bombed, and he was killed and, thousands of people died in the bombing. The new president was Tancrede Auguste.

I got married at sixteen. I was very unhappy. I didn't have a mother, and, with that stepmother, I was very unhappy. So that was what pushed me to get married so young. I met a military man, a sergeant. He was about twenty-five when I married him. He wasn't very good to me, no — not very good. He had a very bad temper, very bad. He hit me many times. I had two children with him, but one is dead. When he grew up, he studied aviation in Port-au-Prince, got married, and left. He had problems in the country, so he went to Venezuela. In 1951, he went out in his plane, and they never found him. He was thirty-five, born when I was sixteen. My second son was born four years later.

My husband was an officer; he had been promoted. I had a nice house. I had servants. I lived very well. I was quite a lady! But his character! He was very domineering. There was this thing with his family; they never liked me. He was a light skinned man with good hair. They didn't think I was good looking enough, and I only went to elementary school. I couldn't go to school when I was married. Nowadays, yes, but not in those days. My second son also studied aviation.

When I was about twenty-two, my husband and I separated. That is why I went back to Santo Domingo. He had found another woman, and she took control of him. He got a divorce. I went to the house of some aquaintances when I went back, but I was destroyed. I had to leave my sons with him because I was helpless. My father had died, and so I had nobody. When I got to Santo Domingo, I went through a lot of poverty and misery. I went from way up high and ended up on the bottom and without my children. I went to work as a servant in a house. They paid very little. Very little. Then, about four or five years later, I married the father of Gilberto, my son, who is in Santo Domingo now, the one I'm going to see soon. I never saw my son who died in the airforce after I left. Both of them used to write me, and I managed to send them letters through a friend of mine. Then, when my son died in Venezuela, Raymond wrote and told me the sad and painful news. I didn't see him until 1959 when I went to Port-au-Prince. When I got, there he was married with five children. I stayed there for four years. While I was in Port-au-Prince, my first husband would come and talk to our son. Every time he came, I would leave. I just wanted to be with my son.

I married my second husband in 1929. He had a business. He sold things in the street. Of course, things weren't so good financially, but he was good man, Andres. But he died very soon, and he never saw his son. There was a cyclone in 1930, and he was killed. I raised my son, Gilberto, alone. I did housework at first, and then I sewed. I was a dressmaker. I spent forty years sewing.

I never married again because during that time I converted to Adventism. You can get married, but there just wasn't a man who believed what I believed. I sent my son to school, but I couldn't educate him like I would have liked to because I had to leave the capital where I lived. I went to the east to work as a dressmaker. There, he went to elementary school. In those days, poor people only went to elementary school and then to work. At first, he was an errand boy. Later, when he was thirteen or fourteen, he worked with heavy equipment, tractors. I kept sewing, and he was working. So from then on things started getting better. He was a good son, a very good son.

When I went back to Port-au-Prince, Gilberto stayed in Santo Domingo. He was grown. He had a wife even though he was only nineteen.Very young. His life was better because then he went from being a helper to a heavy equipment operator. They had a daughter who is a young lady now. His wife was a good woman, but they separated because he became an Adventist and she didn't want to. It was easier to separate because they were not legally married, just living together. Many people would just live together without getting married. After he went into the church, the girl he met was also in the church, and he married her. They are still together. They have been married for twenty-three years. They still live in Santo Domingo. (Angela brings out a picture and shows each of the sons and their children.)

After Trujillo died, in 1962, I went back to Santo Domingo. Then, during the time of Papa Doc, since Raymond's father was a politician in opposition to Papa Doc, Papa Doc (Duvalier) killed him. And, when his father was killed, Raymond put in the papers to come to this country. As soon as he got his visa, he left immediately because he was political and against Duvalier. Everyone who was against Duvalier was killed. Raymond came to this country and left his family in Haiti, hidden. He only had a visa for himself. Then, he petitioned for her as a resident, and a year and a half later he brought her to New York with their five children. Late in 1965, I went to Puerto Rico to work there. I had friends there. I did housework because I had high blood pressure, and I didn't want to work in a factory. I got my room, and all my comforts. And, every six months, I would go back to Santo

Domingo to visit with Gilberto. I would go back and forth many times. When my visa expired, I contacted Raymond, and he said, "Come here, mama. I have a house here, and you can come to my house." But Gilberto was sick and I didn't want to leave so I went back to Santo Domingo and lived with him until Raymond came to get me. They told him, you can take her if you get her residency. He did get me it in about two years.

Now, here I am. I could be doing better, but I always have to be sending money there to Gilberto. The children have all gone to school, but two aren't out of high school yet. Gilberto is very important in the church. The last time I went, he said to me, "Ay, mama, I don't know how I am still alive because the cross that God has given me is very heavy. I work so hard, and my wife is sick all the time." I would like to bring her here to see doctors, but I can't because I live off the government.

I came here when I was already very old, seventy-five, and so I have lived on Social Security. I get $400, and I pay $130 for rent. And I have to pay for phone calls to New York and to Santo Domingo. Sometimes I get bills for sixty or eighty dollars. But I deprive myself of everything. You see how I live. I deprive myself of everything so that I can help out because that woman is so sick. He works very hard, but his family is very big. People give me clothes. Look at these. And I take everything there. I take it there myself. I got a special price for three trips this year.

It was through Elisa Ayala that I found out about foster grandparents. I work at Nazareth Child Care Center. It's right here, close by. After I had my eye operation, I wasn't able to work. When I come back from the trip, then I'll go back. Because I like my kids very much. I work with a group of kids. They always need me. I get it for them because the teachers have to stay with the whole class. So it is, "Angela, get me this" or "Angela, get me that." When it's lunch time, I bring the lunch. When it's time for their naps, I would take them to their cots and sit with them and sometimes rub their backs. When we go out for walks, I would go with them and hold their hands. My kids are three years, and two years. I take them to the bathroom and help them wash. I love those kids, yes, and they love me, too. They call me, "Gramma Angela." I have eight in my class. The teacher I work with is wonderful. Maybe I'll go in a couple of days before I leave. I want to tell them where I am going and say good-bye. I'll get lots of kisses.

The forty-four dollars helps since I haven't worked for a while. So many people talk badly about this country! Listen, I get on my knees and ask God to bless this country. When I get back, I'll go back to my kids. Sometimes I see them walking by here, and I want to go to them. I love them. I always feel full of energy when it comes time to go to my kids. I love them. I have lots of friends because everybody loves me here, but I don't speak English. I met Elisa Ayala in the Alianza Hispana, in the elderly group, and we became very good friends. It's a wonderful organization and helps everybody, all the Spanish speaking people.

What I believe is that God has a plan for everybody. So, if that's the way it is, He must have a plan for me, too. Well, I'm so old, what other plan can I have except to prepare for death, to be in harmony with God. When I die, God will take me to heaven to live next to Him and the angels. That is the promise that Christ made. I have preached the gospel. I have been in charge of churches. I have prepared many people for baptism. I have walked very far preaching the gospel in my country. And I have worked hard in that way. I always say that I don't live for myself, I don't live for myself.

When I go to Santo Domingo, of all that I take, clothes, I give it to the people. I give it to my brothers who need it, the neighbors. An Adventist brother takes me to the airport. And my son picks me up in Santo Domingo. Sometimes I stop in New York and visit my son, Raymond.

But listen, I feel good. I go out in the morning even if it's snowing, if there's ice. I put on my boots, my coat, and I walk. I take the train, I take the bus, I walk. I feel good. Sometimes I go to the doctor, and he gives me a physical, everything. I say, "Doctor, are you going to give me some medicine?" He says "You're in better shape than me.

You say you are eighty-two." Because I was eighty-two then. I say, "I don't *say* it. I *am* eighty-two." He says, "You are set to live to one hundred. According to your record, you can live twenty years more." It's God's blessing, God's blessing.

* * *

Angela lives in elder housing which features a lovely lobby where much socializing goes on. Her apartment has that easy welcoming atmosphere. When we walked in, every stick of furniture was covered with clothes. She was packing three huge cartons, and she had already filled an enormous duffle bag, all stuffed with clothes. Here is an 84 year old woman whom everyone awaits. She is a woman, symbolic of the culture of her land and her language. Despite all that happened to her, she is still full of love. She escorted us down into the lobby, and all the people got up to shake her hand. Even though she doesn't speak English, they seem to be able to communicate with each other. She carries so much in her mind and in her heart.

David Peguero

David Peguero

I expect to finish my life peacefully. I'm a Catholic, but I'm not a fanatic. I've always thought that fanaticism was bad. I've always had the philosophy that you have your beliefs, whatever they are, and I respect yours as well as mine.

I'm very proud that the children love me. They are four and five, and, then, there are some who have finished and are going to school, and I don't even recognize them, and they come up to me on the street and hug me.

I was born June 23, 1918 in the Province of San Francisco de Macoris in Cotui, in the Dominican Republic. My father had a store where he sold cocoa beans and other provisions. There were thirteen of us brothers and sisters, and I was the second born. My father lived to be eighty-seven and my mother sixty-seven. They both died in Santo Domingo. Our family lived well for a while, but after 1930, when I was about thirteen, the so-called general Trujillo came to Santo Domingo. Then things started to change. My father had a lot of cocoa beans that he had bought, and the price fell through the floor so my father went into bankruptcy. He owed a lot of money.

It was a hard time, but my parents sent me to school in La Vega, a private school. For Holy Week, I went back home, and a sister of mine invited me to a party in another neighborhood. I was a young man who didn't used to go out anywhere, but there, I met this friend of my sister, named Zeneida, who was separated from her husband. He was there, too, and when he saw me, he thought I liked her. All I heard was, "They're going to kill you!" and I raised up my arm. There is still the scar there. He came at me with a knife that was sixteen inches long. But I took it away with my other hand, and I knifed him. It went in one side and out the other. His cousin, who saw what happened, knew what she had to do. She wrapped up my wound and took me to a small town where we hid. It turned out that I had killed that cousin of hers, and their uncle

122

was the mayor of that town. She told me she would talk to him, and she did. She said, "Don't be scared. He will have to kill me first before I let anything happen to you." Her uncle followed us to that little town. She told him that her cousin had gone too far and that I was the nephew of the governor of San Francisco de Macoris. She said, "If you are going to do something with your machete, you can start with me." She was very brave and very intelligent.

I was in the hospital for a week when the prosecutor ordered me to jail. But I was still a student and only seventeen. The warden there was a friend of my uncle so I was never treated like a prisoner. Every day, a guard would come and take me to school and then to my house and, in the evening, back to the prison. One day Anibal Trujillo, the only one of that family who was any good, came to our province to buy cows from my uncle. They told him what happened to me. That very day, he sent a captain to get me out. He took me to his farm, and he asked me, "Do you know how to milk cows?" I said, "Yes, of course." He said, "You are no longer in jail, but you must continue school." Then, that captain told me that, as of that day, I was a corporal in the Army. Later on, General Trujillo took me out of the farm and made me a guard at the Army headquarters. Then, I started going out with friends and doing everything. I hadn't ever smoked or had a drink before that. I forgot all about school.

But Anibal was looking out for me all the time. As soon as he could, he took me back to the farm and told me that I would drive the truck each day, taking milk, 5,000 bottles, to the capital. Anibal was a really good man. He would give work to all the prisoners when they got out, and he would pay them well, too. Soon after, there was a big battle at the farm over the animals, and it ended up that the brothers were fighting each other over that farm and the animals. General Truillo sent soldiers, and they killed everyone on the farm. Fortunately for me, I was on the road or I would have died also. When I came back to the farm, I brought back no animals that trip, so I just left quickly and went to Santiago. I met Pedro Trujillo, another brother, who took me to his farm which was not far away. I didn't understand what was going on. A week later, he ordered his men to take me to the prison where he had his office. I found out that Anibal was completely wiped out and had to leave the country.

I stayed with Pedro and served in the Army. I became a sergeant in the traffic police at first, and, then, Pedro transferred me to the National Police. I stayed there until 1959 when I had completed my service, and I retired. I was forty years old. I was in Trujillo's army because I knew his brother, Pedro. That saved my life because it was so easy to be in the wrong place, and I never understood what was going on — lots of killing. I didn't know anything about government. I just was poor and needed "comida" (food).

I had married a very young girl, Flor Maria, when I was about twenty-eight. She was only fourteen. I met her through her sister who lived in Santo Domingo, but she lived in Puerto Rico. We had three children. We separated in 1949 because she wanted to go back to Puerto Rico, and I wanted to stay in Santo Domingo. She lives in New York now. Well, I was smart. I bought her a ticket, and I took her to the airport. From there, I went right to the court house, and I made out an Act of Abandonment by a mother. Later, she came back with her sister and a lawyer and asked for the kids. They went to court, and the judge asked me why I had taken her children away. Then, he wanted to know where the children were, and I told him with my parents in Cotui. When he found out how old she was, only nineteen, he said she was a minor with no rights. The judge asked me what I wanted of her, and I said I wanted nothing. It was over, and I had my children. Flor Maria went back to Puerto Rico. Later on, though, I had to let the children go back to her. It was too hard for me.

Now, I always see her, now that we are older. Just two weeks ago, she was here. She has had to go through a lot. She complains that the older children (ours) don't love her. They were raised by a Chinese woman and, for them, that woman is their mother. It was hard for her and for them. She comes to visit, and we all three get along.

After our separation, I married Ignacia del Carmen who had a daughter, and we had a son together, Pedro David. He lives here now and has two degrees in engineering for computers. He's very intelligent. I left Santo Domingo in 1971. I had been in and out many times. I lived in Puerto Rico, I lived in New York for about two and a half years, and then I went back to live in Puerto Rico. During those years, I worked as a mechanic. That is my profession, fixing cars. I had a garage there. I came to the U.S. in '78, to my sons. I had references from the Army here because I had worked for the Army for one year in 1965, so my son, my second son, came here first, and, later, he petitioned for me. I didn't have any problems getting here. I brought my wife and my other son, too. Antonio, Santiago and Pedro are here now. But I am not a citizen because I don't know English. If not for that, I would be.

I lived with my sons, all three of them. My son Pedro had two houses in Jamaica Plain. I told my sons, "I'm not going to work as a mechanic anymore. Just look at my hands." But I also knew a lot about cooking. I went to work at The Magic Pan, downtown Boston as a dishwasher at first and then at salads. Then, they asked if I knew how to make dressings, and I said yes. And, finally, they asked if I wanted to work as a cook, and I said yes. They gave me a job making Italian soup. I stayed there for three years. I had started at $2.85, and I ended at $7.00 an hour. Then, I had a breakdown. I was sick, getting along in years. I had a doctor who had been seeing me for eight years. She recommended that I not work any longer.

I've always had this thing. I don't know if it's good or bad, but I've always liked to live alone, not with family. I didn't know how to speak English, but, at The Magic Pan, I found out about the Boston Housing Authority so I went to the office with a young woman who worked with me and filled out an application, and they gave me a place in the tower. (It is a tall building in the Spanish area providing housing for elders.) I was there for five years. Then, I moved here, just near Jacobo. While I was living in the tower, a woman there told me about the program to work with children. I still didn't know any English, but they told me I could work with children who spoke Spanish. I've been working for six years now.

Now I have a problem. I want to bring my daughter here from Santo Domingo. She is living with my brother there now, but I want her here. She is a daughter I had with another woman who was killed by a car, but Ignacia loves her, too. I adore her because she is my only daughter. It's different with us Spanish men and women. Ignacia is never jealous.

Now, since I've gotten old, I'm taking care of my kids, the little kids at the day care center. I took Jacobo there, and he loves it, too. I do so much that I don't know how to tell you. All those things (pointing to children's paintings, little clay figures) I do with the children in the school. I'm very proud that the children love me. They are four and five. Then there are some who have finished and are going to public school, and I don't even recognize them. They come up to me on the street and hug me. At the center, I sit on the floor with the kids and help them build blocks and make towers. I tell stories in Spanish, and I just love them. They are all so beautiful. If I go to Florida one day, I will find another day care so I can be with children there.

I've had a lot going on in my life — a long time. I'm a Catholic, and I believe, but I'm not a fanatic. I've always thought that fanaticism is bad. I've always had the philosophy that you have your beliefs, whatever they are, I respect them. I am not frightened of death, no. I've never thought that I was going to die. I'm just not scared of it. When God wants to take me, that's it. You just have to wait for it, whatever day it is.

Ignacia's mother is ninety-seven and Ignacia is only fifty-nine. Her mother lives alone in the country and does everything herself. She doesn't even wear glasses. So you never know what is waiting for you. Ignacia, my wife, never says no to me, to anything. She always says, "Whatever you say is good." So I think I am here to love everybody. I loved many women, and I still do and I love the children. You know, after I left the army, I lived on the road, and so I had a love at every town. I think that because I loved, I was able

126

to survive. Now I am happy with my own children and the little ones at the day care center. I have what I need in my life.

Jacobo Vasquez

Jacobo Vasquez

When I was six, I started making little guitars out of sticks and pieces of wood. So I knew how to play a little. I kept getting better and better. I played folk music on this guitar which is called a "cuatro" (a small guitar with four strings). I learned to play by myself. God showed me.

I'm there for any child who gets knocked down or hurt by another child. I go right over, and I rub him, and I play with him until he quiets down. I'll tell you, I feel so happy because I'm with children, innocent children.

I was born in Calle, Puerto Rico, on April 2, 1919, and my parents were born there also. My father worked in the farm, and my mother worked in the house. I had a sister who died before I was seven, and my mother became what they said, sick in the head. I had two brothers who died before my sister so my mother didn't have any more children, only me. My mother was sick the rest of her life, but she lived to be about eighty. My mother lived with her brothers in the countryside some of the time and then with us sometimes. I was always with my father. Then, one day the San Filipe Hurricane came, and my father was knocked into a tree, and that left him handicapped.

We left for Guayama to find work. I was only twelve then, and I had gone only through a few months of the second grade. My father was not able to do too much, but I worked in a furniture store. We didn't stay too long. There were some problems. We left to go to the coast to a town called Arroyo, and I started to work in an engineer's house as a gardener. My father worked for a lady as her gardener. We were there only four months when my father began to feel worse. The lady he worked for helped me, and we took him to a hospital in Guayama. I think he had cancer in his throat. He couldn't swallow. He was probably about eighty at that time, and I was about fifteen. I'm not really sure of ages somehow. He was in the hospital for a while when I decided to get a job so I could at least buy things for him. I went back to Calle for about one week. When I returned he was dead. Now, I was on my own.

I really loved my old man. He was very close to me. I went to work in a house selling what they call "empanadillas," (turnovers usually with a meat filling. It is common in Latin America for people to cook things like this and sell them on the streets.) I did this for about two and a half years in Guayama. I could see that I couldn't live on that so I decided to go to the coast, to Colonia Julia and work cutting cane. I had an aunt there. I could stay with her, but I had bad luck. She had sixteen children, and I got what they called yellow fever. But the boss and the mayordomo really liked me and took care of me because I was an orphan. The boss took me to his house, and I lived with them about three years.

I haven't mentioned something. When I was six, I started making little guitars out of sticks and pieces of wood. So I knew how to play a little. I kept getting better and better, and by the time I came to the coast, I was a musician. I played folk music on this guitar which is called a "cuatro" (a small guitar with four strings). I learned to play by myself. God showed me. I have two tapes of hymns that I made for the church. So, when I lived with that man, I already knew how to play. His name was Aurelio Ortiz, but we all called him Yoyo. When he found out I could play, he really went nuts. He was so excited! We had a party, and I played for everyone.

Some time later, I moved to Guayama, to the house of the Galimanos. They were very rich people, millionaires. I worked in the garden and in the house. I was over twenty by that time, and I stayed there for four years. I fell in love with a girl in my hometown which was not far away, and I kept seeing her. She was having problems with her parents and wanted me to take her away. I did take her to live with me, but her parents came and took her back. It seems she suffered a lot because her parents were so strict and sometimes cruel. I just went on by myself. I was again without work. My father had told me not to do what he did, not to work on the land. So I learned to be a carpenter, and I got married to Luisa. We had six children; two of them died very young, and I don't know why. They said it was a teething disease, but ... The other four are grown now; my daughter is a teacher, the next boy is a master plumber and a minister in a Pentecostal church. The next one is in New York. He is an interpreter in a factory, and he works as a mechanic. And the youngest is also a minister, an Adventist minister.

They are all married. Well, Luisa and I got divorced. There are certain things that happen that one should not talk about. I was living in Calle, my home town, and I started working in Bayamon where they were starting to build a building like the Prudential, big, and made of glass. I had some good friends, good people with influence. On Christmas Eve, I went to a party and there I met that lady right there (pointing to his wife). I was about thirty years old, I think. We've been married thirty-eight years now, and we've raised ten children, two were from Julia's first marriage. Now, they are all married except for Miquel. He's the youngest.

In 1983 or '84, we decided to move from Puerto Rico. I was building a house for my mother-in-law, and I was tired, tired. I said to Julia, "When I finish this house we'll go." Our daughters were here, and we could join them. I never finished the house really because I had a fall, and I broke four ribs. So my sons finished it, and, then, when I felt better, I said to Julia, "Let's just start travelling, even if it's just here and there." Because after that fall they gave me social security. I haven't worked since. That was about 1975. Well, we came here to our daughters, and we went back and forth between them, until finally, we talked to someone from the government, and he helped us. We got this place, and we pay $315 a month. Between the social security and SSI and the help I get for my son who can't work, we get along. We don't need anymore.

My religion teaches me a lot of good. I have come to know a God of love, a God of mercy. I have always liked to do good and help people. I think that, when one is born, you bring something special to the world. I thank God for the happiness in my life, for the many people who have helped me. I never expected to have so much in this life, a lot of happiness, many good friends, and my family. There are people who look to God, but while looking to God, they also look to the world. They mix up the two things. They look to the Lord and to their family, but the minute there's a party or something, they go right there. I mean parties of the world where they start to drink and flirt around with other people's husbands and wives. I look to the Lord to save my soul. It is prohibited to drink, to smoke and to bet. And we have learned that there are certain things that do harm to the body. The word of God says that one's body is the temple of the Holy Spirit. We must make sure that our bodies are clean for the Lord. We know that caffeine is harmful, so I stop drinking it. I take juice, decaffeinated coffee or chocolate. I must not eat pork either.

I have my retarded son. He is 24 years old. He goes to Morgan Memorial, and he calls it his job. We are trying to teach him how to write his name, and we are trying to prepare him for the future so that he can deal with people because right now he won't even talk to other people. With us, he never stops talking but with others he is very shy. He has a social worker. I hope they will help him so that he can live his life.

When I am at the Day Care Center, I feel such a lot of love. It makes me think of when I was raising my own children. And, when they come to me, it makes me want to cry from happiness. They call me Jacobo, Jacobo. They all come running to me. I'm only like a grandfather counselor. The teachers really take care of them. I'm there for any child who gets knocked down or hurt by another child. I go right over, and I rub him, and I play with him until he quiets down. I'll tell you I feel so happy because I'm with children, innocent children. When I'm with those children, I never get bored because how could you? Yes, I play for them sometimes and we sing. I love every one of them. I hope I can be with them for a long time.

* * *

Jacobo lives with his wife and son in public housing in the South End of Boston. Their apartment is small and filled with many decorations of their religious and Spanish culture. While we spoke, Julia fixed a lovely supper for us; a crowning touch to all we felt there.

Chapter 2
At Our Public Schools

At Our Public Schools

Twelve of the thirty-one Boston foster grandparents who chose to work in public schools were interviewed for this book. Among them, three were language specialists; one spoke Chinese, one Spanish and one, Olga Yi, spoke both those langauges. Explaining her experience with the children in the kindergarten, Olga says, "They don't know how to write their name, but, because they're small, I can teach them. We have Chinese and Vietnamese in my class - the other rooms have others. Because of my background, I work with those kids. They sing Chinese songs, and even the American kids sing Chinese. Some kids are so nice. They are so good when they ask me something — what is that? I like it. One kid asks me why I speak Spanish, and I have to explain everything."

Besides the children who need the "language specialists," others need help in reading, math or appropriate school behavior. Some students also need help with speech and language, especially if no "special needs" teachers are available. Those grandparents who select a public school usually prefer to work with older children and in a setting where the students' concrete results are their reward.

The emphasis on "teaching" diminishes the time for personal exchange; nevertheless, "the magic connection" finds its way into the one-to-one relationship that develops. In an elementary school, Florence Plovnick works with a second grade child who "may be demoted to the first," she tells us. "I sat next to him and kept complimenting him. . . he did all his work and wanted to know if I was going to come back later. Then, I found out that this particular child is seven years old, and he has a key to his house. Nobody is at home when he gets back from school. This is the reason this kid is this way. When I have any extra time, I go down to that classroom and ask the teacher if she needs me, and she always points to him. I think, if I can give him this personal attention, he could come right back to where he should be."

"Mrs. P." as the kids call her, is a "floater," used in different classes for individual children who, for any number of reasons, are slow in learning. Often foster grandparents find themselves filling in where professionals used to be. They observe their children carefully and consult with the teacher for follow-through. The tiny duo they form with the child is a flexible base where the teacher can participate directly at her discretion.

Inner city students come from varied backgrounds and cultures and many are bused long distances each day. Since most public school foster grandparents also must use bus systems, neighborhood connections rarely occur. During the four hour day, two children, selected by the teacher, have a grandparent by their side. A "resource center" or the library affords quiet time alone. The grandparent may also sit with the child in the regular classroom and help her or him grasp what is going on, what is being asked and how to begin to participate. Whenever possible, grandparents reach out to the entire class to extend communication and stimulate common interests.

Dorothy Bibby tells the children in her fifth grade class about the boys' clubs and boy scouts. She says, "Some parents are never home. They work, and their children don't see them much; it's sad, it's really sad. They're up against it. You'd be surprised to know how many children at school only have one parent . . .It's hard for a woman too, to raise children by herself. One little girl wrote a sentence for the word `grieve'. 'I felt deeply greeve when my father died.' She spelled it wrong, but I felt something so deep, it touches you; the things that go through their minds. She's about ten or eleven."

Each foster grandparent is encouraged to use his or her particular talents to help the children learn. There are testimonials aplenty, both oral and written, to their ability to "tune in" and get close to a child who has been withdrawn and insecure. Their work is seen as a divine dedication.

In reading their life stories, one can easily fathom their choice of "being with the kids;" the gratification of indulgence in the children of their time. "Are you coming back tomorrow?"

Dorothy Bibby

Dorothy Bibby

I don't feel, in any way, remorseful, nor do I have regrets growing older with my incapacity. I shall ever believe it was a part of HIS perfect plan for my life for me to find the foster grandparent program, and have you accept me as I am. My life is richer by far than it was in my earlier days.

I was born in Boston in 1923, and graduated from Girl's High School and went right to work. I'm the oldest of six children, four boys and two girls, and I lived with both my parents in the South End. My mother didn't work until the youngest was in high school. My father always worked - the same job all his life. Ironically, he had a stroke, too, like me. There wasn't much known about strokes in those days, about teaching them how to walk, so he just vegetated. It was a sad ending to his life. I saw all of that going on. When he died, I wasn't there. I wasn't living at home then.

I have only one brother and one sister alive now. She lives in Seattle, Washington. In fact, I've just come from seeing her. My brother is in Connecticut. I have loads of neices and nephews. I don't know know how many. I lost three brothers in the span of ten years, all of bad heart conditions. All of them died before they reached forty. I went to see my sister because she had a heart attack. I never would have gone this year because I couldn't afford it. She still has three of her eight children at home. She's better now, but she can't do much. She's only fifty-four.

I was fortunate, in a way, when I was young. I used to go to Newport every summer with my brother who was two years older than I. My grandfather was there, and I got the treat of all the kids. They couldn't send us to summer camp because there was no money. But that made me happy, going to Newport. I still have a lot of friends there. I don't like the changes I see in Boston. Oh, it's awful. All the beautiful views shut off down at the waterfront. I go to Bay State Lobster to get fish, not too expensive, and I see all those changes.

I am going to see a new doctor, new to me, to see if he can help my eyes because, if I don't do that, I won't be able to continue in school. My vision is terrible. I can read, but I have to hold it almost to my nose, and I'm not seeing it too clearly then. My other doctor offers nothing. All I know is that, when I used to pay cash for things, I used to get better service. Now, I'm on Medicaid, you take what you get. Oh, I don't know if that's really honest, but I'm so nervous about losing my sight.

When the war started, I put in a lot of applications to the Telephone Company, but by the time they called me, I had gone to New York. I did come back to Boston. I went to steno-typing school, but I never got any work in that field. I didn't know the people to look for or the right places to go. You know what I mean? I worked in C. Crawford Hollidge for years, and it just kind of ruined me. I couldn't afford those things that I saw. We were working for pennies. I worked there about twelve years. I left and went to the Bell Shops and after that to the Olympia Flower Shoppe, and I stayed there forever until I got the stroke. And then, they refused to take me back. I was just told by a man who I know that I could go back there now if I wanted, but I don't want to work like that now. I can't. I told him that I enjoy being around the young people in the school atmosphere. It's really wonderful. It makes me wish I had studied to be a teacher when I was young. I have many cousins who are teachers, but it never crossed my mind that that would be what I wanted. I really wanted to be a social worker, and I had no one to advise me.

I guess I was different in lots of ways. I really didn't want to get married because all I could see was a house full of babies. I never wanted that because I was around babies all my life when I was young. I didn't get married until I was forty. I don't like to think about it. My mother and father were dead, and I had an apartment alone, and I didn't know much about being alone after such a big family and all. My sister was married, and, I don't know, he seemed to have a lot to offer. We went a lot of places I had never gone before. After we got married, we went overseas, and I just thought it was wonderful. It lasted that way for about ten to twelve years. Then, all of a sudden, the same old story. He's been gone twelve years, I do know that. I've been paralyzed for eleven years. He did have someone call me to say he wanted a divorce. I said, "I won't help him, and I won't hinder him." So nothing happened. I don't miss him anymore. I don't. Everything is going the way I like it, at my own pace. I don't have to answer to anyone. I do what I want when I want. At the time, I didn't know what effect it was taking on me but the very next year, the stroke.

Actually, when I look back, I think I might have married younger, might not have stayed in Boston. Perhaps I could have gotten more education and a profession of some kind. It's hard to know, after all the years. Discrimination is what held us back. That's really what it was. I went to school with a girl who was a straight A student. She graduated without any scholarship aid or anything because they didn't tell us about scholarships. She came out and went to work for some law firm but not as a professional. She could have been so much more. They didn't counsel us either. They didn't. Discrimination is still there, but some places it's a little more subtle than others. Boston, it's still there.

There's my teacher I work with. I've been in that man's room since I went there with the exception of one year, and every year he has a little different tactic. He always had the black children in the last row, and it wasn't according to height or last name. If you come in there now, the entire last row is black. I don't know why. Another teacher and I were talking about it the other day. He says he doesn't think the man is conscious of it. I had reached that conclusion too. It's subconscious. As long as he keeps things going well and he teaches each child, I won't complain. In fact, now there's one little black girl almost directly in front of his desk. She's bright, and he seems to give her an extra lot of attention this year. It's that the seating plan is so strange.

It was never one of my dreams to be a teacher, but this kind of talent is what I didn't know I had. You know it's so funny.

Recently, four of us got together and went to see our first-grade teacher who was at the University Hospital. She told us we had been her first class out of college, and she was so happy to see us. She told me, "I kind-of thought you might become a teacher when you were my student." You know, I think about it, and I realize that I never found myself until I was about forty-five. Too late — almost too late.

I used to have thoughts about my purpose for being here. I still have not really found out what that might be. I have been in situations with people who couldn't read, and I've been able to assist them in some way or another. That used to happen when I was young, too, but I never thought much of it. When I went to the Rehabilitation Hospital after I did therapy for five months, they said they could help handicapped get back into the working world. They never, never placed me, didn't give me any idea of where to go or anything else. It ended up with their telling me I'd be better off staying home because, if I went to work, I'd lose my disability check.

Do you know that when I had the stroke, I stayed in the house alone for three whole days. I fell off the bed and just lay on the floor. My husband happened to come in on the third day, and I think he came back for that purpose. My little dog had been licking my face. I didn't know anything. That was the beautiful thing about it. I guess I was kind-of comatose. He called the City Hospital, and I got the best therapy in the city there. After that, I was at Mattapan Chronic Disease Hospital. There, my therapist, Joanne, worked me like a dog. She would walk me to the elevator with my chair and then walk me through that maze of buildings. She's a photographer, too, and she comes here now and then to take photos out of my window. Mr. Bibby did come to see me in the hospital, and his daughter used to come all the time. She took care of all my affairs. I was there from July to November, but it was all right. I was meeting new people, learning a lot of new things, like how to walk. I never did regain the use of my hand. When I came back home, I just didn't know what to do. This business of homemakers and visiting nurses was really tough. I stayed home for six years. I didn't know what to do.

One day, I happened to be listening to the radio and heard a quickie ad for foster grandparents. I said to myself, "I wonder if I could do that?" I called the office, finally. I was so afraid of rejection. Someone asked me, "Can you get to the office?" I said, "Yes," because I had found out about The Ride. "If you can get to the office, no problem."

Well, I went to a second grade class first, but the children were too young for me, and so I was moved to the fifth grade where I could relate to the children much better. The fifth graders are really young adults now. They're very smart because I am with the advanced class. You know, the teacher has them watching the news every day and talking about current events. They know what's going on in the world. It's wonderful, interesting to be around them.

And I've made many friendships, too. I'm friendly with the school secretaries. Since I get up around five, I go in early and help them sometimes. It's funny, when I go to bed, I go right to sleep! My therapist told me I'm working with one half a body. So I don't realize how very tired I really am. You know, I still have friendships with some of the children who were in the fifth grade when I first went to that class, four years ago. We traded telephone numbers. I have one little girl, October 31st is her birthday, and I never forget her. Every birthday, I send her a card.

When I was in the hospital, I met a girl who lost both legs, and I stayed in touch with her. She was my newest and dearest friend. Just before I got into the Program (if that hadn't come along, I don't know whether I'd have taken the gas pipe or started drinking), Agnes got so bad she just dragged me down more and more. I tried to keep up a good front for her, to keep her from getting worse, but I couldn't. She suffered so much, and, finally, she died. The Program really saved me from going crazy.

This year at school, I have a boy with terrible penmanship; his mind is good, very good, but his penmanship is horrible. I started with him today. We have the old-fashioned Palmer method on the black board, and I copy them down for him. I told him to do five rows of each a night. I love to see the letters when they're pretty. Then I have another little fellow, his math is bad. I said, "Ernest, you just have to stop and think and watch before you mark it down." He wants to write as fast as he thinks. I said to him, "Take your time. You don't have to be in a big hurry." He did a beautiful paper before we left today. It's the age they're living in; everything is a hurry now.

This past Sunday, my minister mentioned what I am doing from the pulpit. I was embarrassed to tears. It's all right. I like to do things, but I don't like to have a big horn blown about it. It takes all the good out of it. He told people that if I can do something, there's so much more that they can do with their whole bodies. That's not the way to say things. But I think people respect foster grandparents when they know what they do.

I try not to use my foster grandparent stipend money because I really don't want to get used to it. I like to keep it for little luxuries for myself, like to go and see my sister and when I want a decent dress . I certainly can't buy it from my social security check. I worked since 1941, so I built up a little more than some. Still, it's not what I could have gotten if I had a better job. I never made a good week's wages. I lived in poverty most of my life, yes. It's a part of me. But, still, it teaches you to appreciate the good things, poverty does. I think so. I don't feel any bitterness, no. I probably wouldn't know what to do with money if I had come into it, really, except travelling. I loved that.

I talk to people about coming into the Program. Some of them say, "I've had enough of children." My cousin wanted to do it, but she gets just a little too much of an income. It seems foolish to say no to her. And, you know, she might play some important part in a child's life, just talking to them in a very quiet way about drugs, illicit sex, and all; you never know when you are shaping a child's mind. Some children don't have anyone at home to talk to, and they don't have any spiritual life.

I tell them about the boy's clubs and the boy scouts. Some parents are never home. They work, and their children don't see them much; it's sad, it's really sad. They're up against it. You'd be surprised to know how many children at school only have one parent. There's an awful lot of that, an awful lot. It's hard for a woman too, to raise children by herself. I think we fill a void in their lives. One little girl wrote (you know, they have these spelling words and make a sentence, ten words a night) a sentence for the word "grieve." "I felt deeply greeve when my father died." She spelled it wrong, but I felt something so deep. It touches you that those things go through their minds. She's about ten or eleven.

I don't feel in any way remorseful, nor do I have regrets growing older with my incapacity. My Lord goes with me from moment to moment. I can do no more than it is His will for me to do. I shall ever believe it was a part of His perfect plan for my life for me to find the foster grandparent program and have you accept me as I am. While the present day educational system leaves so much to be desired, I still feel fortunate to have paired up with my teacher at the school. He is a bright, friendly and compassionate person. My life today is richer by far than it was in my earlier days. I think it is partly due to the fact that we have time now to reflect on things that might cheer or help others. I don't have time for self-pity. I am quite satisfied with things the way they are.

* * *

Dorothy Bibby lives in public housing on a main street that overlooks the Christian Science Park, a site that visitors to the city will often stop to see. The view from her lovely living room window is breathtaking. That sight is the focus of her eyes for long hours of many days when pain or excessive fatigue keep her from going to school.

Dom Eno

Dom Eno

In the North End then, you know, I really didn't know it was so hard because we were just living. Everybody in the North End was Italian, and none of them knew how to read or write. I remember my father digging the streets for the telephone lines, and I was a water boy. I would take a bucket of water and go to all the ditch diggers and ask them if they wanted water. I was making ten dollars a week then, and that was a lot of money. I was only fourteen years old.

My mother and father came from Italy together around 1907, and got married when they came here. I was the first child, born in 1910. My father had a job at a shop in Essex Street where they made leather belts. We lived on a little alley street. The homes were very small and tight, and we only had two rooms in the North End. My father died when I was about three, and my younger brother died of pneumonia when he was a baby. My mother had a hard time.

In those days, she did a lot of washing for people who was wealthier than us. She got fifty cents for a tub of clothes to wash. And I used to deliver them when I was about ten or twelve years old. Then, my mother remarried. She married a man that didn't have any children, and she had three children with him. I call 'em brothers, two brothers and a sister, the loveliest girl. She was a seamstress, and my two brothers owned a sportswear shop in Boston.

In those days, when the mother of a family had a baby, everybody brought chickens to make soup because chicken gave you strength, they thought. I remember this crate of live chickens in the kitchen. You had to kill them yourself. And the men didn't have regular jobs — they were construction workers. They dug the street for the telephone lines sometimes. I remember my father doing that. I went to St. Anthony's Catholic School that is still there, and then I went to Commerce High School. From there I went to be a printer. I was obssessed by printing — I wanted to put my own shop up, you know. I used to go around selling invitations. I would read the Globe and see which girl was getting engaged, and I would visit them. In those days, I would charge them ten dollars for 100 invitations. I used to work in the daytime and go selling invitations at night. I wanted to put a shop in my cellar, but I couldn't because of fire laws. I learned the fundamentals of printing at Commerce High. Not that I want to put a halo over my head, but seeing the printing to me was like some of these musicians and their music. I worked for some nice concerns. I still get letters today asking me to come and help. I tried, but I got tired.

We, my half brothers and sister, we all grew up together really, and it was O.K. My step-father was good. I just lived and obeyed the rules. If he loved me, he never showed it, but maybe I'm at fault; I didn't show it either like you would your own father, sit on his knee. But that didn't make any difference with Sam and Tony and my sister; we were together. I was in business with my brothers, but I didn't care much for that so I went to work for the government. I had been a printer for private industry. Then, just before the war, I took a civil service exam. I heard they had a wonderful plant in Washington. I was hired, and we moved there in 1940. My wife and my daughter came after I found an apartment just across the street from the Catholic University. I had two sons born there.

One day, my son and I were picking dandelions on the grounds of the college. A group of students, all dressed in habit clothes, came along and asked me questions about what I was going to do with the dandelions and where I was from and so forth. I guess they were doing some kind of paper for school. I told them we would clean them carefully and have them for dinner. A few days later, I invited them to our apartment and had a dandelion salad for lunch. The very next day, I saw several students picking dandelions. I laughed. I had started something.

I wasn't used to making money. The salary that the government gave us when I was in Washington was about $1.36 an hour against sixty or seventy cents an hour in Boston. A lot of us worked double time so, when I got paid, I used to put my money in the shoe, fearing that somebody was gonna hold me up. I don't know the city, and I'm putting my money in the shoe. My wife, she would write and say, you'd better put it in the bank. So I put it in the Hamilton Bank, and that's where we saved the money to buy this house. We moved back to Boston after seven years in Washington. My wife really wanted to be near her family. The house we bought is this one we're in. She wanted me to buy this house because she remembered her father had built it. And this is where my seven grandchildren were born. When we came back to Boston, I kept working as a printer in various places. If one place didn't pay me enough, I moved to another. I was pressman and composition so I could do that.

I don't like to sound like a braggard — when you're poor you save when you can and you help others whenever you can. I just gave my son a car because he was having trouble — it's just the way to do. And we had a certificate of deposit, and it came due, so I was able to buy myself another car. My wife loves it. So here I am a foster grandparent, and I have this nice car. What a father or mother does to help a child is always good. Now he's smiling, and I'm smiling.

My son Phillip, named after my father, married a very nice girl. They lived here in this apartment. I lived downstairs then. Later, they moved to New Hampshire. One day, she was on the phone talking about fixing the alter of the church, and she stopped talking and her friend kept hollering, and so they went to the house. There she is, she's sitting on the stool, the phone is dangling. They touched her and said, "Isabel, come on," and she toppled over. She was dead. She had an aneurism. That was a tragedy. They had three children, and he raised them. He just remarried about a year ago. He met her at a church prayer meeting. They are so happy, and we're going to their house for Thanksgiving. His sons are ready to get married now and have their own family.

My daughter married a nice man. He works for the Blackstone Electric Co. When I asked him how come he married my daughter, he said, when he looked at me and my wife and saw how poor we were, he thought he'd give us all a break. She's smart. She works for "Hit or Miss" in the office. I always go by and bring her bran muffins. She jogs because she doesn't want to lose her figure. My granddaughter trains horses — she's in love with horses. She's at Amherst now.

Remember Andrea, the accordian player who was a foster grandfather in East Boston? I went to his house several times. I was taking accordian lessons, and he helped me. Now, he's gone. A pity. He was such a nice man. So, in my spare time, I go down the cellar and study. I wouldn't dare play it up here. I know how to play three little songs Andrea taught me. Now I get out of her way and go downstairs and play.

I'm seventy-seven now, and I'm starting to feel it. We try to smile. But she's had a bad time. She had shock treatments, and, then, she said, "No more." She was smart enough to stop it. Now she has another doctor who has really helped her. We go out a lot, especially in the summer, and we go to New Hampshire. We like to go to the fast food places, like pizza and hamburgers. I love to walk all the steps up here. It does something. You feel tired when you land here, but it's good. My wife likes it here, too, so I guess we'll stay. When we went to the Faulkner Hospital for her check up, I said, "Mummie, let's walk up this hill backwards. It's good for you." "You know I feel tired in my legs," she told me. "That's good for you. Breathe hard," I said. She made it.

Last year, I was so sick, and they couldn't find out what was wrong with me. But I don't figure I'll be around too much longer. They put me in the scanner, and they found out I had a diseased gall bladder. No pain, but that's why I was turning yellow. But the kids keep me going through everything.

These kids. You should see what I do with these kids. When I first enter the school downstairs — I work with the kindergarten

kids - I dance with them, - "and a one and a two and a three" —
singing, "I turn you around, and I turn around myself, and where
did that angel go?" They go and hide. And they're waiting —
they're waiting — the girls and the boys, too. When the teachers
come in, they say, "Everybody looks happy." They eat breakfast
in the school, and then we go in the classroom. I help them to
write their name, show 'em how to color. For happiness, I like the
little kids best. Some of the homes they come from are not too
happy, but they fight for being with me. They laugh, and here's
Mr. Eno. Once in the class, it's different. They learn to spell with
crayons. They're learning the alphabet. There's no fooling in the
classroom. But that time in the morning, it's just joy.

I'll ask this little girl if she went to the store with her father, and
she'll say, "I don't have a father." And here I am, making her
laugh and joke. And my own children and the little boy downstairs. I play with kids, I buy them balls, I buy lollipops. I'm not a
psychologist — I just do what I do without thinking.

I was that way with my children. I played ball with them, even
up to fourteen and fifteen, and I used to umpire the games. Now,
I have two Spanish kids living right here, from Honduras, and the
mother is teaching me Spanish. Their kids are going to bilingual
school. I love those kids. We speak to each other with both
languages.

All my family is very religious. You know, what Jesus said to the
children when the Roman soldiers were chasing them away from
Jesus? He said, "Suffer not little children, please come unto me."
I tell my wife, "God is good to me. I'm sick, he heals me." Maybe
I'm making these children happy and the good Lord is good to
me. Maybe God put me on this earth to make these children
smile.

I don't like getting older. If I had to stay home and not go out, no!
I've got to go out and see those kids and make them laugh and
help them with their lessons. I have to achieve something. I want
to teach children what to do, and I want to learn. Let me be free.

Let me go to the school. I want to see little Harry make his H and little Maria make her M.

If I was working in private industry, I'd be looking for a raise. It isn't for the money that I work with the kids. I don't want money. I'm too old for that now. I have all I need. Making my foster grandchildren sing and dance with me — that's more than money. My kids think I'm fortunate to be doing this.

I want to accomplish playing my accordian, and I don't think I have the time. I want to take my accordian to one of our meetings and have a good time. Let's dance. I want to play a waltz or a fox trot. If I get enough strength mentally and physically, that's what I want to do. I feel that I don't have the time. I think, is that all I can give now? Is this it? I think I have to give more. I want to say, "Come," like Jesus, and bring happiness.

Celia Epstein

Celia Epstein

My father had a terrible time around 1907. It was what they called "the panic" in those days, a depression. He couldn't get work, and, when he did, the conditions were horrible. They had a market downtown where they used to gather with a machine on their backs, waiting for someone to need a stitcher. It was like a slave market. When he got involved in the union, he slowly saw conditions improve and working hours come down.

My father was born in Vilna which is now Lithuania but then was part of old Russia. My mother was born in a very small village nearby. My father left there to avoid military service and went to Manchester, England in 1905. My mother came shortly after that, and they were married there. My mother had two brothers and a sister in Manchester.

My father had an aunt and uncle here in Boston so they came here in 1907, and I was born that same year. I just celebrated my eightieth birthday. My sister Bertha was born six years later. By that time, my parents had moved to Roxbury. I spent most of my youth in Roxbury and part of my adult life. I went to Boston Latin School and then to the conservatory for two years. I got a piano teacher's diploma and began to teach. That was before the conservatory gave degree programs.

I graduated in 1927, and I was married in 1931. It was depression time, and we couldn't afford to get married. Then, we decided to go ahead anyway. We had each other, and we lived with my folks because we couldn't afford an apartment. Later, when we could afford it, there were none available because they hadn't done any building during the war years.

My son was born seven years after I was married. My husband had worked in a dry goods store. When the depression came, he lost that job. He opened this little fruit store. During the Second World War, it was good, but then it fell off. He went into another business in Malden and lost his money. Anyway, we survived.

Growing up in Roxbury was very nice. We had originally lived in the West End of Boston. When we were going to move to Roxbury, I told everybody we were moving to the country. It was an exciting community. On Saturday night on Blue Hill Avenue, it was like old home week doing the family shopping there. It was hard to take a step without bumping into someone you knew. My mother would buy herring from a barrel, I remember. Friends used to say the greatest times were when my mother served potatoes and herring.

We got a very good background in social history, so to speak. My father was very active in the union he belonged to, the ILGWU, International Ladies Garment Workers Union. I think it was formed after he came to this country. He had a very tough time when they first arrived here. Working conditions were horrible, and the pay was what we would now call the poverty level. But, later, he saw working and living conditions improve.

That's why, when people tell about horrid conditions, I know what that means. We went through terrible times economically, but we always had this loving unit to fall back on. It was a struggle, but they sent me to school and that helped me the rest of my life. The desire for education was intense.

Bertha, my sister, was a drama teacher. She loved it all her life. She was an actress, too. She acted in some very well-known plays, like "Waiting for Godot." Then she got lupus, and by the time they discovered she had it, it was too late. The damage was done. She died of a stroke in her fifties.

My grandson is in law school and his wife also. My son teaches music. He's been doing a good bit of composing and recently has had several performances of his work. My daughter-in-law works for the welfare department in child care. She's a supervisor of day care centers. It's a tough job, but she loves it. My children will be married thirty years in 1988. It's hard to believe. They told me a few years back that when they got together with other couples, they were the only ones with the original mates.

I started to teach music when I was in my senior year at the Conservatory. Then when the depression hit, people couldn't afford to take piano lessons, and it kind of petered out. I did play for the Jewish People's Chorus, but I didn't teach much. I helped my husband in the store for the years he was in Roxbury. I worked hard there.

Bob, my husband, died when I was sixty-three. He had given up his business; well, actually, he went bankrupt there. After that, there wasn't much that he could do — he ended up driving a cab. He did that for about sixteen years. It was his heart that went. For about two years, he had symptoms. He and your father were playing chess when he got his first attack. Your father drove him to a hospital. They didn't think it was that serious, but when he came home, he had another attack. It was terrible. I think, if it happened now they would have done surgery, and he could have lived. It was thirty-nine very happy years — a wonderful man. That's the way it goes.

When my husband died, I was working in Sears Roebuck taking telephone orders and then later in the cashier's office. I moved to Hyde Park to live with my friend Esther after he died. She eventually had Alzheimer's. It was terrible. Then, when I was sixty-five, I had to retire. In the beginning, it was a relief not to have to get up early and rush out of the house. Then I began to be bored. I went to work as a senior volunteer one day a week but, after a year, I said to myself, "This won't do. I have to have do something more." That was when I heard about the foster grandparents on T.V. I entered in '74 with a whole group. The whole gang of us went to Wrentham State School. Fortunately, we were only there for four years.

You know, when they took us out to Wrentham the first day, we all said, "We're not coming back here." We were there on a Friday. Monday morning, everybody showed up, and we all stayed. I worked with a boy who was in a wheel chair, paralyzed. I used to help him with his lunch, and it got so that if I went to another child, he would cry, really howl. He felt that I belonged to him. But I was glad when we moved out to the community schools.

This was such a fortunate coincidence for me, to be able to work at the Ohrenberger School right here in Hyde Park. I was so happy when that change took place. The school is within walking distance. It's been just wonderful. The administrators and all the teachers are so appreciative of what we do. It's a challenge, and it's so very rewarding.

Let me give you a typical day: I wait till the children start trickling in. I talk to them. They are six to twelve years old. Ohrenberger is an elementary school. I work with individual children in different classes. In the first class I go to, I work with this little boy, a Vietnamese boy, and I help him with some of the motor skill development tasks. When he first came in, he couldn't talk English at all, but now he speaks. He's retarded, but not so badly. When we needed to go to another classroom, I would take his hand. From then on, whenever we needed to move, he would come over and take my hand. I have that much of a relationship with him. I work there — it's not fun and games so it's hard to develop strong emotional ties with the children, but we do get close in some ways.

Actually, I work with all retarded kids. In the other class I go to, it's the worst really. I'm not denigrating the children, but we have children with difficult emotional problems. I try to do the best with them. It's hard for them, but they try the best they can. It's hard work for me too but so rewarding. I get through at 12:30 when the kids go to lunch.

You know, my friends think it's fantastic that I am a foster grandparent. I have one friend who lives in Swampscott. She boasts to her friends about me, "The woman who doesn't sit home by herself and goes out to work every day." I want to tell you that, for my eightieth birthday, friends of mine gave a very generous donation to the Ohrenberger School to be used for the benefit of the children. They bought a computer game that teaches them how real computers work. I felt so wonderful about that. My son and daughter-in-law and my nieces and nephews made the party. There were forty-five people there including my grandchildren, of course.

You know getting to eighty, well, I never expected to reach the age of eighty. When I was younger, if someone would tell me that I would reach to be eighty, I would think they were crazy. But I made it. I lived through wars and the holocaust and the depression and all sorts of things. Now that I'm here, I really don't feel like the image I had of a person of eighty. You know, there are days when I don't feel as I did when I was forty, for sure, but I still enjoy life. I still enjoy my family and seeing people. I can't get out as easily as I used to, to theatres and concerts so I have my T.V. and radio. And it shouldn't be any worse till the end. Unfortunately, I can't get much pleasure from the state of the world, but, truthfully, there are some brighter spots. Medicine has made advances, certain diseases are under control. If I had many years to live, I would still be optimistic about things getting better.

I'm not good at dealing with death. Of course, you hate to lose your parents. My father was eighty-three and my mother seventy-eight. But, when I lost my husband, I felt that it was like losing a limb. I later learned that I wasn't original in that. Psychologists say that now about loss. You never really get over it. When something happens, in the back of my mind is the thought that I have to tell Bob. At the beginning, it went on all the time. When I think of my own death, I have the hope that I won't linger long, that I won't be sick and disabled and a vegetable, like my mother. That's my hope.

It bothers me that my children are so far away — in Philadelphia. This year, I spent some time with them on the Cape. They came here for the party. Now, I'm going there for Thanksgiving. I'm going to Hartford where my grandchildren are and then drive down with them. They both are at the University of Connecticut. And Christmas, I'm going down to Philadelphia again.

I love to travel. Now I'm hesitant because it's tiring. I have to take a cab from here to the airport, and it's expensive. About thirty-five dollars. But I love to go. And, when I go for Christmas, I always travel Christmas day so it's easier.

The Program, being a foster grandparent, has meant really my life in these past years. It's thirteen years now, and I hope to go on and on. I don't know what I would have done if I had to sit and twiddle my thumbs.

One more thing. No, I don't think I was put on this earth for any special reason. I feel that the only ones responsible for my being here were my parents. If my life has any meaning, it is thanks to my upbringing. My parents imbued me with a set of values which I never forgot and which I tried to pass on to my son, and he, in turn, to his son. I am very proud of my work as a foster grandparent, but I do not believe it was pre-ordained.

* * *

Celia Epstein and I grew up in the same area of Boston. Our parents had much in common. My father also left his home town in Russia because he had been drafted and had no intention of serving in the Czar's army. I took drama lessons from her sister, Bertha.

Margaret Gray

Margaret Gray

When I told everyone that I was going to be a Foster Grandparent, they thought I was crazy. A job for you at sixty-nine? Sean was so small, I fed him with an eye dropper. He couldn't eat but he could smile. I loved looking out for him.

I was born in Scotland on February 27, 1898, and I came to the U.S. in 1924. I was the oldest of ten. Only two are still alive, and they are twenty years younger. The other seven are gone. When I reached seventy, I thought it was special, and now here I am ninety. I have enjoyed life — it's been grand! I have four wonderful children, fifteen grandchildren and twenty-nine great-grands.

When I was a child in Scotland, we had a very strict school. We marched in at nine in the morning. Roll was called at 9:45. Kids came from big families. Many of us worked, but we had to do exactly right in school. Girls learned cooking and sewing; boys, carpentry. I got a practical education. If you didn't show up to school, the truant officer came after you. The janitor of the school, who was a retired sergeant, put us through setting up exercises every day! I also got a course in Housewifery. I enjoyed school, got everything I needed. The same teacher taught all the subjects through the standard grades in our public schools. Some left at twelve years, I left at fourteen and became an apprentice to a dressmaker. I hated it! But I did learn to make all my own clothes.

My husband went to what they called Marine College for five years, beginning at twelve or fourteen. They gave national exams and sent reports to the local school board so he could get the work he wanted. After his apprenticeship, he went to work in the shipyards.

On New Year's, everyone would have Open House in Scotland, and nobody would come empty handed. The religious holiday was Christmas, called Hogmenay. New Year's was the treat time, carry gifts to houses everywhere and to all friends and relatives. It was a grand holiday time.

Work in the shipyard was really sporadic. It was tough getting by so my husband left Scotland and came here in 1923 and got a job as a millwright. He installed heavy machinery and engines. He got a house for us, and then I came in 1924 with the three little ones, Peggy four and a half, Gilbert two and a half, and Agnes ten months. The crossing was about thirteen days, but the others on board took the two older ones off my hands. That was a help.

I enjoyed life — it was a good family, and my husband was strict with the children. The younger ones were put to bed early — no late shows. He would take two of the kids to the beach at Castle Island on Sunday — no nonsense! We laugh about it now, but there is nobody like the family.

I've made one trip back, the year of the Coronation, 1954. I stayed in Rumford and travelled around a bit. Scotland — England and into the highlands — I loved it. The biggest struggle of my life was the passing of my husband. He got tumor of the colon. He was in agony. Doctors didn't seem to help him. When they opened him up, it was too far gone, and so they did nothing. I said, I want him home. I was glad I never let them take him back to the hospital. He was wonderful to me all my life with him. I enjoyed the kids — all the kids were good; there are no bad kids — they've all got good in them.

When I told everyone that I was going to be a Foster Grandparent, they thought I was crazy. A job for you at sixty-nine? My daughter Agnes heard about it. So I applied, and then I waited. Then, I said, "I told you, nobody would hire me." But they did call me after a few months — you know Herb Jerauld, he was Director then, and I started at Wrentham State School in 1967. I enjoyed it there. They were wonderful to us. The kids there had braces, couldn't talk, and some couldn't walk at all. Sean was so small, I fed him with an eye dropper. He couldn't eat. He was microcephalic. But he could smile. I loved looking out for him.

When it was time to leave the state schools, I went to Children's World Day Care in Mattapan, and there we taught the kids a lot. I had the kids ready for the first grade. I liked that a lot, too. Then, I went to the Grew School and had both the first and second grade children — the ones who were slow. I taught them their ABC's and numbers. I had to leave in '86 because of the ulcer in my leg, but I guess I did about nineteen years.

Now I don't go out. I'm fine from the waist up, but, from the waist down, I'm dead. I have a walking stick with legs, but I use a cane. Agnes comes to get me when I have to get out.. My eyes are good and my hearing. I don't need any of those aids. I like folks to remember me running down the street!

About dying? Oh, I've lived my life, and I've enjoyed it. Today, tomorrow, I live one day at a time, enjoying life. Everyone of my kids — they can't do enough for me.

* * *

Margaret Gray wanted me to remember her running also. I interviewed her on the telephone and agreed to use a photo of her with the children at the day care center. She was an active participant in the Program, attended legislative hearings at the State House, and was one of the actors in "Lives of Foster Grandparents."

Eva Madeiros

Eva Madeiros

I do not like the idea of being interviewed and think I would rather not have my photo taken. Now that I'm old, I'm wiser and maybe more beautiful inside, but I don't like my picture. It's a real privilege to grow old. I am a very private person, and I do not wish to speak of my private life at all.

I was born in 1909, in Fall River, Mass. My family is Portuguese. I was the next to youngest of twelve children, eight of whom grew up. Four died of childhood diseases. The older ones helped with the younger ones. I knew I couldn't be a teacher because you had to be rich to go to college, but I always wanted it. I started work at the age of fourteen in Fall River at the American Print Works, and I worked all my life. My first check at APW was $11.21 for forty-two hours. I stayed there about five years. Then I went to a hat factory making straw hats for a few years. After that, I worked at Honeywell for over twenty years soldering, wiring, and building cable. We built the cable and then laced it behind the big computers.

I did get married, and I have one daughter who lives in California. She was a dental hygienist, but now she has just completed her Ph.D. in Sociology at the University of California, San Diego (UCSD) at the age of fifty-two. I'm proud of her. She has three children.

When I started in the Foster Grandparent Program in 1969, we were getting only twenty-eight dollars a week; now we get forty-four. Not too much. I certainly don't work for the money. I have been at three different sites. When I entered, I was sixty, and I started at Wrentham State School and left there when the young ones were being moved out in 1978. I went from there to Children's World Day Care with all Black staff and all Black children. It was a big change, and it was great! I liked Wrentham, also, where we fed the kids and took them for walks. I loved working with those kids. They were so helpless. My friend Margaret Gray fed one child who was about a foot and a half long. She fed him with an eye dropper. She and I went to Children's World and the Grew School together. What I do now at the Grew School in Hyde Park is real work in comparison. I went to the Grew in 1981, and I am really tired when I get home. I've had it. I have a wonderful teacher; working with her is a pleasure. She appreciates any suggestions I may make, and she cares about the kids. I watch how she handles the children and how she teaches them, and then I copy her.

The kids come in the morning, and I help them with their clothes, get them seated. It's only the kindergarten, but it's like first grade used to be. By February of each year, the class is expected to recognize and sound each letter of the alphabet. By the end of the year, some few kids may be reading. I push them, and they learn; they seem to really enjoy it, and I do get close to them. When the end of the year comes, I don't want them to leave.

Now that I'm old, I'm wiser and maybe more beautiful inside, but I don't like my picture. It's a real privilege to grow old, and being a foster grandparent is wonderful. It gives me something good to do, some place to go; without that, my life would be dull. I would surely miss it if I couldn't go to school each day. Helping the kids at school is a challenge. I miss the children each year. Some people enjoy just being retired, but I have to keep busy. At the end of the year, if even one child does letters well, I feel that I've done something.

I'm a Red Sox fan. They are disappointing to me this year, but I'm their fan, of course.

* * *

At a later date when I called Eva, she seemed in better spirits. She told me that her grandson had called and asked for her photo.

She went off to a department store and had one taken, after all! It seems her daughter had been able to reach out to her since she'd completed her doctorate which had kept her in isolation for quite a while. All this had had its effect, and Eva was able to speak more enthusiastically about her life.

Marian Magaldi

Marian Magaldi

I took a job in defense. It was a steel foundry, Walworth's, in South Boston, and we made valves for the ships. It was a job for sure. You took a man's job then. And you didn't get that much doing a man's work. We got sixty-five cents an hour in those days, the late 30's and into the 40's.

After Phil died, I was working at the Baptist Hospital, and I heard somebody say they didn't like to work with old people, and so I said to myself, "I guess I'd better retire." If someone said that to me now, I'd say to heck with you.

I was born in Lynn, Massachusetts in 1914. I lived with my grandmother for a while because my mother and father were very young. When my sister was born (she's five years younger than I am), I went to live with more distant relatives, but I called them Grandma and Grandpa Queen. They lived in Wakefield. I loved them very much. I had my own room. They had chickens and an apple tree and a pear tree. I remember I made a swing on the pear tree and broke a branch and got a spankin'.

My mother was born in Nova Scotia and my father in South Boston. My father's people came from Ireland and my mother's from England and Scotland. So I have all three. Our family were sea-captains in England and sailed the seas. That was why my Grandma Porter, my real grandmother, always thought there'd be a legacy for her, but there never was. I loved her, too. She lived in Lynn and worked in a shoe factory there, and my mother, when she was young, worked in the factory also. My mother was very pretty, a pretty woman.

When I was thirteen my father died. He was young. Thirty-three. He had a heart attack. So my mother had to go to work, and I'd come home from school and put the supper on. I put the wood in the stove, put in the gasoline, and lit the match. It's a wonder that we are here today.

I went to work early; left school after the eighth grade. A few years later, I found out about what they called "laboratory kitchens." They were restaurants, really. One was on Washington Street, near our house, actually. That was where I worked. The people who ran it would get these young girls right from the school department because they had to leave school to go to work. We served all the newspapermen and the stock brokers and the lawyers with all that nice home-cooked food. You would follow a recipe (that's why it was called laboratory, we were learning) that you were given.

When I came, I was sixteen or seventeen, 1930 or so, and I stayed there until I was twenty-one. I could make all kinds of tapioca, not just a quart but fifteen quarts, and chocolate meringue, a pudding. We had all the best ingredients, and all the puddings were made from scratch. I learned to make all kinds of sauces too, blueberry, lemon. It was an experience for us, and it was good. We worked very hard, went to work at 7:30, and stayed until after 5:00. And, then, came the National Recovery Act (NRA), and so we had our hours cut down. In the beginning, I earned eight dollars a week, and, then, I went up to ten dollars, and, then, it went to twelve.

By 1935, I had to leave because my heart got enlarged from workin' too hard at such a young age. I stayed home for a while. Later on I got work in a tea room in the Franklin Square House which was a place for girls to live who worked in the city. I liked to work with food, but I didn't stay there too long.

A woman that I met from a settlement house kinda liked the family and wanted to help us. She had evidently found out about us because my sister got hit by a car. They took care of her, and, then, they found out about Billy and me. They kinda took a shine to me. That woman, Mrs. R., got sick and asked if I would come and take care of her, and I did. Then, in the late 30's, she left for Detroit to live with her daughter. I was able to get a job in a defense plant.

I went to work on what was called a demler machine. Actually it was a steel foundry, Walworth's in South Boston. We made valves for the ships. It was a job, for sure. You took a man's job then. It was sand that went into the machine, and you made the molds. Then, they went on to the casting where steel was poured on them.

That's where I met my husband, Phil. I worked nights, and he worked days, and I met him in the changing shift time. I went to work at 3:00 in the afternoon until 11:00 at night. It was hard. Just work and sleep. And you didn't get that much doing a man's work. We got sixty-five cents an hour in those days, the late 30's and into the 40's. I worked there for two years. I married Phil, but I continued working until I got pregnant and had the baby. Then, I stayed home with my daughter, and I loved it.

Phil had a heart condition. When he tried to get into the service, they refused him. He died in 1972. I had no insurance, nothing. My daughter was grown up then, and so no social security either. I had to get a job as soon as I could.

My brother had a friend at the Baptist Hospital. I went there for an interview, and they hired me. I became a dietary aide. I worked one whole floor, in charge of twenty-nine patients. I served them their meals and made sure they were getting the right diet if they had diabetes or whatever. It wasn't very good pay. Then, I heard somebody say they didn't like to work with old people. It was one of workers, not the head of the department. I did work better than any of them. I said to myself, "I guess I'd better retire." I felt, maybe somebody else isn't saying it, but they feel the same. So I left. Then I was at loose ends. If someone said that to me now, I'd say to heck with you.

I was really at loose ends. I didn't know what to do, I really didn't. Nobody knew what to do with me. They were all getting upset with me. They didn't like me in fact, nobody. They didn't understand how I felt because they didn't go through it. I'd get up early in the morning when I worked at the Baptist. I was up at five in the morning, and I used to love it. I'd be the first with the virgin snow, the first birds would come, and they'd say, "Well, here she comes." Oh, I really didn't know what to do. I wanted to give away all my things.

I was at my daughter's one day, and the woman next door said to her, "Why don't you have your mother go to see the foster grandparents?" I said, "Oh, Ruthie, I'll go today." I went, and poor Susan at the office, she had to erase everything. I forgot my telephone number, I couldn't do a blessed thing. I made more mistakes on the form. I thought, "Oh, they'll never hire me."

Then, when I got called, it turned out that my sister-in-law who works at the Grew School found out that I was going to be with the program. She didn't understand that you had to go through channels so she got them to take me for three days. They really needed a teacher. Then, I said to my daughter, "Gee, I'm not signing anything." Well, I figured I botched it, I'm done.

One day, I was gonna make beef stew. I had the meat out on the table to cook and all of a sudden a phone call from the office. "How soon can you come to the Grew School?" I left everything. I said, "I can be there in two minutes." I changed my dress and went and Mrs. Amis, the principal, I loved her. She was lovely, and everything was cleared up. So that's the way I started.

I look at all I have done and I think, well, I've done it. There were hard times, but I did get through it. I gave my mother money, and I have a good daughter, and I have good grandchildren. Christine, my granddaughter, is studying to be a nurse. She comes every Tuesday to have supper with me. Every day, since they were very young, those kids delivered the Boston Globe. The money they got went into the bank for their college. My daughter lives in West Roxbury, and she calls me twice a day. She has a boy, Gregory, who goes to Latin School. She, herself, subs at the school but not regularly.

I love to read. I find it's relaxing. I just finished "The Fitzgeralds." I also like Rabbi Cushner's thoughts and Leo Boscaglia. In the summertime, I read Agatha Christie. I go to bed at 8 o'clock. I get up very early, and I listen to the talk shows at night. If there is something good on Channel 2 (the educational channel), I stay up and watch it. I go up to The Most Precious Blood, a Catholic church up here.

I guess I was put on this earth to work hard. You know, I've never talked this much in my life, but Shirley McLean believes it. I mean about being here for a purpose. I don't know about myself; perhaps to be the very best I can. Just the kids, I just love the kids. I help them all at school. Right now, we've got this new boy, Morris. He comes from Jamaica. There's a certain tribe there, they don't wash their hair. I think he wipes his hands when they're dirty, on his hair. So Morris, because he came only a couple of weeks ago, I am with him constantly. I teach him his letters, how to write the numbers and all that. I'm in the first grade with them. I'm there five years now. I sit beside him, take his hand, and he is something! I think, just for now, until he grasps everything, I'll work with him, but, later, I'll get other children. I can't stay still so I go around the room and help all the children if they're having a problem with their math or their phonics. I say, "What is this picture? See, this is it, you know. Now let's try it again and see if it's easier for you." When the grades change, I get sad. But now I've been with them so long, I'm used to it. I've seen them graduate from the school. Each year I get some special child.

I remember when we had this little boy, Gerry. He was a terror. We had him last year. I guess his mother was on drugs, and he went to live with his grandmother. Then his grandmother's house caught on fire. He came to school filthy dirty, and he comes to me, "Wash me up, wash me up, Mrs. Magaldi." So I got him by the sink, and I scrubbed him up good. He was all right. He did have a hard time, but he's made of tough stuff. It always makes me feel better when I can see that I can help a child.

You know, I feel terrible about getting older. I really do. I said to

Judy, my teacher, "I don't want to have any more birthdays. I'm seventy-three now. I don't want any more. No presents either. Look at all the wrinkles I'm getting, and my hair is getting thinner. I just want to stay healthy so I don't become a burden to my daughter." That would kill me right away. Of course, I've learned a lot. I've learned to adapt. When I get sick, I can't wait to get better so I can get back to school. It's true. Now I'm worried because Gregory would like to go to Texas to college, and my daughter can't see him go away like that. He can get a $50,000 scholarship to go to the school of his choice. I'm proud of him, though.

My daughter and grandchildren are proud of me, too. I can't even stay home in the summer time when the school is closed. I get placed at a summer site. I have to have some children to look out for so it's so nice at this new summer place in Roslindale. I don't get too much social security. Phil's wages were low in those days, and, when I worked in that laboratory kitchen, we worked forty-eight hours for eight dollars a week. Can you believe that? I got very little from the Baptist Hospital. None of us works for the money, but it helps me.

It's different now. When I was young, I had one dress, one pair of shoes that were run down. We really had nothing. And my mother had a hard time. She died of cancer. Now I have a brother and sister-in-law who are very good to me and live downstairs. All my in-laws are very good to me. I'm very lucky. You know, where we lived in the South End, there was a true League of Nations. We had Jewish, Italian, Lithuanian, Irish, Black, everybody. Now the South End is so expensive, none of us could live there.

I've never been to Ireland or England. The furthest I've been is Washington and up to Maine. I really don't want to go. I'd rather stay here. I'm very easy to please. There are times when I get depressed, but I think everybody does. If I can find something to laugh at, it will make me feel better so I wait for that.

I still think of that time when I thought I'd never make it in the program. I was so sad. When I got the call to go to the Grew School, I knew that day was . . . well, I can't describe it. When I came home, blood was dripping from the meat I left on the table, my dress that I changed was on the floor, and that's not like me. I just lickety-split went up there. I said to my daughter, "You should have seen me. I never went so fast in my life. It was the beginning of five beautiful years."

Phil Magnus

Phil Magnus

I was drafted one month after Pearl Harbor, and I got the worst of it. I was in active service for three and a half years. There was lots of anti-semitism in those days. A lot of the officers were O.K. but the enlisted men....

The kids I work with are the ones who are slow in reading. If those kids don't get their reading skills from the beginning, they're in bad trouble. I take my work with them very seriously. I believe in kids, and they should get what they need to grow up to be productive.

I was born, May 20th, 1916. My father and mother were born in Russia. They had a little property, and he had a barber shop, but they were havin' problems — the pogroms* were startin'. My father came over first, and he got discouraged because he had trouble with the language. He was ready to go back, but my mother was too smart for that. She sold everything, took two kids by herself, imagine that, and came over here. One was about three and the other about four. It was tough in the ships in those days; they weren't pleasure ships. She came over with some money, and they wound up in Boston because they had relations here. I was born in the South End. I can remember the street, but it isn't there any more. Then we moved to Dorchester where I grew up.

My father was down at the Hotel Somerset. He gave haircuts and shaves to the managers of the hotel. He worked, but he didn't know how to handle the situations too well. He worked for all the hotels later on and still didn't like it. Finally, he got his own shop on Commonwealth Avenue, and he was happier.

I went to school. Graduated Boston English High in '34, and I didn't take a book home. Why? 'Cause I was workin'. I came home eleven o'clock every night. Just imagine the marks I could have got if I was studying. I didn't. I didn't have the opportunity. I just made it by hook or crook, and I did it in the four years. I wanted to go further, but you can't do that with six kids in the family. In those days, in the depression years, it was out of the question. I wanted to go to college. I worked for some of the theatres after I graduated high school, and, also, I sold novelty jewelry. Then, the war came, and one month after Pearl Harbor I was drafted. I got into the worst of it.

There were four of us who were drafted, and we all went overseas. Only one came back bad. He was on a flyin' fort over in the Pacific. They shot the tail off, and he didn't have a parachute. Luckily, he came out of it. After that fall, he'd say, "I can't level off, I can't level off." I had four brothers and one sister. I lost three brothers inside of six months. That was about eight years ago. My sister is the only one that's left. One brother lived out at Fort Lauderdale. We all used to get together at his daughter's house out in Holliston. His son went to Brandeis and studied psychology. My sister's kids are both living in Silver Springs, right near Washington. They do really well, too.

I went to Africa in '42, and then we went to Sicily. When we were in Africa, the colonel decided he wanted to see what the mines were there — the place was really mined! We got some out. They were booby traps, and, when that's the case, they may be connected to three or four other mines. If you just trip over one of the wires, it sets them off. While he was looking for some of those mines, one tripped and no more. That was the end of him. It was scary. We didn't have any equipment — a trench knife, on your hands and knees, learning to find these mines. If anyone hit a wire? Bang! You're gone. We didn't know anything. Then, this buck sergeant, he was too industrious for his own good. He dug around and picked up this booby trap — he picked up the top one. The top was connected to the bottom. They didn't even find the pieces. He was a good kid, a hard working kid. That was awful. Afterwards, they got the mine detectors, but that wasn't sure proof either. They started to make some of the mines out of plastic. One man has a white tape to show the ground that you went over, the second guy is using the mine detector, and the third guy disarms the mine. So, if anything happens, it only happens to three. It was tough there.

On the ship that was taking us to Scotland, I contracted yellow jaundice. I was sick as a dog, laying down in the hold of the ship. I finally saw a doctor. He said I had a bad throat so they sent me to sick bay. One week later, I saw the men on board, and they said, "Hey man, you're yellow." Down again to sick bay. Yellow jaundice. I was laying there weak as a bird. Now, we get onto a ferry to the trains, and, then, finally, we got into a town. Some time later, we were playing soft ball, and I jumped up in the air to catch the ball and got it in the nose. It was broken.

There was a lot anti-semitism. I felt it a lot. I took the OCS (Officers' Candidate School), but I missed by one point. Then, I took a shot for the Air Corps, but they had to block the holes up in those days so they put me in the engineers. Being an engineer was not me, but they had to have men there. They got 'em and they trained 'em. I passed the exam for the Air Corps, but they pigeoned me, put me into different things, kept moving me around. Every time there was a promotion, I didn't get it.

I felt there was not much I could do. I just kept my mouth shut. In spite of that, I knew a lot of officers who were really O.K.. They never bothered me. It was the enlisted men who gave me a hard time. It was ignorance, stupidity. They were all Georgia, North Carolina, and it was tough. The best thing that could have happened was for me to get out of the outfit, but that didn't happen. One guy called me, and I let him have it — they pulled me off of him. But he never bothered me again.

So we were in Glasgow and Falmouth. Engineers do everything. We built huts for the troops coming in. We were always the advance troops. There were plumbers and carpenters in our outfit. Then, we were in Bournemouth, England working on the LCI's — the landing barges. On June 6th, we landed with the First Infantry Division. It took us three trips to finally make it into France. I was lucky all the time with all this stuff. Lucky!

After the invasion, we went to Belgium and Germany. We were beyond the Seigfried line. I never got wounded — all those years. By that time, there were very few of my original outfit left. When I got to Czechoslovakia, I had 110 points, and that entitled me to go home right away. I just loved that country, beautiful country, attractive girls, small, petite. I had been in active service for three and a half years. Imagine. I was lucky, and I wanted to go home. I should have looked out for myself more, but I didn't. I could have gotten a whole truck load of stuff that was coming through, war-surplus, it was called, but I didn't think of all that. If I had done that, I could have been ready to go into business after I got home. Maybe it's just as well.

I hated the thought that he, Hitler, did those things. For the things that they did, that were never done ever on this earth, they deserve so much more than what they got. We fought the war, and, when it was over, they started to make it easy for all those Nazis to come here and go to South America and get covered up. We had to fight that war, for sure. There was a madman there. I really didn't think about why we were there because I wasn't in a position to do anything about it.

When I got out, I even did a night club job. I used to come in, do the ordering, set everything up. We had a night club show. I never had anything to do with night spots. As far as running it was concerned, I had never done such a thing, but I did it, and I did it well. At seven o'clock at night, I was gone. I did a day job. I was the day manager. I took care of getting the maintenance of the building. I recommended the women for the show. Then, the boss would see them. All the wheels were turning during the day. We also had one show during the day. I was there for quite a few years. It was late 50's when I left there.

I can't say that I didn't have an interesting life, but it could have been more exciting if I had done things differently. I've seen so much, and I gambled with the highest stake, my life. If you get a good start in life, you have the chance to run your life. For example, to live here in this building for elderly. They check on everything you've got, and they make the decisions. They have to do it, I don't blame them, but I wish that I had done better so I could be in control of my own life.

I wish I lived in California, but I can't make that change now. I'd like to get up in the morning and have a short-sleeved shirt and easy going, but ... You have to start new roots, and at this stage of the game, it's not too easy.

I never married. But when I get acquainted with someone, it's not just a passing fancy — it lasts for a long time. Usually, it takes a long while. You meet somebody, and, if you have a mutual interest, then it can work. It's either the person I really connect with or it's nobody. It's with me, and it's in me, and that's it. I don't only get physically attracted. There's a lot more to it. There was a girl waiting when I got back. I got twenty-one dollars a month then. But, now, I have a relationship with a woman that's good, really good.

I was stupid. I could have gone to school after the war. I was thinking of optometry, but I didn't do it. Someone gave me bad advice, and I didn't think for myself. In spite of everything that did happen, I came out O.K.

I always liked kids. When you don't have them, you know, there's something you're missing. The sincerest and most truthful attitude comes from children. Whatever comes out, comes out spontaneous, truthful — it's something that you rarely find in grown-ups. Adults figure things. Kids just react. I love that about them.

I've said it quite a few times — just to see the honesty in their faces. We go up to the fifth grade in our school. I help them with their papers, correct their papers, help them with their work books. The teacher I'm with teaches those who have reading problems mostly. She works hard with those kids. I wanted something to do in the morning, and I found the perfect thing. I didn't want to stay in bed. If your body isn't getting any help from you, yourself, you're in bad trouble. I wouldn't enjoy sitting around doing nothing. What better thing could you do with your time? The kids I work with are the ones who are slow in reading. We have a mixture of black and white children. The teacher may get ten children on a particular day, and she will give me four of them to work with. If those kids don't get their reading skills from the beginning, they're in bad trouble. I take my work with them very seriously. It's so important. The older I get the more I realize the value in reading well.

When you see the reading set-up in our school, you know there should be more money appropriated for education and for our foster grandparent program. You have to know how to read and write. And, if kids don't get that chance, they're bound to have trouble. There is going to come a time when people will not elect those same people to office anymore. We used to believe, live and let live — and now it's gone bad. We have to make some changes. I believe in kids. They should get what they need to grow up to be productive. I know what it's like when you don't have enough education.

I feel that I'm losing my memory sometimes. I hope it's not Alzheimers. I know that no one gets a second trip around. I don't believe in an after-life. I know when you go, you're gone, and, if they open up the box, they're just gonna see a pack of bones there. I know that definitely. I know I have my body, my mind. I can express myself. You open that box up a year later, those bones aren't going to talk to you. I am thankful that I am up on my feet. As long as I have that, I can do something.

I go to the school all the time, even in the summer. I love it. I appreciate a lot more things now. I don't take things for granted anymore. Now every bit that happens is something. When I was young, death was impossible, and now I feel vulnerable. About dying — there's nothing I can do about it. When I'm gone, I'm gone, and that's it. I don't have any real fears about it. Somewhere around the place, there's a witch and a broom. I'm a person who believes in facts, but there has to be somebody over all of us to make all that we know and see. I would certainly not go upstairs after all the things I've done. I don't want to go up there 'cause all the fun is downstairs.

* pogrom: A word used by the Jewish people in old Russia to signify the attacks by the Cossacks (Russian mounted police) directly on their persons and homes.

Florence Plovnick

Florence Plovnick

After I left Teachers' College, I went to work where my father worked, in that bake shop. I was there from six in the morning until six at night, and I made six dollars a week.

I think I was put on this earth to produce and nurture children. And, also, I must say I see the children at school more often than I see my own grandchildren, and there's a closeness. I try to be, not like their teacher, they're afraid of their teacher; I try to be their friend. When the year ends and I can't see those children, I miss them.

I was born in Malden in 1915. We lived there for a short time and then moved to Roxbury where I spent the rest of my young years. I was the youngest of six. I had four brothers and a sister. My father and my mother came from Russia. He came here when he was about twenty-one, and he died when he was ninety-six. My mother spoke English very well. She learned from listening to the radio and talking with us. She couldn't write though. They married here through a match-making service. Yes, that's the way it was. I don't know how much my mother was in love with my father but with six children years ago, devoting themselves to the children and keeping the family housed, it was hard, hard work. She really didn't see him that much. But often enough to have six children, I guess.

I graduated from Roxbury Memorial High School in 1932. My family was what you might call lower middle class. We always lived in a neighborhood with lots of children. My father was a baker in a huge commercial bake shop called Freedman's. We hardly ever saw him. He'd leave the house about three in the afternoon and come home in the middle of the night. He belonged to a union, but it didn't make any difference to him. He always worked overtime. We had no relationship what-so-ever with my father. But I was happy when I was young, growing up. It seems so long ago.

When I graduated from high school, I started at Boston Teachers College, but, at that time, if you taught in Boston and if you were female, you couldn't get married. I student-taught for two months. I quit because I didn't want to be what they called "an old maid." I didn't want to spend four years studying. I went to work where my father worked, in the bake shop. I was there from six in the morning until six at night, and I made six dollars a week. In 1932, that was a lot of money. A loaf of bread was a dime then and a dozen rolls twelve cents. I worked there for about a year and then went to the office of my brother-in-law who was a jeweler. I stayed there until my mother died.

My mother died when I was about twenty. I quit my job, and I stayed home and took care of my father and my three brothers. When my husband proposed to me, I hesitated because he was living in North Carolina. I was concerned about taking care of the men! My sister had married before, therefore, I was it. I did the cooking, cleaning, laundry, everything. My brothers were very kind and treated me as if I had a regular job. They sent me off on vacation for a couple of weeks during the summer. I used to spend a lot of time at Franklin Field playing tennis, meeting dates in the afternoon and just enjoying myself. My time was my own. Nobody ever complained about my cooking. They were all good about it for after all I was the kid-sister. And, strangely enough, when I did decide to marry, my brothers married also and my father as well! I always felt that, if I hadn't married, they might not have either.

When my father's second wife died, he came to live with me. I didn't even know him. He was a total stranger. He couldn't speak English, and I could hardly speak Jewish, so there wasn't too much communication. He was nice. He lived with us for sixteen years. His two sisters died at ninety-six, too. I just realized that, though we hardly knew each other, we lived together for a good many years.

When I got married, I went down to North Carolina. My husband was a chemist and was exempt from the service because he was working in an asbestos plant that did defense work. We lived there seven years and had our first three children there. When my husband wanted to start his own business, we decided to go back to Boston. My mother-in-law owned a large house in Roxbury, and we moved in with her for seven of the unhappiest years of my life. It was never my home. Finally, we moved into our own place when I became pregnant with my fourth child. I really enjoyed my boys a lot. I used to go coasting with them, play ball with them. They were really fun. Whenever we had a vacation, it was planned around what the boys would like to do.

You know, years ago people felt they had to stay married whether they liked it or not. So you don't think about that. At one time, my husband's business went into bankruptcy, and I wanted to go to work. No wife of his would work! I think it was his pride. But my marriage was really good. I was happy. My husband was a very good person. Today, if a young woman wants a man, they can just live together. You don't have to get married. It's not like it was years ago. If a woman said that she was thirty-five or forty and wasn't married — oh, oh, like a sin! Not now. My son just got married, and, at his wedding, he had two of his woman friends. One of them had lived with him for a year. Then they decided that they weren't compatible. The other woman lived in Maine. She also had a close relationship with him but never would move down to Boston. He has remained friends with both of them, and they both came to his wedding. This is the way he is. He's the type who likes to go camping, bicycle riding and such. One of his friends said, "Bernard's idea of a gourmet dinner is opening a can of spam." At the ceremony, the Rabbi from Brandeis referred to them as "a couple of characters."

I'm happy about all my kids. They have each put themselves through college because our financial condition was not that good. I think I was put on this earth to produce and nurture children. I must say I have the same feelings toward the children at school as I have towards my own. I see the children at school more often than I see my own grandchildren, and there's a closeness. Lots of times I should say we don't even read. I have them tell me different things about themselves and their interests; what they like to do, things like that. I think it relaxes them so I have a little intimacy with them. I know more about them.

I try to be not like their teacher. They're afraid of their teacher; I try to be their friend. When the year ends and I can't see those children, I miss them. During the regular school year, I am at the Baldwin Elementary School. The teachers and the principal, Mr. James, have been wonderful to me. Now the school is over-crowded. They've had to make two classrooms out of one. There's hardly any space for me to work. I am in the lunch room now, in a space the size of a closet. I work with these Chinese kids. The teacher told me to try to get them to talk, plain conversation. There were no chairs, and so I went with the three of them and sat on the floor. This is how we worked. I will always find a corner somewhere or other where we can work. I guess it's because I want to do it. I do want to do it. It's really not work.

The kids are in the fourth grade and they can hardly speak English though they were born here. They were in a bi-lingual class up until this year. Now, they're trying to learn the language, reading and all. They live in a Chinese community, and their parents speak only Chinese. I seem to see a lot of the same problems my parents had. It's a kind of isolation, separation.

Yesterday, I worked with a child in his classroom. He is in the second grade, and he may be demoted to the first. I sat next to him and kept complimenting him. All the children like to have a one-on-one relationship. He did all his work and wanted to know if I was going to come back later. Then I found out that this particular child is seven years old, and he has a key to his house. Nobody is at home when he gets back from school. This is the reason this kid is this way. There is little time for love or affection. I feel so sorry for children like that. When I have any extra time, I go down to that classroom and ask the teacher if she needs me, and she always points to him. I think if I can give him this personal attention, he could come right back to where he should be.

I also work with two Cambodian children in the fifth grade and another in the fourth. They can pronounce all the words, but when you ask them what the story was about, they don't know. I teach them to use the dictionary to help them begin to get the understanding. It always makes me feel good if I'm walking in the street or if I'm in the street car and one of the kids says, "Hi, Mrs. P." with a nice smile. They remember me. I didn't realize that it's almost ten years that I've been there.

This past summer, I was working with four boys from Cambodia. They could hardly speak English; two sets of brothers, the oldest fifteen. They had recently come here. They knew no English at all. I had to teach them the sounds like, cl, sp. One of the words was "spank," so I took the biggest one, and I put him over my knee. Then, every time they were acting up I'd say, you want spank? And that word stayed with them. I would perform for them to show them what a word meant. They really wanted to learn, and they were fun to work with. I think they made a lot of progress. That was at the site I work at during the summer months when my own school isn't in session.

The years go by so quickly. I think many times I don't want to live as long as my father did. Right now, I can take care of myself, but you never know. I don't think about tomorrow. Who knows whether my children will want to care for me or not. I don't know. I'm happy that I don't need them now. Sometimes I think if I had a daughter, maybe there'd be a closer relationship. Maybe. The only time I think of my own age is when I look in the mirror and see the change. So I avoid the mirrors. Thank goodness, my health has been good, and I don't feel old yet. I really don't feel different. I do think one becomes more mellow, but I've always been more or less mellow, sort of a home-body. I used to be very happy just to stay home with my husband. My oldest son would say, "How come you're always in?"

But we were happy holding hands, watching T.V., talking, and, once in a while, we'd go to a movie or visit with friends. So that's the life I'm leading now, happy to go out to spend some time with friends or take long walks. My interests are centered on my children, my grandchildren and the kids at school.

The kids at school give me so much. So much. My own children realize how much my work means to me. When I told them I was going to be interviewed for a book, they thought, "Wow, a celebrity!" I don't do anything for that reason. I just take it for granted. I do what I do because I enjoy doing it. Some of the foster grandmothers worry about whether the checks have come in. I keep telling them, if I didn't get a check, I'd still do it. I'd still do it. I enjoy it so much. It makes a difference to me, too. I can buy a few extra things because of that check, but I would do away with those extras and still do it. I enjoy it. It's so great!

Somebody else might think kids are a nuisance, but I have discovered that children are exciting in so many ways. When I attended the training we had at Lesley College, they showed us the value of putting words to music. Just the other day, I was having trouble with this same little boy in the second grade. I took him out of the classroom, and I started singing to him. "Ricky, come over here I want to talk to you," in a melody. And he started singing back to me. "All right I'll do it if you want me to." It works. It really works. When I'm with them, I'm on their level, I think the way they think — a little like a kid — and that's why I don't think about my own age anymore.

Lillian White

Lillian White

And, now, I'm a foster grandparent after all those other jobs. I had a boy this morning who finds it very difficult to multiply. He's slow, and I have to be slow with him. It's not his fault that he's slow. He would like to be able to do it, but his brain can't. And I understand.

This is my tenth year as a foster grandparent. All these years at school with the kids. I was born in Malden in 1910, graduated Malden High in 1929, and I'm now I'm back in school in Malden. My parents both came from Russia about 1906, I would guess. My father came first, and then sent for my mother. Two of my sisters were born there, but they were infants when they came. They were three or four years older than me. One sister passed away. My other sister lives here — we're all in Malden, two brothers and a sister. We were a close family. We still are. About 60,000 people in Malden but, of course, they are building more condos and the population grows.

My father, as far back as I remember, loved horses. He worked in a stable grooming the horses. Then he bought his own horse and wagon and went into the ice business. And he worked very hard. You had to put a card in the window to let the ice man know how much ice you wanted that day, and he would cut that size for you. That was long before refrigerators. It was very hard work delivering to peoples' houses. But his family always came first. We had neighbors who were even worse off than we were. My mother would tell people, if you order a quarter of a ton of coal whenever you have the money, you can pay us later. My father delivered coal as well as ice. There were always people giving of themselves. Things were bad.

I remember, after my father died, I passed a grocery store one day, and the owner was outside. He said, "There couldn't have been a more wonderful man than your father." You know what he used to do? There was a family that was very poor, as if we were rich, and he'd come in and buy a quart of milk and leave it at their doorstep. They never knew who left it.

My two sisters were both sales-ladies here in Malden. Unfortunately, Malden Square is not what it was. We had Jordan Marsh, we had all beautiful shops, and, now, there's hardly anything left. When my brother was going to high school, he worked in a market after school. Then, the range oil business began, and my father had a little tank on the same ice team. But it didn't work out too well. My mother decided that as soon as my brother graduated, he could get a truck and put the tank on that.

My father didn't drive. My mother was the book-keeper. She could read a little bit of English and write very little. She used to take the phone calls and write it in Jewish, and my brother could read it. That's how the oil business started in our home. She was cute. She'd answer the phone and say," Hello, Sher Oil Co." She never missed a call, and the business grew. Later on, they rented a little office. My father would say to customers, if you need credit (at that time there used to be a lot of credit accounts) that was O.K. He'd give them credit and always speak of the business that everybody owned. He used to even loan people money if they had to pay some other bill that was overdue. They all paid it back. Some paid one dollar a week. But, of course, things are done differently today.

My brother stayed with it and got married and had one daughter. My other brother was what they called an inside man. He lives here, too. I couldn't think about moving out of Malden. I was always over at my mother's, every day. Sometimes I'd be there twice a day. My mother got older, and she needed different things done for her. I always drove a car but going out of Malden, I just couldn't imagine how I would do all that I wanted. My husband and I once saw some land at the Cape, beautiful, for $300. I said no again because how would I get to my mother. I figured she was going to live forever.

I have a tendency to like sewing of all the strange things. One of our neighbors had a sewing machine, and she taught me. I was fascinated. There was an ad in the paper for a person who could stitch. They asked me if I was experienced and I said yes. The minute I sat down there, I knew I wasn't experienced. But I was a good kid and, by cracky, it turned out that I became their supervisor. It was a furniture slip cover company that I worked for. Now we are talking about the early war years.

While I was still working in Malden, Uncle Sam took my brother into the service. Every time we got a driver, the army took them. Soon it was just my father and he couldn't drive. He said to me, "You've got to get into the truck and drive it." It was winter-time, and the road was a glare of ice. I said, "I'm really afraid, Pa." He said, "I'll sit next to you." (laughter). Poor man. He really killed himself. At that time, they didn't have the automatic wind-up hose. You had to pull it, and then wind it back by hand. And that was something! I had to back into everybody's back yard. My father would be up front saying, "Cut 'er this way, cut 'er that way, straighten 'er out." and I'd do it. I had two rocks here in my arms for muscles. It was a 600 gallon truck. I sat on a pillow. I never put a scratch on the body. One place I had to back up to, there was a huge post, and only a sheet o' paper might fit between the post and the truck. But I did it.

And, then, suddenly, our supplier saw that my brother wasn't around. He began to cut down on our oil. It was a very cold winter. I took the phone book and called every supplier. The answer I got was "Sorry, nothing we can do for you." There was only one place, Tidewater Oil Co., where the man who answered said, "Sorry, but try us again." That was the man I married! Well, I went to the Rationing Board, and they said, they thought they were going to be releasing the oil. So, I called Tidewater again. This same man said, "I'm sorry I don't have any such news yet, but give me your number, and, if I get it, I will call you." Which he did.

And so we had two trucks and one driver, then. I wore slacks and little flat shoes. When I arrived to load my truck, there were so many in front of me, and, I had never met this man before of course. He was the dispatcher, at the time. He tipped off all the men who worked there that there was a girl comin' in, and he wanted no hanky-panky. I paid him (I had taken my place in line just like all the others), and he said, you pull up to that ramp, and we'll load the truck. I did. Well, he worked there only three long days a week, then he'd have the other two days off. We were telling him what a difficult time we were having getting a driver for the other truck. He said, "I'll come down on my days off, and give you a hand." But there was no romance at the beginning. It took a long time to develop.

One of the men who worked at the Malden Slip-Cover Company called me one day. He was a salesman. He said, "I'm going into business, and, since you are a know-it-all, I'd like you to come and help me set it up." It was on Lincoln St. in Boston, and it was to be the same business — slip covers. Who wants to go to Boston? I hesitated. When I got home and talked about it, I made the decision to try. They had bought all these machines from another company. First thing I said was, "Throw that one out, throw that one out." I said, "You can't produce with anything like that." So they did whatever I suggested, and it became big, The Lincoln Textile Co. I was there for four years. Now, they are in Pennsylvania.

My husband-to-be continued to help out in my parents business, but now they didn't need me to drive the truck any longer. I wasn't dating too much because I was too busy but, then, just sort of naturally, I married him. He was a very refined gentleman and treated me royally. He gave up his job at Tidewater to come to work with us. He had a duodenal ulcer and so wasn't drafted, but, when my brother came back, there really wasn't enough for the two of them. During war-time, if you left your job, they'd never take you back. He found a job with Zarex Syrups and stayed with them for a long time.

You know, I like to cook. So over the years, my husband put weight on. He was very slim when I married him. Later, he went on a crash diet, and, when he got the flu, it seemed he had no resistance. Suddenly, a bad cough ruptured the varicose vein in his esophagus, and in one week, he was operated on four times. But it didn't help. He bled to death. My son was fifteen at the time. It was 1968, and my husband was in his fifties. It was terrible, terrible. I lost my voice for a while, and I wouldn't socialize with anyone for two years. But I did go to Malden Business School to brush up on my typing. Then, I got a job in the State Street Bank doing the clerical changes for the computer. And that I loved. That was in 1969. I stayed until '71 when they moved to Quincy. Of all the jobs I had, that's the one I really liked.

I want to tell you a story about my son. He had a photo developing set-up in the basement of our house where he and some of his friends learned to develop the pictures they took. One day, he got the bright idea to try for the Malden News. He found out that if he got accident photos, he could get them printed in the paper. One night, I'm in bed sleeping, and he wakes me. "An accident! Quick!" I jump into my clothes, get into the car. Every policeman knew me. Out he'd jump, and take the pictures. He had a short-wave radio, and he would hear the police calls. That's how he knew. Some of the other kids got their mothers, too. So mothers were competing with mothers to see who got there faster. This went on for over a year. He continued doing this accident chasing even when he drove. But when he graduated, he went to Wentworth and Northeastern and became an engineer. Thank God. He does fine.

I also go to Fernald State School, as a volunteer, of course, where I am a Building Representative. I inspect the building. I just reported that the rain water still collects in the driveway. It needs a drain installed and that the nurses' office needed a fan installed. And now they have it. I meet with the Building Reps whenever there is a meeting, and I make my reports. I also help with the Spring Ball which raises money for the School. When I examine the buildings, and if any of the staff is there, they'll say, "Tell Mrs. White. Tell Mrs. White 'cause she gets things done." And I do. I keep after them — sometimes on the telephone and some-, times in person.

And I'm a foster grandparent since 1977. It's funny, as the years go on, the children are getting a little fatter and a little fatter because I'm always making something. Last year, my teacher took a leave of absence so I went to work in the Resource Room. The children would come up to me, and I would help with their writing and their phonics and yes, their math. We'd work together on it. I'd read stories to the children while the teacher was at her lunch. I was involved in their work in all their subjects. The children were six, seven and eight. Then, my teacher came back this year, and I'm at the Learning Center, at the Emerson School. I take one or two children. They have a little computer, called the Math Man. I'll work with them on that.

I had a boy this morning who finds it very difficult to multiply. He gets confused. So I sit and work with him. He's slow, and I know it's not his fault that he's slow so I praise him when he does it well. He would like to be able to do it, but his brain can't. I know all that and I understand. I have another little boy, too fast, so he can't print. I try to slow him down carefully and help him that way. I love them, and it's a mutual feeling. There's something nice about each child. When you find something nice about a child, you help to bring it out and you make that child feel like a king or a queen. That helps them in their work.

My own granddaughters are six and two and a half. I have toys here for them because, of course, they visit often. I love all kids. When the kids at school graduate, I have a hard time. I miss them. At the Learning Center, the children come and go, but, at the Resource Center, they come for a long time. I have contests. I buy great big stars and put them on their good work. Then, when the school term ends, I make ice cream cone cup cakes and home-made fudgicles. I got coupons at McDonald's, and the winners of the contest, the children who did the very best, got two coupons. The others all got one. That way no one was left out. "We all have a present," they said, "She's the best teacher in the world." I make Santa Claus cupcakes for Christmas with three colors of frosting. It takes me about two days because I make about twenty even though I only have eleven children. I give some to others.

I love children. I love to see their eyes when I give them something. Their happiness — my reward. I was brought up to give of myself. All my life, this is how we are. It's my pleasure to make a child happy — my reward for everything. Money is great but not everything. The children have given me more little things. Sweet. I enjoy what I'm doing. It just makes me happy. I know I must get there early so I get up with a vengeance, straighten the house up, and off I go. The minute the first child walks in with a smile, it's great.

Well, I'm getting older, but I just want to go on. I've slowed up a little bit, but I see life as always. I've been involved in a lot, but I don't like to be in the limelight. I couldn't get up and make a speech, but, if I hear that somebody needs a hand, I'm right there. I know that I'm getting older — I'll keep fighting as long as I can. And I thank God for all my days. We never know what the end is, but, as long as I can, I will keep going. Yes, I guess I'm proud. It's certainly not a lot of money, and money is not the motivation, but it has helped me. And I thank everyone for that.

* * *

Lillian White is a tiny woman who one would never guess could drive a 600-gallon truck or organize a stitching shop into a successful business. She told her story in such a matter-of-fact way, hardly conscious of all she had contributed to her original family and later to her own.

The Foreign Language Specialists

Beatrice Feliciano

Beatrice Feliciano

When I came to Boston, everything was different. I had no husband, no work, but I always have my family. And I like to be with the children in school We give love to them, and they give us love back.

I was born in Puerto Rico in 1916, in a little town called Guanica. My father worked on ships, but I don't know what he did. Both my parents were born in Puerto Rico. I had three sisters and five brothers. I was the fifth child. My mother worked in the house. My father supported us. That's the way it was. I went to school but only to the eighth grade because Papa wanted all his daughters in the house with our mother. He said, "I don't want my daughters working because I don't know what can happen to them." I stayed at home until I got married.

My husband came from Yaoco, a small town like Guanica. I met him when he moved to our neighborhood. We believe it is where Christopher Columbus landed. He worked in a store, and he lived with his parents. He was twenty-two, and I was nineteen when we got married in 1936. At first, he was selling. Then he got his own store where we sold clothes and hardware and other things for the house. My father didn't even want his daughters to get married. He said we were still little girls. My husband was a very good man.

Later we went to live in San Juan, the capital. I had three children, two boys and a girl. We had a store in San Juan. We sold it in 1952 and came to the U.S. My brother was here, and he kept saying, "Come, come." Almost the whole family came. We came to the Bronx in New York and bought a store there. We stayed there twenty years. At first, it was nice, and he did very well, but then it got bad. We could go to the park when it was hot and bring some sheets and even sleep there. Later, it got very bad. They started to vandalize the stores everywhere, and so we sold ours.

206

I must tell you that I always lived near my daughter. She is my only daughter. In New York, she lived in the apartment above me, and we had the store below. When we had to leave New York, my daughter moved to Detroit. We went there to be with her, and that is when my husband started to be sick. It was his heart. But he had to go to Puerto Rico to see his mother. When he was there, they told him that he couldn't travel any more. So I went there and stayed there for about a year and a half. Then he died. It was 1975. We brought him to New York to be buried there. He was very good to me. We had a very good marriage.

I have one son who works at the Post Office in New York. He is married but doesn't have any children. My other son works with television cameras in New York. He goes out with reporters and works the cameras. He is married and has four children. Both my sons have wives of Puerto Rican families who were born here. When I came back from New York, my daughter and I moved to Boston. She married a man who they made a minister in the Christian Church. They have three children. When they joined the Christian Church, they sent him here to Boston. She has one daughter, twenty-seven, another twelve, and the son is almost 10. At first, they only wanted to have one. But, then, they became Christian, and it was a sin to use birth control. My daughter is almost fifty.

I like to be with my family when they get sick and need me. I always go to take care of them. But, when my husband was alive, I worked in the stores. And I worked for a little while at the Post Office in New York. I really needed to be working, and I always liked to be taking classes. So I took classes in how to work in a post office, and I took a course in English. When I came to Boston, everything was different. I had no husband, no work, but I had some money from my husband's business. And I have a son who gives me money, the one who works in the Post Office. I won't take money from my other son because he has children. I have Social Security from my husband — not too much — and I have Medicaid. My children don't want me to work, but I don't like to be in the house. I like it when I'm working now because I enjoy being with the children. I love the children.

When we came here from Detroit, I didn't know where I was going to be. But my things arrived at the same time as my daughter's. The woman who was the manager here was a Christian, too, and she found me an apartment right away. Soon my daughter will be moving to Fitchburg to a veteran's house. She's moving because she hears people using bad language, and she has children. I'll go to visit her, but I'll stay here now. My married granddaughter is staying here. She has one little girl, four years old, and is separated from her husband. They broke up because he started to drink a lot. A lot. He was in Vietnam, and he used to have those attacks of craziness. He would break things, just go crazy. Now, he has another wife, but he still calls my granddaughter and tells her everything. She doesn't want to live with him anymore, but she talks to him. And so that she can go to work, I take the little girl to the day care in the morning, and she picks her up. I take her to a school not too far away, and, then, I take the bus for ten cents, and I go to my school.

I used to work in another day care center further down. So there I would do circle time with the children. I would teach the first hour, their little lessons, and then play with them. But, since it was pretty far to go there, I wanted to change to the Blackstone School, which is close. They put me in the first grade. I work with six-year-olds and like it where I am, but there is no time to play with the children. I get there at 9:00. I correct their homework. I try to show them what to do. Then, some of them do their work there at the school, and I correct that, too. There isn't enough time for me to work with the reading, but, when the teacher has a child who is slow, I can help him.

The school is bilingual, but the math books are in English. Since the children are just starting and they don't know how to read, I teach in Spanish. In the afternoon, they teach in English after I leave. In the other school where I worked with the little children, I didn't teach in Spanish. I worked there for a long time. I like it better teaching in English because then I learn too. I don't like

208

bilingual schools for the Hispanic children. They never learn the language that way. I think that the children who go to bilingual school are going to have problems. They have to first learn the language. In our house, we speak to the children in English. I know a little, but I feel like I'm losing it.

Well, I believe, like everyone else, that our Celestial Father is Jesus Christ. We have to be like him. Try anyway, because that is very hard. Try. That is what I must do for my life. We believe that those who are dead, who are born believing that our Lord sent us his son, Jesus Christ, will await to wake again. We have to love each other. That is what God tells us. That's why I like to be with the children. We give love to them, and they give us love back. When I was with the little children, sometimes I had to stay late because they would go to take their naps, and they didn't want me to leave. So I would stay until they went to sleep. Then I would leave. And I would feel good.

I have lived in the U.S. many years. I like it here because I don't have any family there, only one sister. Everybody else is here or in New York. Wherever I lived, I never have had any problems. Never. Even when there are bad people, they aren't bad to me. I never have problems with anybody. If someone has a problem with me, I pretend that I don't hear, and it goes away.

I feel good getting older. I don't really feel old until I look in the mirror. When I go out, I get dressed according to where I'm going, and I feel good. I don't feel the same at seventy as when I was twenty-five. It's different when you are older after living all the years. I am happy even though I can't do the same things I did when I was twenty-five. But, when I was very young, I felt a great love for my husband. That was different than now when I'm alone.

* * *

Beatrice Feliciano lives in an area that was developed in the late 70's with a good deal of community input. The intention was to

209

offer good, low-cost housing to the growing Hispanic population in the Boston area along with the opportunity to continue to participate in the various forms of Hispanic culture.

Kam Kew Lee

Kam Kew Lee

I was born in Toy San in Canton province in China in 1908. My father lived in the United States and worked in manufacturing. My mother was a housewife in China. She never came here. My father-in-law lived here, too, and my mother-in-law, in China. But their son lived in the U.S. with his father. When he wanted to get married, his mother arranged for me to marry him. He came to China, and we were married in 1929. Then he returned to the States. I had one son born in 1930, and we both lived with my mother-in-law until we were able to come here.

I went through high school in China and then to teacher training school, but I couldn't work as a teacher because that was the time of the war. I was a farmer during the war and planted rice which was the main food we had. When the Japanese attacked China, we all ran from city to city. We had a very hard time then. I was about thirty-nine, then. It was very bad until I left. The revolution was just starting when I left for this country.

We were not able to come here until 1949 because, before the war, Americans did not allow Chinese men to bring their families here. When I left my country, I went to Hawaii and waited there until I could enter the U.S. I came alone because my son was studying, and he stayed to finish school.

I arrived in Boston in 1950 and lived with my husband. It was hard at first to get used to the new country. I worked in a laundry when I first came here. Then my husband died in 1977. He died of kidney failure. They didn't have the machine, at that time, so they couldn't save him. My son married here, and then went to live in California. He passed away in 1985. Now I have a daughter-in-law and two grandchildren, a boy and a girl. My daughter-in-law comes to visit me in the summertime each year.

I do not really feel lonesome. I tell my daughter-in-law I do not want to live in California. I like Boston. I had two brothers and a sister in Canada, but my sister died when she was young, and now my brother-in-law lives here in Boston.

I became a foster grandparent one year after my husband died. At the school, they have many immigrant children who have recently come from China or Vietnam, and they do not understand English. When the teacher teaches them, I tell them what she is saying in their own language. And then I also help the little children, five year-olds who don't know how to go to the toilet or how to be in this school. They don't know when to ask for something or how to understand what is happening. I show them everything. I love the children, and they get attached to me. "Hi, grandmother." They learn something with me every day. I am so happy to help them. My own grandchildren are far away in California, and so I love these children. Everybody needs love, and the children love me.

Now I feel that human beings were made by God for otherwise we wouldn't have life, you know. God granted me the right to do this teaching because, before, I never had that opportunity, but now I do. My husband wanted me to be a nurse, but I didn't like that. I really like to teach children. It was an unconscious wish for a long time. It is something I wanted to do. I can do it well. I am happy with what I am doing now and satisfied with my life as long as I can continue to do this.

I don't have too much time to socialize when I come home. I leave the house very early, and sometimes it is two o'clock when I come home. I read the Chinese newspaper, and I read short stories, but I don't go out. My friends in the building go out sometimes or they have other things to do so it's only on the weekend or holidays that I see them. I am happy to stay home. Too many crimes in the streets.

* * *

Kam Kew Lee's teacher, Janet Shih: I have worked with Kam Kew Lee for ten years, and she is so wonderful. It's so important to

213

have a grandmother in the class. She's here all the time from 7:45 to 2:00. All the school day, she works with the children. Whenever we need her, she comes with happiness, so willing to help. You don't have to tell her what to do, she sees it herself and does such a fine job. We all learn from her. She never claims any credit. Many old people in this country are being wasted. It's so important to have older people with the children. They themselves don't realize how important they are. They are needed in our lives. They are not old-fashioned and unimportant. No. They are the most important to give us the sense of where we come from and so we know where we are going. Kam Kew Lee does all that.

Olga Yi

Olga Yi

I learn from people. I no like to go to school. I learn to take care of my father's money that way, and I learn English at the school from the children.

When they see me in the corridor, they say, "Hi, teacher." They call me "teacher" and the real teacher in my room, she says everybody is a teacher. She's very smart, and the kids respect everybody. But she has no special time for each child. She tells me to help every kid here that I can. And I do.

I was born in Havana, Cuba in 1917. My father taught me Spanish. Then I went to the San Jose School where I learn everything. At night, I go to Chinese school. There were so many Chinese there. My father and mother come from Canton Province. Many went from China to Cuba. My father had a market first, and later he had a restaurant in San Raphael Street, a main street. He had Chinese food and everything. He had farms, one in Mantanza and another near there. He grew his own Chinese vegetables, and later he exported those Chinese vegetables to New York. I had a very comfortable childhood. For the Chinese, it doesn't matter how rich you are. As soon as you can, you must go to work.

I didn't go too far in school because I no like to study. My brother graduated from Texas military academia. He is still in Cuba. I call sometimes, and he call me sometimes. He is younger, about fifty-seven. My other brother live here in Braintree. He bought a house there. My niece picks me up sometimes, and we go to visit him. He's about one year younger than I am. (At this point she identifies the family photos that are sitting atop the T.V. Then she explains the arrangement of her parents' photo and the small bowl of water nearby.)

One of the things about Chinese people, water is very important to make tea because we put the tea in with head bent to help those to rise who have died. When somebody dies, we do this ritual to help those who has passed to rise. Somebody must do this ritual when there is a death. I use water because I don't drink tea. All Chinese drink tea like water but not me, my stomach. The Chinese, in any country where they live, they do that. They always honor the dead. On Chinese Memorial Day, so many people go to the cemetery with all the food and then bring it back and eat it. It is all cooked, and then to eat it makes the person close to the dead ones. Mexican people do that, too.

I went to like, high school. I work in my father's business. I take care of money, take it to bank and do office work. I no went to University, I just learn it. It's better you go to University but I am very nervous. I keep the records, and I do a good job. There were seventy-eight people who worked there. I took care of all the records. My brother showed me, and I learned it because I did not want to go to University.

My brothers went to University, but I take care of everything. I can do whatever my father needs in the business. Everybody do something big in my family but not me. My nieces go to University, too. When I was in school, I could not write Chinese so my father put the homework for us, and we had to do it. In our house, we had to speak Chinese so we had to study. He put the time to do the homework, time to do the dinner. He said, "You can speak any language outside, but in the house only Chinese." It was better for me because I learned two languages.

I never get married, no. You know everyone no think the same. When I was younger, I have money, I am well, I can go to vacation. In Cuba, no boyfriends, but friends, amigos, no live together. I have friends, no boyfriend. I have to work, but I have freedom. In Cuba, not everybody have a car, but me, I learn to drive. You know, everybody here like this country. So many people rich here. Everybody has cars. But in Cuba, when you have a car, you have lots of money.

When Fidel Castro come, he took everything — the buildings with apartments, the restaurant business but not the farms. My uncle sold them before the revolution. My father said to my niece who was pregnant, "You go to New York, and then maybe you come back." But, when Castro take everything, what am I going to do there? You have to work. That is very hard for me to work for Castro. It was May, 1962, and I am very angry, but I don't cry because I don't want everybody to look at me crying. I was so nervous, I had to take medicine. Anyway, what we lose, it's so hard because my father work so hard when he was younger _ everybody work so hard. So we leave, my mother, two nephews, and my niece. We all leave. My father say maybe six months and Castro go down. But it's not true. He stayed, and then he come about a year later.

There were five of us at first, and I didn't know about welfare. If somebody tell me, I would go. My niece, she has two boys born in Cuba, and then one was born here. My sister-in-law came and my parents. Twelve of us lived in one apartment. I couldn't sleep there because I am so nervous. We lived like that for more than six months with no heat, and we couldn't keep it clean. I got job in factory. Then the government took the building, but the landlord, a Chinese man, bought a big house, and we moved there. He was very nice. We live there sixteen years. After that, I come here to Chinese elder housing. My father came in 1964, April. My mother died just after, in July. My mother said, "It's killing me," and she died. I saw the eye, you know when the eye doesn't move. I called the doctor, they took her to hospital and doctor told me, bad. The next day, she died. Then, my father died just three weeks later, the 28th of July. I take off from work when my parents die, I don't remember three or four weeks. It was terrible. I lose everything.

I worked for Garland Sweater Company on a machine. I never worked on a machine before, but they teach you at Garland. They had a bus to take us to work. I worked for them for eighteen years. I had three weeks vacation after ten years, and I have a pension and twelve holidays. They still pay the health and life insurance for me. If I worked hard, I got money. We did not need a union. The company was good to us. I work fast, piece work they call it, and I make good money. Now, I have the little pension and my social security and the little from the program, and I can get along. I don't have too much, but a little here and a little there, and I get along.

I want my own house, not if I marry, but my own house. I would like that. I am happy that my mother never had to go to work. She never work in Cuba, just in the house. My father and mother teach me everything I do, everything. I like cooking, and I have a garden on the Fenway, just near me. Sometimes I work six hours in my garden. I don't think I here for a special purpose, no. I never feel that. I used to go to visit my family in New York when I was younger, but now I don't go. And some of them have moved to Texas, too far. I have cousin in California who come sometimes for a week, two weeks. She ask me why don't you come? I no like planes.

I like the program (FGP). It is so nice for old people. Every year, the teacher at the school have twenty-five children, every year. I'm working for four years now at the school. Every year, five or six kids need help even in kindergarten where I am. We try to teach them. I don't understand why the mothers who stay home not teach them? They don't know about 1,2,3,4,5. They don't know to write their name. But, because they're small, I can teach them. We have Chinese and Vietnamese in my class — the other rooms have others. Because of my background, I work with those kids. They sing Chinese songs, and even the American kids sing Chinese. Some kids are so nice. They are so good when they ask me something — what is that? I like it. One kid ask me why I speak Spanish, and I have to explain everything.

Some kids are very smart, and some kids are slow. Last year we had two kids, very hard for them to learn. The mother does not want to hear about it. Some of them are new here. The teacher say the kids need help, but they watch T.V. every night and come to school tired. When they see me in the corridor, they say, "Hi, teacher." They call me "teacher" and the real teacher in my room, she says, "Everybody is a teacher." She's very smart and the kids respect everybody. But she has no special time for each child. So she tells me to help every kid here that I can, and I do. Now I go to computer room every Tuesday, and I teach them from the computer, the alphabet. The computer shows "A" then, I say, "What comes next?" Then I say, "'A' for what?" and they say, "Apple." Then "C" for what and they say, "Cat" and sometimes get mixed up with "K." The computer is good for the kids. If some of them are slow, I sit with them and help them more.

My family think I do good in this work. This is the first time in my life working with children. Well, maybe because I like the kids I can do good. Sometime the mother bring the kid, and I talk with them, and I say, it's good you talk Chinese at home because the children learn it. It's good for them to know more languages. I never knew English when I come to this country.

It's hard to learn, but I learn at the school with the children. I don't know grammar, but I can talk a little. I speak Spanish or Chinese with my family, and sometimes I speak Chinese with the children. I don't need too much English because it's only the kindergarten. I teach the ABC's and the numbers. In Garland, I don't speak English too much because so many Cuban ladies worked there.

I think growing older is nice. Yea, it's nice. I have a brother here. Everybody has good job, making good money. My brother is always good because he says he has his health. Everybody is O.K., and that's good. I'm not very ambitious, but in my life, I have everything. I am happy. The kids, my family, no drinking, and I can enjoy now. All day, I'm busy. My garden, the children at school, I'm busy. I go to the school, then I come home, take something to eat here and go to the garden. I like it. The teacher say to me, "Why you come early?" I say because I take the bus so I meet the kids for breakfast. I not lonesome. I have a full day. Some people say, nothing to do, nothing to do. I no understand that. Stay in house with four walls, no, I can't do that. Some people say my phone is broken because I never home. I have three phones, one in every room, but I never stay home. When there is no school, I go to the garden, but when snow comes I go to my family's home. Sometimes my nephew sends a ticket to come to Philadelphia, and I say I have money to buy ticket, but I don't go there too much now.

It's so far. I'm very happy, and very lucky.

Chapter 3
At the Hospitals

At the Hospitals

Clyde Forde and Mary Morris are the two foster grandparents interviewed for this book out of a group of nine who worked in Boston hospitals in the late 80's. Clyde made his path to the world famous Boston Children's Hospital, nurturing children with diseases of long duration including cancer and AIDS, attending youngsters who were separated from their primary source of security at a time when they needed it most.

Applicants who expressed preference for working with children in hospital were interviewed extensively by a staff person and many times by myself as well. We encouraged them to speak of their apprehensions, of their previous experiences with children who were ill, and their concerns about working in large and complex structures. Mary Morris worked at Boston City Hospital, a very large inner-city medical center serving a cross section of the metropolitan population. "City" is primarily resonsible for providing medical care for low-income people. The children in the pediatric wards are largely from poor families and one-parent homes.

The administrative staff provides group discussions of department procedures and professional functions so that the grandparents can comprehend how the medical staff and management work together to provide the best possible health care. Each day the grandparents have access to the head nurse or a nursing staff member. It is the head nurse to whom they report and from whom they receive assignments and information relative to each case. The patients' rights to privacy is an especially important issue for the grandparents who frequently encountered family members at the bedside of the children. There, they came to know the varied interpretations of "privacy" for each family. In addition the grandparents are seen as a superb support, particularly when family visits are limited by distance and/or work schedules. In some cases, parents felt replaced or supplanted and "sensitivity" became a watch-word. Thus, the grandparents were cautioned to recall that a nursing staffer was always available.

Relating to parents, children, nurses, doctors, social workers, the whole complex system and guarding the confidences of every family, the foster grandparents continue learning and enlarging the meaning of their own lives. Clyde Forde from Barbados and Mary Morris from Georgia tend the children at two of the largest hospitals in Boston's world renowned medical center.

Clyde Forde

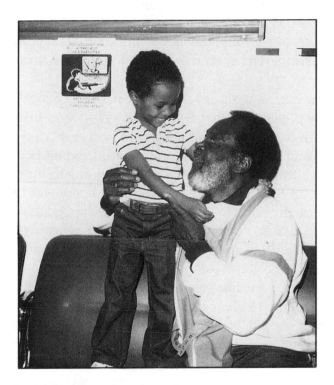

Clyde Forde

I'm seventy-two, but I don't feel that I am older than sixteen. I would like my life to end up showing that, well, here's a guy who comes from nowheres, and he ends up doing something good - a contribution toward helping people!

Recently, I have been questioning myself. First, I wonder why God, if there is a God, why God should create a man to die? He made stars, everything, the moon, the earth, everything seem to be everlasting. Why is it he made man not everlasting?

I was born on the 26th of July, 1916. It wasn't what you would call a very pleasant time. I had no shoes to wear. I used to go to school with bare feet. My parents were very, very, very poor. But my schooling was second to none. I could remember telling my mother as a little kid, what's the point of going to school because I don't see anything to gain by going. All I knew was that I had to get up every morning to tend the cattle, sheep, goats, pigs, cows. You had to earn it. You had to work for it. They were my mother's animals, yeh. Well, that was all we knew. My mother was self employed. She didn't work for nobody. I think her mother was the same way. All the generations lived in Barbados — all in poverty. We had really a strip o' land, and all the family used to live on that strip. Up to today, the land, it cannot be sold. It's handed down from like seed to seed. My mother's house is still there, it's liveable. I made a lot of improvements, electricity, water. When I lived there, it was kerosene lamps and an outhouse. Most of the people there lived in poverty.

Speaking of my family, you would have to say, we were rich comparatively. We had food, we had land, my mother had her own business. In that sense we were rich. She had a shop. It was a food shop, and she had a specialty. She used to make pudding and souse from the head of the pig. She used to cut it up and pickle it. She had clients come from all over the place to buy pudding and souse. The fowl, eggs and milk, we used to sell. I used to work all the time, all the time, from a little kid. That was all I knew. I grew up that way. Going to school or working for somebody else and things like that was completely out of my mind.

I went to school up to the fourth standard. When I go to the next standard, I couldn't make it. I leave school. I couldn't study the lessons. Arithmetic and algebra were the hardest thing for me. I could read, but I couldn't understand mathematics. I could count the money, but in those days it was pounds and shillings and pence, English. Every night, when I used to count the money from the little shop, I used to steal about sixty cents worth and hide it. So that accumulates, and when my mother go to the races (she used to bet heavily on the horses), when she lose, I used to turn around and give my mother that money to keep her going. She didn't know where it was coming from, I could tell you that. But eventually, I was aware of what I was doing that was wrong. I tell her, and she didn't believe me.

My mother, you wouldn't believe how interesting she was. She was something. She was in contact with my father, but I don't think there was much love in that. They never lived together. I don't think she ever wanted to get married. My mother was very independent. From the time I know my mother, she was always dwelling in her family house, her mother-house. She was very strange in that respect. She never looked to anybody for anything. She worked night and day. I believe it was an accident my coming into the world. It was an accident.

I knew my father. I was told, and, certain little acts I got to understand that he was my father. For instance, he was sort of a carpenter contractor, a builder. When I got a little bigger, he used to take me to work with him, what you would call an apprentice. I used to go to the railway 'cause he used to repair all the canvas tarpaulins that cover the freight cars, and I would help him. But I never got any money from him. The most I think I used to get from him on Saturdays was two shillings, forty-eight cents. So I recognize him. He's my father and well, I accept that until I grew big. Then, I realize that he was taking advantage of me working with him. He's drawing all o' this money and never give me anything. I think it wasn't fair. But I respect him as my father.

When he began to get old, he began to lose his sight, and he got married to another woman. Eventually things began to catch up with him. He used to come in the shop every day, and my mother used to feed him. Oh yeh, my mother would give him food. And I think he had another son, but that wife died. When he died, his son, well, couldn't bury him. So I had to go home and bury him. Yeh, I buried him, and I buried my mother. But I didn't put them in the same grave. I believe that whenever I die, I would be buried with my mother. Most of what I have comes from my mother. I have a lot to thank her for; a lot of me is my mother.

Well, I quit the Wesley Hall Boys School and the most part of my education came from after I leave school and start to read books. I begin to learn and learn. And, even when I got here, well, just a few years ago, I got my high school equivalency. But, in me, I didn't know, but I thought there was other ways to live. I'm sorry now that I didn't get my mother's advice and go to school. You see, I was smarter than all the kids around me when it come to subjects on what's going on in the world. So the guys who was in the school, they always looking to me for what's going on. I read the newspapers and listen to conversations. Believe it or not, the little shop that my mother had, had doctors, lawyers, shoemakers. It was like a university. Every day, from the time the shop was open, teachers, only talking or arguing about something. You would love to be in there. People coming in, they don't want anything to eat, they just sit down and listen. I felt secure, you know what I mean? I didn't have any way to go. There wasn't any way to go until when things begin to change.

Well, first my life begin to change with girls. I was fourteen and fifteen, and I began to see changes, despite what you would call the low profile that I kept. Girls began to get interested in me. Truly, I don't think that that was really part of my life. I just began to get drawn into this atmosphere. I'm being sought after because of my mother. She used to keep me real neat. When you dress up to go to school, bare feet, and even at dances, bare feet. Imagine going to church in bare feet!

One of the remarkable changes with me, I began to get tired going into the shop, serving people everyday. The same thing over and over again. I began to get pressure from my peers 'cause it was very feminine to be in the shop. I was leeched onto my mother. The chores I used to do was more in keeping with what a woman would do. There was not running water. You had to go out to the public pipe outside, get a bucket, put it on your head or in your hand and carry it home. And I would help with the making o' the bread and the souse. So I used to get comments from my friends, "What kinda boy you is?" It irks me. After a time, it get to me. So I said, I got to get out o' this, but how?

In those days, sail boats, not ships, used to come into the harbor. They used to sail around to the other West Indian Islands and bring in wood and rice and all that sort o' thing. So I went down to the shores, "the walk," they used to call it, and got a job as the captain's boy. Now, I was still in my teens. I remember the captain's name was Marshall. I didn't tell my mother anything about this, did this on my own. I told her after I got the job. She said no, but I leave in the night with a little bundle of clothes. The little boat was called the Lillian Heir Barnes. It sailed from Barbados to British Guiana and carry wood, rice and coal back.

My first voyage from Barbados, there was a very nice crew. I had to be obedient to everybody on board. I didn't know anything. Nothing. It was about half way between Barbados and British Guiana, they decided to initiate me. In those days, there was no electric pumps. You used to have a hand pump to get the water out. Well, I had to drink that water, bilge water, that settles in the bottom of the boat. It did make me sick, so sick that when I got to British Guiana, I couldn't work anymore. When I came back to Barbados, I had to go straight to the hospital. I nearly died. I had all sorts of rashes on my skin and a very high fever for a very long time. I don't know how I got over it. I do know that the nurse who attended to me, she became very attached to me and attached to my mother. She was a Seventh Day Adventist, and the church was on the same street as my mother's shop. She would come by the shop to inquire about me.

I had a Raleigh bicycle, in those days, and she wanted to learn to ride. So I taught her, and, eventually, this thing began to grow and grow. I think she fell in love with me, but I couldn't think of her as someone I could love because she was much older than me. To me, she was like a woman and I was a little boy. There was about ten years difference between us. I respected her, but being in love with her, no. Anyway we were becoming close, very close. We had a relationship develop, and it became so intense that I ran away. Now, my mother encouraged it. She felt that it was good for me, and she liked Ruth very much. With Ruth in my life, it would sort of stabilize me. It would make a better person out of me. Everything would be very good for me. She was nice in appearance. She was well off, and all that sort of thing. But I was young and not ready for this kind of responsibility. I was only about twenty or twenty-one.

I signed up to get in the air force, but my mother put her foot down on that. She had a very close friend, a doctor, and you had to go to him for your physical. She tell the doctor, and he said, "Well, you leave it to me." because they were really, really close. So he turned me down. Not only turned me down, but he talked me out of going. But, as time goes by and this pressure begin to build up again, I got a job in the central foundry where they used to repair ships. I worked there for a while, got acquainted with using tools and that sort of give me a mechanical background. I got bigger and stronger, and eventually I got into the Navy. When I first left, my mother didn't know. It so happened that the ship leave Barbados to Trinidad and broke down. We had to come back to Barbados for three or four days. That's where my mother got to find out. She was angry. Ruth was angry, but I did finally leave for Trinidad.

Ruth had an aunt in Trinidad who was a big wheel. Through corresponding with her, she introduced me to her aunt and her aunt's daughter who was a school teacher, working in the country side. So I went to visit, get to know them. I don't know if it's love at first sight or whatever it is, but she fell in love with me. Her mother now, who is Ruth's aunt, wanted me to marry to her daughter. Well, that can't be because I got introduced to them through Ruth — kinda weird. Her mother seemed to think I was a very good catch. "No," I said, "I can't do that." "Oh, forget about Ruth, I'll take care of that for you. You don't have to worry about that," she told me. She was very rich. She had a chain of theatres and a bus service there in Trinidad. I'm not talking about an ordinary person. Incidently, Ruth and her aunt was more white than black, you know what I'm talking about. In those days, in those kinda thinking, you wouldn't think. You didn't have it clear to think about it. I didn't feel that I fit in, in the first place.

When that proposal was made to me, only a fool would turn it down. "You don't have to work. It's not a question of money. Just marry my daughter and this is yours. You can have it."

Then the aunt told Ruth that I am going to be married to her daughter. That's what she did. She wrote and tell Ruth that. Then, she send her daughter to Barbados to convince Ruth that it was O.K. When she told me that, I took up my hat, because I was still in the Navy, and I walked out of the house. Never went back. Never went back. I took a leave of absence and went home to Barbados. I went home, now, to marry Ruth, to convince her that I wasn't going to marry her cousin.

When I got to Barbados, I didn't propose to her. We wasn't engaged or anything like that, but I bought my suit and everything. But then my aunt, my mother's sister, put me to sit down and tell me what I didn't know about Ruth. In those days, you couldn't do anything because the place is small. Everybody knows who is who. While I was away, Ruth was going around with an inspector, a big police inspector. So it's no use. I confronted her with that, and she didn't deny it. So I said, "I can't get married to you." I was so hurt and so disappointed, cut me up. And that's when I met my wife.

Up to this day, I don't think I have really married out of love. I don't think so. I was a very confused guy. My life was complicated. Not in any way that I treat my wife bad, or I didn't respect her, 'cause all the kids that I have was from my wife. I married her. I respected her until she died. I have three girls and one boy. It was unfortunate because my life wasn't easy. In my wife's family, I wasn't accepted because I was a poor boy. Her family couldn't see in me what she saw. After I got out of the service, I got a mechanical job for Texaco Oil Company oiling machinery, heavy duty work. I wasn't a little boy playing with pencil and paper. All of her family, they were lawyers and doctors and what not. Her father was an architect, a big wheel. So I was a little on the dock side.

After the death of my wife, I couldn't live there any more, of course. I had to take my children away. Then, I really had a hard time. The eldest was about seven. They were little kids. A lady used to board me during the week, she and her husband. Now, my kids come, and they had to sleep on the floor. No beds. I got on a boat and went back to Barbados. I had to. The last kid, the fourth, she was very fortunate. An uncle of my deceased wife was the manager of an estate in Trinidad. His wife begged me for my last kid, Debra. She begged me. They were well off, and I said, all right. My son and two daughters came with me to Barbados. Hard times. Hard.

Small as our place was, my mother, their grandmother for the first time, for she never saw my wife and kids, my mother took them. I leave the kids and come back to work. My mother took care of those kids until they were big, until she died. I used to work and send money to my mother and the kids. After the death of my mother, I went about getting my kids with me here in Boston.

Once, I took a vacation from Trinidad and went back to Barbados. When I was coming back they put me on the wrong plane and instead of coming to Trinidad, I was brought into the States. They put me up in New York for one night. The sight that I saw from the air! My God, I thought it was heaven. I thought to myself, I have to come. I have to come back. But, thereafter, I was still working for Texaco. The time came I want to get out of this place. I was there fifteen, sixteen years. It was going very good. I had my own bungalow, that's what they called it, had my own vehicle, sending money for my kids, but there was something else calling me. I got in touch with an agency. You used to pay them X amount of dollars, and they would fix you up with a sponsor here. I did that. I got the sponsor, and I got my mother to agree, and I took off. I leave my job. I leave everything. If I hold onto something, I'd come back, and I didn't want to — a new adventure, a new adventure for me. I was in my forties then, late forties. I landed in New York. I spent a few months in Brooklyn before I came here to Boston. My sponsor was in Boston, but up to this day, I never met him. Anyway, luckily for me I got a room on West Concord Street in the South End. I went to Westinghouse Electric and got a job there.

I did become a citizen, took out my citizenship for my kids, to get them up here, for me to sponsor them. Then, they didn't want to come 'cause they were quite happy. After the death of my mother, my eldest daughter, she went to England to live. There was a guy who wanted to marry her. I wasn't in favor of it. She was too young, I thought, but she was very stubborn. It was my mother who forced me to say O.K. Then, they came back to Barbados. They both lived in my mother's house until he built a house, and they moved in the country side. He's a contractor, and carpenter.

My other children were here in the States. Phillip was in the service. He was stationed in San Francisco. My other daughter, she was here in Boston. After my married daughter move out of the family house, it remain empty for quite a while. Eventually, I fix it up and kept it for a vacation place. I could go home, and it's there. It's still there. Now they have three kids, two boys and a girl. I do visit them, and the children were here on their vacation and spent a month with me and my daughter. The big girl is studying to be a doctor now. The boy, he wants to be an architect.

My daughter Sandra, the one here, is a nurse at Youville Hospital. Part of the time they spend with Sandra and part of the time with me.

Phillip is still connected with the Navy in California. He's married, and they came here once to visit me, his wife and a beautiful little girl. So, he's doing pretty good too. But I never went to visit there. Maybe some day.

I think still, to this day, that I am here for a reason. I haven't given up that feeling. I feel that there is something great that has to come out of my life. The amount of up and downs, the experiences that I had, I feel that my purpose is to do something that is unique. Whether it be presently what I am doing now, I mean, helping the kids, I don't know. But I believe something big is going to happen. I don't know if it's going to be in the health department, I don't know, but I believe that it will be connected with kids. My life is not going to be completed until, until I have done something that everyone will be able to look and say, a miracle. A miracle. I have that feeling from the time I was a little child that I was put here to do something for humanity.

I reached a point, at one time, that I used to be able to heal people, but it wasn't lasting. Now, I'm being reminded, now, at the hospital not only by the nurses and by the parents, but even by doctors. Well, a child would be medicated and having pain, restless and things like that, "Hey, get Clyde to hold him." The pains would subside, irritation would subside, and they'd go to sleep in my lap, wake up feeling good. These are not like what you would say things that happen far apart. It's something that constantly happens, practically every day. Nurses would come to me, "Clyde, rub my back for me," you know. "Come, Clyde, rub my shoulders, rub my leg." Don't ask me what it is. I can't tell you. You know I suffer from high blood pressure. Well, the last doctor I had, he recommended open heart surgery. Now, up to this day, I'm still going on. I have no surgery, and I don't intend to have any. I take my medication, but I feel that the time would come when I wouldn't have to take it. I eat, I drink, I feel good, go about my business as usual. I don't think I am a special person, but I feel I am here to do something good.

I would like my life to end up showing that, well, here's a guy who comes from nowheres, and he ends up doing something good — a contribution toward helping people! That's my strongest desire, to help people, regardless of who they are. I saw it in my mother. Give and give and give until it hurts, and that's what she was, a giver. I can't remember my mother asking anybody for anything. She was always, always giving. And I think I can say for myself, I don't think that I will ever be rich because I'm really happy when I'm in a position to give something.

I'm seventy-two, but I don't feel that I am older than sixteen. If I catch myself feeling that kinda way, I feel there is something wrong. I'm not exercising enough, I'm not doing something right. So I check up on myself. I don't feel that I have to live with a cane in my hand and be very grouchy. I feel that, if I am one hundred tomorrow, I have to sit up straight, I have to walk straight, I don't have to fear anything. It's like the world, everything changes, believe it or not, but you accept it or you don't. The world keeps changing all the time. People keep changing all the time. And I change.

I think I am more tolerant now than I was before. I think that comes from a deeper understanding. I can't be tolerant and appreciative of you if I didn't understand. That comes with the years. I might have changed my life, maybe yes, maybe no. But I'll tell you this, I don't think that I would have liked to change my mother. At the time of growing up with my mother, maybe I was a bit resentful of the way in which I was treated, but, when I see the behavior and attitude of other kids, people in other families and I look at mine, I wouldn't want to change it. I used to think, why do I have to go through this, why do I have to dress like that? But looking back, no. I wouldn't want to change it. You see, my experience with my family was unique. I couldn't get that experience nowheres, even if I was the next door kid. And, if I had to do it all over again, I would. I was not what you would call an outward expression of love. I wasn't that type of person who expressed myself to someone else. I had friends, but they were at a distance. Now, I'm more outward than I ever was. Maybe it was fear.

Recently, I have been questioning myself. All these years, you know I came up believing I believe in Jesus Christ. I got the conception that there is a God, there is Jesus, the things that he did. But, recently, I have been questioning myself. I am beginning to wonder. What I felt about Jesus is what I hear. I don't know the man. It's just from readings, from the bible. First, I wonder why God, if there is a God, why God should create a man to die? Why should he go through all of this trouble to make me and then for me to die? He made a world. Up to today, we are still in this world. He made stars, everything, the moon, the earth, everything seem to be everlasting. Why is it he made man not everlasting? They're still there. Trees, they grown for hundreds and hundreds of years. Even sands upon the shores, they there, for an unlimited time. Why? He made man of his own image and likeness. Why such a short life span? If you think there is something better coming later, then it can give you a different view of this life. I would like to feel today or tomorrow that I can either keep my body and live in it or, if I lose it, get another, even a little better. That is my idea. I feel pretty good in my body. It's not at its best, but maybe, as time goes on, it might improve. There's a lot of things I used to do with this body that I don't take the chances of doing now 'cause I feel that it might hurt.

So I don't worry regarding death and burial and reincarnation. It's hard for me to believe that this body shall be reincarnated. I don't think so. My beliefs about that is not so strong. So, I'm here. I know that I'm here. I'm conscious and aware that I am here. Why should I have to leave this consciousness to go somewhere else? You know, let's face it. Does it make sense? I try to live very simply. I don't go around trying to impress anybody, and I make sure that what they think about me do not effect me. There is one thing I do feel, that I was rejected by grown-ups, big people in the world. I wanted to be of some use to people, in general, but they didn't not only ask, in many ways they wouldn't let me. And I don't find that in kids. I find in kids that they was more open. There was more room, there was more of everything that I really wanted to do. I felt that I could freely reach them and freely give to the kids!

* * *

Clyde Forde has been a foster grandparent at Children's Hospital in Boston for five years. He shares his very nice home in the Mattapan section of Boston with a woman friend whom he introduces as "my partner for life." He contributed to the FGP by serving on the Advisory Board and participating in the theatre production, "The Lives of Foster Grandparents."

Mary Morris

Mary Morris

Believe me, I took anythin' to keep my kids together. The idea I got six or seven kids and everyone by a different man, I couldn't stand that, an' I just prayed to God the Lord, let me, I used to use the words, let me keep all my eggs in one basket. Young as I was, if I came off and left with him, I couldn't have nobody, and so I just stayed with him.

An' I talk with the teen-agers 'cause you know this generation, havin' their babies, they're too young, they hadn't had their childlife lived before they become a mama. When that baby starts squallin' and hollerin', first thing they think about is fightin' like they fightin' other chillun, an' they hit 'im because they don't want to be bothered. There's a lot goes on there at that hospital.

I was born and raised in Tarlton, Georgia; born in 1923. I stayed with my grandmother until I was about thirteen, and, then, I went to live with my mother and step-father. They reared me up. My mother, she was but fourteen years older than me. She was raped when she was about twelve. See my mother's mother died when she was a baby, and she gave her to the uncle. He took her, and his wife wasn't too well so my mom had to do things in the field like a man. So this time when she got raped she was in the field, plowin'. She was fourteen when I was born. He was an older man, in his thirties. She was nothin' but a child. Anyway, I was born and my uncle and aunt took me, an', later, my mother got married to her childhood sweetheart. I went from my aunt and uncle to my grandmother, and, when, my grandmother died, that's when I went back to Tarlton. I went through high school, an' then I got married to a boy. Me and him kinda grew up together, and I start having kids. I was sixteen. I'm seventeen years older than my oldest son, and I'm the mother of seven.

I had Rosco, Marianne, Rosebud and Barbara, and after her my husband went to Brunswick, to the shipyard. I stayed with mama, and, then, we did go down there. I got pregnant, and I come back

242

to deliver. I was staying with mama, and I didn't feel that baby move no more. I was seven months. I tole my mother I hadn't felt it since Saturday and this was Monday. She said, "Oh, he's sleeping," and just shooed it off like that. I went on for a week, and again I tole my mother. She said, "Oh, Mary, you sleep, that baby moves. You'd be sick if it wasn't moving." So it went another week, the fourth week now. He kinna mean, my husband, so he didn't pay too much attention, and I didn't have a doctor there. So about the fifth week he came, my husband and he taken me to Butler to a doctor. When we got there, he said, sure there was no heart beat. And my husband ask him what we gonna do. He said, "Just let nature take its course." Well, yet I'm not being prejudiced to say this, but he had a white lady in there going through the same thing, and he put her in the hospital and gave her something to help her. But he sent me home.

And so I went back, and I prayed. I was very prayerful. My husband had to go back to Brunswick. I began to accept the fact that I was gonna die. I looked at my chilluns, and I said, "Lord, I don't wanna leave them, but, if I'm gonna die I will. I understand you." But at that time, I just thought about if I lied to somebody, if I hurt somebody, 'cause I wanted to be saved. So I went to praying for God's forgiveness for everything. I didn't know too much I had done, but I was gonna get back what I didn't know I had done. I done have enough suffering, and I didn't wanna die. It was 1943, and that made me about nineteen 'cause I had chillun every year. When my baby got 3-4 months, I was on the way with another one.

Back to the one that had died within me and the doctor told me to let nature take its course. People began to say you'd a' been mortified if that baby had been dead all that time. I knowed the baby wasn't moving. Finally I prayed all night that night. I just knew I was gonna die and leave my kids so I just prayed and prayed. The next morning, I just was at peace. We didn't have a bathtub. We had to use the tin tub to take a bath. So I heated water every night for the kids, and I bathe myself. That night, I got into bed, and I had to get up to use the pail, what we used for the bathroom, and it was a large clot of cold blood came. My legs felt just like ice. I just knew I was gonna die. I called out to Mama, and she came and she said, "Oh, Mary, you getting sick." (They used to call delivery time, gettin' sick.) She gave me some hot tea. We were loaded with teas. Those teas kill ya. And she made all kinds of sassafras tea and other herbs because they all believe in herbs. She told Papa, and they gonna get Dr. Montgomery. You didn't just get a doctor because you didn't have no telephone. You had to get in somebody's old car or walk ten miles to get to a telephone to call and, then ride twenty miles to pick up the doctor. Then Mama tole me when I feel this pain just get on my knees around her. She was sitting in a chair and I got on my knees. Every time I had a pain I would strain just like she told me she had seen the midwife do. I shut my mouth and strained. Whenever I had a pain I did that and sure enough the baby was born.

It was born about an hour before the doctor got there, a big ole, fine, healthy boy. It wasn't a scratch on him, only a blue spot like a bruise from the birth. But I was the one who suffered. See not suffering before, I suffered after. And the doctor gave me, in each of these legs here, he called them hypodermics. It was just like you take a piece of steak and chop it this way. Oh, I stayed so sick, I was sick about a whole month and finally did get my strength. My husband come got me, and we went back to Brunswick. And I had Kenneth after him and my baby boy after him.

Believe me, I took anything to keep my kids together. The idea I got six or seven kids and every one by a different man, I couldn't stand that. I just prayed to God the Lord, let me, I used to use the words, let me keep all my eggs in one basket. Oh, I had plenty reason to leave my husband. I said one night, he treated me so bad, this was after all of them had come, and I was gonna leave. Another lady was standing by. I said, "No, I don't know whether I would be able to go through." Things that your body may desire, I wasn't gonna go through with no other man.

So I just stayed there and let him mistreat me because after I came to the Lord, we don't believe in but one husband. We don't believe in divorce, and I definitely believe that. So I know, young as I was, if I came off and left with him, I couldn't have nobody. So I just stayed with him. If I'm having more kids, let it be by this one man. Then, after my baby began to get seven years, I said, thank you, God. I would never relax when he was with me. So I think that did a lot to help me not to have any more. It wasn't no consolation, it wasn't no joy, nothing. You was just going through it because you was there. You know that was the only thing gonna make a little peace. Because I hate to hear him raising over the kids and the kids, they was big enough to have their own company and everything, I just didn't want those kids to hear his mouth. I stayed there and took it and went right on, and when I did get ready to leave him . . . Well, that's another story.

I went to work when Mitchell, the baby, he was about two months old. The reason I went, because the kids needed things. They had such as food and a house to live in, but I wanted them to have little things like other chilluns, you know. So, he wasn't making that much, and he was parting that with somebody else. So that's when I first started. I went to work for a lady named Miss C. I think she was paying me about ten dollars a week. Then, after I stayed, she gave me a lot of little clothes from her chillun.

Then, a lady came to my house and me and her was talking, and she was very nice. We were living in a little two-bedroom house. Some of my kids had to be piled up with other kids. She knew I didn't like it. I had the boys sleep in the living room. I wanted them to have a room where they could be. She asked me why I didn't have one of those projects they had just built, brand new, nice, single house projects. I told her I had went, and they wouldn't. So she said, we're going by there to see. So we went, and she asked this lady why? "Mary of all people should have one," she said. So she give her a little bit of history and because her people had money and a big factory and hired a lot of people, the town was getting the taxes and everything, so the lady listened to her. So I signed up for a place. I moved the next Saturday in a big four-bedroom project. This is where I raised my kids up.

All my kids got college education through Mr. C. who gave donations to a college in Morristown, Tennessee because he had a plant there, too. I overheard him talking. See I was doing all the cooking and everything. When they come home to dinner, I would always serve them so I would hear him telling some more people about this college. I got the idea that I was gonna ask him what about financing my kids? And he told me what to do. (My oldest son, Roscoe, was gonna be in the twelfth grade that year.) He told me, when the time come, he would give him some papers and a letter. When Roscoe got out of high school, he did go to Morristown. Then, the next two years, two girls got out and went down.

When my son come back from college, he went into the service. So with his money, what he was giving, made us able to save up enough and make a down-payment on a house. They was building houses, called WPA or something. You had to pay $300 down and the rest you could pay monthly. I was determined. So I saved up enough to pay down on this place, and we moved. Even though she wasn't paying me nothing too much, I was working though believe me, she would stand me for something. I would say I need $100, and she'd come across with it. Things like that because she know I was having a time. So after they got out of college, my second daughter married her childhood sweetheart. I didn't want her to get married then but she said, more money she make, her daddy just borrows it and runs around. He threw away more money which he took from them. That's the reason my oldest son was so bitter when he come out the service. He had no money saved because he sent it, and we bought the house. It hurt him, and he's very hurt now because, after I left my husband, he let the house go. Roscoe felt at least he could've sent him word. He'd a tried to get some money up and kept it in the family. And my husband, he kept what he got for it. He always been crazy about a lot of women. Right now I guarantee he had a lot of women. His sister told me she finally come to the conclusion that he was just what I say he was.

My oldest was born in 1940, and you know how old that make him. He's in environmental protection. I got three grown boys now. By them being my boys, they never has spoke anything evil. Never has raised their voices. They get mad. They have gotten angry, but when I tell them the second time what I believe and what should happen, they do not say one word. The girls is the same. All three of them. They are still with the same husband, even though one of them got a lazy man. But he's kinda friendly. But the other two, one of them is kinda moody but they got some stick-to-it. You might have better words than I but you know it's not because everything is on flower beds and they gettin' every-thing they want. But they got a spirit about them. My baby daughter tells me, "Mama, when I get so mad with my husband and think about I'm gonna leave or something like that, your voice always come to me."

I have enjoyed, but my life was no rosey bed either. I thank the Lord because I appreciate just being alive. And I may not have a lot, but I feels contentment even though you could use extra. But since I don't have it, I'm not gonna worry about it. I'm not gonna let these things make me all uptight. I want to be thankful and grateful for what I do have and try to ask the Lord to help me to get some more. I'm not saying the Lord dropping nothing out the sky, but, if he give me the strength, and then open a door for me when I try to get a job. . . He do works on peoples. An impression can touch a person sometime. That's the way the Lord work. He ain't coming round toll us he gonna drop nothing. I'm not that simple.

Lots o' times, when Miss C. went to New York and stayed a week, I kept her house just like it was mine. I drove her Cadillac, just like it was mine, too. Then I would stay the night with her baby. I would go and pick him up at school, and let him go and play with somebody till I run home and see about my children. Then, I come back, and get his supper and mine. My oldest kids was big enough to take care of the others. And I had taught them how to cook long time before. When they was ten and eleven they was cooking. And they knew the necessity of me making the extra dollar so they wasn't going out and do things they wasn't supposed to. I had one girl washing, one girl ironing and one girl cooking. Then, the next week, change it around. Then, make the boys clean the yard and the mopping to be done, clean the bathroom. I'd call them on the phone. They kinda kept in line, and, today, they say, "Mama, if you had to do it again, I would want you to raise me up the same way." We were like sisters and brothers. You see, I wasn't that much older than they, and I'd get on the floor and take cardboard boxes and make a doll house, fold and cut and make chairs for the dolls to sit on. I bought all these paper dolls and bent them and let them sit in there. We just keep a conversation going. When we was outside, we ran together. My little boy used to say, we called him baby brother, he'd say, "Bun, baby brother, bun!" We thought that was so cute. He tell hisself to run. But all these things that have happened to my chillun, they have taken care of themselves. I'm very proud of them.

I got seventeen grandchillen, and one daughter got ten. When they had the seventh child, I went down and, I said to my son-in-law, "What are you tryin' to do, kill my daughter? You just had the seventh, that's enough." He said, "Come here mother. Has Rose ever been without food and a place to stay?" I told him no. He said, "Has she ever needed clothes?" I told him "No." He said, "Don't I work and take care?" I said, "Yeh." "Well then?" He let me know to close my mouth. They was happy with what they had done. I shut my mouth. Their oldest child is twenty-three this year. He came out the University of Georgia second in his class, in a class of 400. And they all doing good. She got four out the house and six still home. But she'd have been going on right now if the baby, it's a Downs Syndrome baby. Her mouth just twisted a little bit. She, my daughter, sit home and taught that baby and taught her so well. She's just moving on like she's normal.

My kids all know they get me up when they go to saying something about what I believe about the Lord. The oldest son do it, too. I told him one day, I didn't feel good. He said, "Mama, didn't you call on the Lord?" (laughter) He's a believer, but he's on to me. When he get down to a crisis, he'll say, "Mama, you gonna send out a prayer for me tonight?" My kids are something. And I love them, I really love them.

I got my yuppies too, believe me. I don't know that I like them too good either being that way. My baby daughter's tops in her job, a manager, and she ain't changed a bit. She as human, kind and loving, and they love her, and she loves her job. Her husband's the manager of Grossman's. She gets mad with her brother and her nephew for being, every time you see them, it's a dollar sign. She mocks them all the time. How much that cost, how much this and that? My oldest says he like to make good, but it's nothing like living. The material things are not it. He says, "Give me the spirit in human beings." Now, he helps people. They get boys they took out of jail, and they counsel with them. He just got a name for going around helping folks. He come by Saturday morning, and he said, "Mama, we ain't gonna get in no argument about the Lord. I call you every night and find out how you're doing. If you need anything you let me know." So, when he come to the door, I was holding my heart, and I say, "You sure I ain't going to die?" He said, "Why you say that Mama?" "'Cause you come by to see me. I know when the Lord getting ready to call me home." He just rolled.

And my son, Mitchell, he come by every Sunday morning. He take me to Sunday school. I teach Sunday school, and so I have to be there at 10 o'clock, but I goes at 9 or 8:30 because he has to go jogging. Believe me, I be ready. I can't be choosey. I ain't got no car! I just sit there and meditate. Sometimes I dust the piano and cleans the mirrors until the students start coming. It's over in my church in Dorchester.

I have to tell ya about how come I come to Boston. I told ya my husband and me wasn't getting along good because he was very mean and everything. So I had had dreams when I married of growing old together, and our chilluns coming home and seeing us. You know, you see these love stories. It just didn't work out like that. So Marianne, my oldest girl, she came from college, and she came to Boston. Then, she met her husband here. So all the time now, I seen things weren't gonna get no better. And the things I said to him, try to sit down and talk. Ask him how do he feel about love and everything. He made fun of that. Every time he do that, that was just making me know I'm not afraid to face if you don't want me around. Some goes crazy if someone say I don't want ya. But God taught me, if you don't want to be in my company, you ain't gonna hurt me if you just let me know. You won't have no more trouble of me. So I'm working, knowing this in my mind. So my son who was here in Boston, I told him, "Now listen. I'm gonna leave as soon as Mitchell get out of school. I didn't want to bring him in-between terms. I said "When you going in the service in January, you give your sister my fare and Mitchell's fare. Let her put it in the bank. When I get ready to come, she can wire me the money."

I was still kinda frightened of my husband. I thought if I had the money on me, he'd take it. So I worked, and my husband was getting worse and worse. He raised his hand so much there for three months, every day he would curse and raise his hand. Even my thirteen-year-old jumped up one night in the bed and said, "Mama, I'm getting so tired of daddy. Every time I turn around he talk, talk, talk and cuss, cuss. I'm getting tired of it. Why don't he stop?" He didn't like to hear his son talking that way so he goes to whip him. He went to draw back, and the baby son jumped around his neck and held him like that. I scold Mitchell though, like I was mad at him, to make him get off his dad. I said, "Don't you ever let me see you do that again." An' so his daddy so mad he was gonna whip him, but he didn't.

So I come to the conclusion that night. Lord, if I don't do something, something terrible gonna happen. 'Cause this boy, he would stay out in the street with the boys and come home when his supper wilt because he told me, "I'd rather not eat to the table." He did that to weasel through. I couldn't blame him because I ain't been ate something so I wouldn't have to sit down.

Like I was busy washing dishes or doing something that would be keeping the noise so I wouldn't hear him. That was the turning point. If you drive a child to make him so angry, he do something he regret the rest of his days.

My daughter was here married. She had a big place and tole me, "Mama you can stay with me." So this is when I say to my boy, "Mitchell, I know you love your daddy and you love your mama. You can stay here with daddy if you wanna, don't mean I don't love ya. I love ya and I work and send ya some money and some clothes if you prefer staying with him. 'Cause I don't wantcha going with me and you don't wanna. You can go wit me, but I'm letting you know I'm going so you can make your choice yourself." He said, "Mama, I want to go witchu." I wrote my daughter, "School is gonna be out the fourth day of June, and I'm gonna leave the fifth. Don't wire the money until the third to Western Union. They will call me on the job, not call the house." We went on through every day, him raising his hands.

See, my husband, he had a fear about him of the Lord. Before, when he used to say little things back to me, I'd say things back to him. But, after I come to the Lord, I didn't use no vulgar language. I didn't say nothing. I would just cry. When he made me cry, look like he got satisfaction out of it. But you see, at that time, I didn't know how to deal with it. When he made me cry, he would walk around there like he was Mr. It and that hurt. I come to the conclusion, if I didn't do something while I had the power, something was gonna happen. See, my husband knew I was gonna go. But see, he was a very proud man. He didn't want the neighbors to think nothin was going on. When Western Union called, I told that girl to keep it, and I would pick it up on my way back from work. About a month before, I went to Pick and Save and put up on a trunk. I would go by every week and pay on that.

So the day before I was to leave, I got the car and got Mitchell, and we went to Pick and Save. Boy, I was moving like ole clock work. The man brought the trunk out and put it in the trunk of the car, and I went to the house and picked up all my clothes. It was God give me sense how to do. And then that's when I got my money from Western Union because it is right by the railroad station. I bought my ticket and left my trunk. It went on ahead. I was using my head! The next day, I got in the car, and, on the way, the ole car stopped so I had told my son-in-law to follow me. I didn't trust my husband. I didn't know what he had done to that car to keep me from leaving. We was there about ten minutes. You could hear it coming down the tracks, this long mmmmmmmmmmmmmm. It had to start slowing down about ten or fifteen miles from the station and it went to breaking its speed so I knew it was going to stop. I was nervous. I was. Because I didn't know what he was gonna do. When it stopped, I looked back when I got on, and he come up on the train, and I'm sitting there. "Well, Mary, I'll see ya in about two weeks." I wasn't gonna tell him what was on my mind. He said, "I'll be up there to see about you and Mitchell." I said, "Uh huh." As soon as he stepped off and the train give that long hoop because it was fit to move, I settled back and I said, "Thank you, Jesus!" I think I thanked the Lord from Jessup to Savannah.

And he did. He came up in two weeks, but I had done got stronger then. I was up here in my own territory. I was up here where some police was. If he was trying to act up, I could call the law. See, down there, the law just gonna side with who they figured because sometimes they giving their wives a headache, too. But they just figure mens don't give no headaches. "Oh, Mary," they'd be saying. No need of me calling em. Up here, I knew my rights was gonna be exercised. I was working at Deaconess Hospital, and I said, "Lord have mercy." When I came in the house, he got behind the door, scared me like everything. So sweet like there was nothing wrong. So we sit down to the table. My daughter, she fix a steak supper, and he run his mouth like there nothing happened. So come 11-12 o'clock, and I knew I had to go to work the next day. My daughter she played real smart. She took a heavy pitcha and laid it on the sofa so he knew there wasn't going to be no question. So he says, "Mary, where I'm gonna sleep?" I said, "I don't know, I'm gonna sleep here. You can go to Marianne." He said, "You mean I'm not gonna stay here witchu?" I said, "No you sure ain't." He got so mad, but he said, "It look like I better cool my heels."

So he went on to Marianne's. When I come home the next evening, he had done come over again. Same thing. Then, Wednesday, he came back again. This night, Bobbie said, "Mama we're gonna try to can him off somewhere. Let's go to a dinette at Revere Beach." So we was on our way there. Bobbie got out the car for something, he says, "Mary, I got enough money, I could get us a motel. Me and you could go and stay at the motel." I said, "No. Uh uh. I ain't going in no motel. You can go, but I ain't." He was so mad you coulda seen it in him. He wouldn't say nothing because Bobbie is a different child from the rest of them. She's just like him. She would speak her mind, and she didn't care if it was her daddy because she knew that he had mistreated me. He was mad, so, when we come back, he just went out to Marianne. When Friday night come, he tole Bobbie he was gonna leave. He ask me would I walk back to the car with him. So I told Bobbie, keep your eyes out. I walked out to the car and stood outside. He says, "You really mean you're through?" "Yes," I said, "I didn't take all that I did to let you think that I wasn't through."

Then I made a parable to him. I said, "You know, take a glass. You can crack it an' you still hold water. I had 'em like that. But one day, you drop it and you shatter it all to pieces, and nothing can put it back together." I said, "That's the way our marriage is." He looked at me and laughed. You know, he would say I thought I was bein' smart, saying those kinda things, but he know he gonna leave without me. And I knowed that God was gonna spare me, and He did. The only time we had had peace at home was when he'd go on a trip Monday we maybe won't see him till Friday. Everybody was happy. We was having a ball. He come in from the road, I fix a nice duck. "I don't want that." I had to cook again. If I stood him up and didn't, he'd have raised his hand. So I sit down wit him one day and I told him, "Walter Lee, it's evident you don't want me, but I can see you happy wit somebody else. I don't wish you no anger. You're a nice looking man, and

you got a lot going for ya. So why don't ya go wit somebody else?"
He just look at me and don't say nothin'.

When Mitchell got married, he sent his daddy an invitation. I
told my oldest son to get his father a hotel. "And" I said, "if you
need some money to buy him food or pay for the hotel, I will help
you do that because that's all the Lord require me to do." Some
church people say if he want ya back, you go whether you like it
or not. I told them, "No way! God give me better sense than that.
This is what I got to do. If he hungry and I could afford to give
him something to eat, give it to him. If he's naked, I'd do the same
thing. He need a place to stay, help get him a place. Them the
only three things God require me to do. I should be sleeping with
him and intimate with him, God ain't required me that. Because
Paul said, when he was writing to the Corithians, if you and him
can't live together, you can part, but you cannot marry again,
except if he be dead."

When I come here, I didn't know anything about working in these
plants and big hospitals 'cause I always stayed down there. The
old saying "You can take them out the country but you can't get
the country out of them." Well, that's to a mind that wants to be
dead and dull. I always wants to be independent. Independent
enough to know what my rights are and teach my kids the same.
Don't try to overgo the other fella's right, but know what yours is
and stand on it. So, when I come here, I stayed at the Deaconess
about two years. My girl friend, Esme, she's a foster grandparent
now too, me and her become friends, and we been friends ever
since. She was working there, too. Later, she left. She was gone
about two weeks when she come back an brought me an application. She told me that at Beth Israel you didn't have to pay for
your meals. She said, "You'll make more over there too." I filled
it out, and the very next day they called me. It was in 1970 when
I left and come over to Beth Israel.

Miss G. interviewed me. She was excited about the way I was
telling about my life and where I was working at this hospital
down there. She ask me did I know how to make molds. Jello

molds, that's the way she called it. I said, we make congealed salad all the time, and she fell out and went to laughing with the other ladies. She had to laugh because my accent was so southern. She got more kick out of listening to me say words, it tickle me. She started me to work in the kitchen the next day. They worked me nearly to death. After I was there about six years, another positiion opened upstairs which was diet aide, and I applied for it. They tried to give me the run-around, but I went upstairs to be interviewed. I told her I knew what I was doing. If I don't get this job upstairs or the one in the office where they had a tally machine, I'm not going back on the salads. So the next day she ask me which I rather have. I told her I'd rather have the tally machine and she told me O.K. The tally machine run off the menu and count the food.

I did the tallying for five years, too. Then, the position open for inventory and ordering. Then, I was ordering all Beth Israel food from Monarch and all of them. I like Beth Israel, but some people over me in the kitchen was very racial. Then a company came in what did all the food so they broke up what we was doing. A Mr. F. come at the same time. One day, he was teasing, and he used to say a lot of bad words. I would say, "You know you're wrong don'tcha? How do you feel bringing your boy in and your wife and the other boy of your girl friend?" And he didn't like it. He told them that he didn't want me doing the inventory. So he got me switched out of the office into a paper room. There no windows, no nothing. Nothing but a desk and a telephone, and I'm still ordering. He claim they didn't have room in the office. It was a flimsy excuse. So, when he carried me back there, I looked at him, and I says, "Why you do this?" And he said, "Well, that's the best we can do. That's all we got." So about two weeks later, Mr. F. said, "Mary, I come back here to interview ya. I want to talk witcha." I told him I didn't have but one chair, and I got up and gave him my chair, and get me a barrel. He said, "No don't do that." I said, "You come back here to interview me, you sit on the chair." Oh, that killed him. The word of God was killin' him too because I ain't done a thing. He knew I was doing a good job. So he sit there, and he ask me, "Mary are you mad at me?" I said,

"No, Mr. F. I'm not mad atcha. I'm having a ball back here." Then, he said, "Will you forgive me?" I said, "I was hurt at first because I knowed I was doing my job, but I ain't mad atcha. Fact is, I am more free back here." Three weeks later, when I came in that Monday morning, the head peoples at Beth Israel had took his things out and locked his office. One of the girls called back for me to come in the office. He was standing there, and the supervisor says, "Mary, Mr. F. is leaving." He had to go over to the other desk for something, and she said, "He's fired." It made me roll, and I couldn't help but gloat. I walked up to him, and I said, "You reap what you sow." I wasn't glad he was let, but I didn't have no anchor in that they would do that. They put him out like a vagabond.

But soon I retired. They had some operators come from New York. You have read the story of Joseph, when he was down there in Egypt, and Cain didn't know him, and give Joseph such a hard time. Well, this is the way it was with the supervisor. I said, "Mary, looks like it's time for you to make make a move." And this girl, she was being one of these yuppies, she came in there one day to me, and she said something to me I didn't like. I went to the benefit office and talked to the woman there, Cathy, a sweet person. I didn't have my birth certificate so I wrote to Atlanta. They said I needed this form. So I sent the money, but they didn't send the form back. I finally went down there to the County man. He said (he scared me to death), "Well, I'll tell ya the truth. Somebody here didn't have his birth certificate, and he retired for six years. They still hadn't given him, and he died before he got it." So you all know what he telling me! They the kinda peoples there they don't wancha to come back acting intelligent, nice and everything. I wasn't going round there looking like I was dead, jollying and everything and taking life easy. And he looked at me and said, "I ain't even gonna help you to get it."

And Cathy knowed this. She kept working with me and calling back. And when I heard it was August — that is since February it went on, and I was 62 then. They said that my social security would begin January the first. Miss G. accept the fact that I was retiring. She told me they was gonna give me a time. That Monday, when I went up there, I couldn't believe what they did. I mean, she had out all the china, all the chafing dishes, nice food, and my present. They had a bible with my name stamped in gold because they know I reads my bible, and money, and Miss G. made a speech. They had me sitting in the chair so they could take my picture. This was a room full of folks, employees in white, doctors and everything. She said, "Let me tell you this one thing, I couldn't believe, not this Mary was leaving, but she is retiring, and God knows I hate to see her go and," she said, "she can get a job if she want to come part-time anytime she want. One other thing. Nobody, nobody, can fill Mary Morris' shoes." I couldn't even look at the folks. I couldn't say a word, I was so kinda uneasy. I said to myself, Miss G, I wish you shut your mouth and not say another word.

When I first went to City Hospital, they not being used to the Program, [Mary and two other women were the first to be placed at City Hospital] I began to think they didn't want to be bothered with us. Now, there's one there named Jean. She call on you so much you almost have to say, huh? They got used to it all right but I sure was glad when they carried me over there to be interviewed and ask me which floor I'd like. I'm with a baby, this little baby, I feel so bad for it because it's mother just ain't doing right, and they gonna give her away. I gave her a bath this morning, a bed bath, and I put her in a stroller, and I took her for a walk in the garden. About one and a half hours I stayed out with her. They was glad for me to do that. They don't want to let the mother have her back because she's got a drug problem. They told me to ask around church. You know, you got to go through the agency to get her. Yet and still, they want somebody to have her. And then everytime you turn around there's an accident. They had a boy there, seventeen, he got shot the night before, looked like he's paralyzed. Another little baby, so sick, they had to send him to Kennedy Hospital for special tests. There's something there all the time. Some is very seriously ill, and they don't ask me to come to those. When you see them, it almost make you cry. But I get along with them beautifully, and I loves it.

I can take a leave-of-absence when I go back home. The nurses said, "Let me tell ya, when we like a person, we like them, and we want you back." When the mothers come to the hospital, "Oh, Miss Morris, would you go in and talk with them?" One girl, I talk with her. They weren't gonna take her baby away, she was improving so much about her duty, and they finally went along with her mother being in the house with her. I carried her some tapes that I had telling her, trying to build her up and everything, and she agreed with me. You don't have to be that way. You just don't have to be that way. I almost crying telling her because I have feeling for what I'm saying. And I convinced her so she's ashamed then. Now, she don't come in any more. And I talk with the teen-agers when they there. Some of them, they try to psyche you out. Lot of times we talk, and I share things that I see in the comics and try to talk on their level. But you know this generation, having their babies, they're too young. They hadn't had their child-life lived before they become a mama. When that baby starts squalling and hollering, first thing they think about is fighting like they fighting other chillun. They hit him because they don't want to be bothered. There's a lot goes on there at that hospital.

Well, I have always felt I was born for a purpose. We all born for a purpose. But some of us don't use the purpose, and some of us can go further. If I had applied myself more in school and stuff like that, I feels that I could do better. I makes a lot of speeches now in our church, but, when I'm talking about the business of the Lord, it can be broken English or any kind of English long as I get my point across. I know them that's really highly educated — "you know she said this when she shoulda said that." It don't bother me.

I am a missionary. My pastor made that. We got about twelve. If anybody's sick and we know we can help them, we goes. When I first came here, I thought about marrying again. There's nothing like a nice marriage when your husband and you enjoying and go places together. I like that. I like cooking good things for him. It gives ya something to do. Then, too, companionship. I like that.

258

One man did come to see me for a while. He could never tell the truth. I told him I didn't need him. If it's something ugly you had done, I wanna hear it, but don't come telling me no fibs. But I feels good, and I don't want my life pulled apart. Caring for somebody else, see, that's my life. Caring, and not just for myself. I wanna put myself and care for the other fella. We sing a song, "Use Me Lord Till I'm All Used Up."

Chapter 4
At Two Widely Disparate Sites

At Two Widely Disparate Sites

The life stories of two foster grandparents make up this fourth and last chapter. The contrasts of the two sites are intriguing; the one similarity speaks to the persistent state of disfunction in our large cities. Chauncy Moore and Daisy Dawe worked at institutions which provide care to our most injured children. Children are placed at both these sites according to what is available, bearing in mind the location of the family. At Fernald State School (Fernald), Daisy Dawe refused to go to a community school for she said, "they need us the most." She was devoted to her "little David" and felt it was right for her to stay with him. She stayed until she could no longer make the journey.

The children at Fernald need full-time care, the type families are too burdened emotionally, physically or financially to give them. In the 70's, when it was recognized that large institutions like Fernald were not the best for helping a number of those children, many were moved to smaller pediatric clinics or "group homes" where it was also possible for them to attend public schools with special needs classes. But David and many others as incapable as he, remained at the institution.

Chauncy Moore volunteered to work with the young men who had been placed by the Department of Youth Services in a Youth Detention Center. There, teenagers (13 to 18) who were found to be guilty of anti-social behavior are evaluated by professionals who determine their potential for reentry into society. The facilities provide regular school programs, programmed recreation time, and psychological help. Moore is a minister who believes in living his life in poverty and bringing his message to those less blessed. A perfect person for those youngsters, he may even by his example rescue a few from years in prison.

In the 80's Chauncy Moore, working as a teacher's assistant, was the only Black person in that capacity at that Center. The Black youth had only the child care workers and the maintenance men for models. All the professionals were white. But Brother Moore, as he was called, did not shirk.

262

Daisy Dawe and Chauncy Moore, a most unlikely pair, destined to meet as over one hundred foster grandparents gathered monthly to socialize and participate in discussions on new developments in child care or on Boston politics and ageism. As unlikely as are Margaret Gray from Scotland, and David Peguero of the Dominican Republic, sitting side by side on stools, telling of the most significant moments of their lives in a foster grandparent theatrical presentation. Foster grandparents tell us, in both the theatre of their lives and the reality of their work, how they reach across cultural borders, erase sterotypes, create bonds, and arrive at a new consciousness of themselves with the children they have chosen.

Daisy Dawe

Daisy Dawe

I want to tell you about bein' a foster grandparent. The first three days at the state school, I was sure I wasn't gonna stay. I can't stand it. I can't stand it lookin' at these children. The supervisor told me not to worry. "You'll get used to it," she said. This was 1973. They gave me David. I called Martha that night, and said, "I guess I'll go tomorrow." She said, "I'm not goin' in till Monday. My pressure is still up. I don't know if I can take it." I went back. David, a little bundle, he was so cute and soon I was lovin' every day.

I grew up in Newton and Brighton. We didn't have much. We were poor, but we always had enough to eat. My father worked for the city of Newton. My mother made all our clothes and stayed home until my youngest brother was ten years old. Then, my father was home for three years with rheumatoid arthritis. He was on crutches and couldn't do anything so my mother had to go to work. She was a practical nurse. She worked for doctors and in peoples' homes. I was born in 1904. As my Swedish lady friend says, "God bless you, daughter dear!"

There were four children. I was the oldest, and I am the last one still living. My mother knew I could baby-sit my brothers and sister. Later, my father got insurance for being out sick from his job, but she never allowed us to baby-sit for others. She believed if we were off school, we should enjoy our childhood. But I always used to start the supper, and I never really played much outside. My sister was a regular tomboy. She was in to all kinds of sports. She lived to be 75. She died of tumor on the brain. I miss her terribly. We were so close. (Daisy's sister Martha was a foster grandparent also. They were always together and had joined the program at the same time at Fernald State School.)

After I graduated high school, I went to work in a little real estate office, but my parents didn't like it so I found a typing job in a big office with lots of girls. I had learned typing in high school, and I ran with all the girls. We'd go to the movies, and we'd go watch the boys play football or baseball, but boys never entered my mind. Then, I met a fellow at a house party when I was twenty-two, a very lovely young man. He was Swedish. I went with him for two years, and I got a beautiful diamond. He was an interior decorator for stores and offices and a lot older than I was, but I liked him. But his family was rude to me because of our different religions. They were very bigoted. Just about that time, I met Tommy, the man I was going to marry. I met him at a party, too. He asked if I was still going with Carl. I said, no, because my mother and father don't like him and his family was very rude to me. My father had told me, "Stay home where you belong and keep away from him!" My family never really interfered, but they knew that I felt terrible. I told Carl, "Don't come near my house because my family is very mad. After all, I am a lady, and I don't go any place to be ignored. If they would ignore me now, what would they do to me if I married you? They'd crucify me. So I'm giving you back your ring, and let's part as friends." He wanted me to keep it, but I insisted and gave it back.

I wasn't in a hurry to get married. I used to dance a lot, and I loved it. I went with six other girls. We'd go dancing and bowl-ing, and we had lots of fun. But when I started going with my Tommy, I had to stop dancing. "You only go to dances to have another man put his arms around you," he said to me. "No jealousy," I said. "If you're gonna be jealous, I'll break it off now." My mother used to say, "If any of my children are jealous, I'll knock their heads together 'cause that's a sign of insanity." My mother said, "But you're not going to dances." That was the end of it. But we had lots of fun bowling. One night my friend Peggy said, "Let's go out to the new alley in Dorchester." I said, "I'll get killed for going this far," sure as hell that something was gonna happen. We come out of the bowling alley and sure enough the car just wouldn't start. So I called Tommy. I could hear my mother say to him, "Now don't you call for her, let her come home the best way she can." She always took his part. "We don't know how to get home from here," I said, and Tommy laughed, "You'll learn." Finally, he said, "Just stay where you are." Well, we took

Billy home first, and this time she went around the back door. Tommy said, "That's funny, isn't it?" We all thought she seemed to be in a daze, her mind somewhere else. Just as we were getting ready for bed, the telephone rang, and Waldo, her husband, is asking Tommy where she is. He said, "All her clothes are gone. Suitcases and everything gone." They got along wonderful, we thought, but she was in love with some doctor who was married. They both disappeared, and nobody ever heard from them from that day 'till this. How any girl can do that! Of course, she's not the first one that done that, but I don't know how anyone can leave children like that.

My family loved Tommy. The day he died my mother took a shock. It was like losing her own son. He was so good to my mother. When he was off from work, he was a bus driver for the MTA (Metropolitan Transit Authority), he would take my mother out shopping. They were close ever since they met him. Before we were married, he called up one day and said he had no heat or hot water, and the landlord had gone away. My father told him to bring his clothes and move in. "But," Tommy said, "I'd have to take her room, and she'll have a fit." My father, "Oh, don't worry about her. We'll worry about her. You'll be married soon anyway so you're allowed to finish your time here." We were married the following September. It was 1931. I was twenty-seven.

On my first Christmas, 1931, I was taken out at four in the morning with acute appendix. Twelve o'clock come around, and I thought I was gonna die. The pain! No matter what they gave me it didn't stop. Finally, they got a Dr. Keenan in, and he operated. The next day our neighbor, Dr. Smith, came in with Dr. Keenan and said, "He has bad news for you." He sat down by my bed and put his arms around me and said, "Daisy, I hate to tell you this, but you're not gonna become a mother." "Oh, how could you say that to me, doctor? That's the reason I got married - to have children." "You have no bottom to your womb," he said, "It's just like an empty pail." Oh, I cried and I cried. I had to stay five days longer because my pressure went up, and I was throwing up all the day. My husband was very shy and very quiet. I could see the expression on his face. The doctor said to him, "You can have your marriage annulled." Tommy told him, "Listen doctor, I didn't marry my wife for sex. I married her because I love her. We can always adopt children." He said that, but I was sick for almost a year. I didn't have any strength, and I couldn't hold my food. I just went all to pieces. Then, one of my brothers was killed in an auto accident, and he left three babies, and that will tell you the way we adopted children.

I did go out to work because I had to do something for myself. I worked at the Kennedy Butter and Egg Store for thirty-one years. I started in Newton. Then I managed the Watertown, Waltham, Allston and Brighton stores - the whole circuit. I loved doing it. One day, not long after my brother died, my husband called me at work and said, "Where's the bank book?" "It's in the drawer under my underwear," I said. He never said why he wanted it, and I never questioned him. When I came home that night, my mother said, "Don't bother changing your clothes, just sit down." My husband leaned over and put his arm around me and kissed me and said, "We bought a house today." I said, "Without me?" "But you'll love it, and you've always liked the neighborhood, and I wanted to surprise you." Well, we fixed it all up, and my sister-in-law came with the children to live with us. We had two bedrooms upstairs, and she had her own living room and den. She and the children lived with us for sixteen years. My husband taught them their religion, and he was a non-Catholic! He turned Catholic when we were married twenty-five years. But that's another story.

The Monsignor called me up one day, and said, "I want you to come to 12 o'clock mass on Sunday." I never went to that church but . . . I get there and walk down the whole length, and everybody's looking at me. When I got down in front, there's my whole family. "What's going on?" I said. "Don't you know why you're here? Tommy's turning Catholic today." I couldn't believe it! So after he received communion and hugged and kissed me, we got to Martha's and had a lovely party. She had sixty people there, some of his people and our friends. A week later we left for a two-week vacation in my favorite small town in Canada.

Now, I'm alone. When my husband retired, they were making small money working for the MTA. When he died, his pension died with him. Now all that's changed. But I have a good social security. Good thing we have that, and Reagan would like to cut it right in half or do away with it if he could. He's cutting down in medicare, medex. I don't think he's any good at all — not for the poor people. He's for the rich. But now, I'm happy. I'm very contented. I don't allow myself to get lonesome. I read or watch T.V. I wouldn't change a thing. I'm not interested in men. One day, I said to this man I meet every morning at the bus, "Everybody is talkin' about us. If I was younger, I would make a play for you." He said, "You wouldn't have to make a play for me, 'cause I'm tryin' to make a play for you," laughing.

When I lost my husband, they threw the mold away. I had a wonderful husband. I have to say that. I lived with my mother all my married life and got along very good. I had no complaints although I had a lot of surgery. But God was good, and my husband was always there. When I had my gall bladder out, he had died just three months before, I told the doctor, "I don't care if I get well or not." Mind you that was 1967. But my sister Martha and her husband and daughter were right there for me.

Just after that operation, I was going for a check up and suddenly right in the station, this fella came from nowhere and dragged me down eight steps and left me bleeding like a stuck pig, unconscious. I woke up in the hospital almost dead. That guy took sixty dollars from me. Well, I had to be operated on again to sew it up. Oh, God, I don't know. I've had other times when I was robbed in the street. But I'm not afraid here. We have tight security.

I want to tell you about being a foster grandparent. The first three days at the state school, I was sure I wasn't gonna stay. I can't stand it. I can't stand it looking at these children. The supervisor told me not to worry. "You'll get used to it," she said. This was 1973. They gave me David. I called Martha that night and said, "I guess I'll go tomorrow." She said, "I'm not going in till Monday. My pressure is still up. I don't know if I can take it." I went back. David, a little bundle, he was so cute, and soon I was loving every day. Martha came back, and she had a little boy she taught to speak five words. He never spoke a word before. Oh, God, how could anybody not love these kids?

You know, there were forty-two of us who started there. Some were there before us. I think they started in 1966. We had a lovely bunch out there. I never believed I'd be there this long, for sure. I'd say every December, "I guess this is it." One day, I'm talking to little David, "You know the cold weather is coming pretty soon, and Nana won't be able to come." He looks up at me and begins to whimper. "What's that mean? Do you think I'm still gonna come?" Then, he's all smiles. "Did you miss Nana over the weekend?" He can't shake his head, "Yes," Everything is like no. I just look forward to getting there and hugging him in the morning. I really love him, and I never thought I could. But I talk to all the children, and I make of them. When they bring him in the dining room, I put his bib on, and I hug him, and then I say, "When you get through eating, Nana will wash you up and put a clean top on you, and we'll go out." He smiles. I go over to Timmy, and say, "You gonna smile for Nana today?" And he laughs. There's a lot of coming and going there. Changes all the time, and they always say to me, "Hope you're staying. These kids need you."

I guess I was put here to take care of children. One day, I said to the priest at the school chapel, "I like children so, but I'm disappointed that the Lord didn't give me any." He said, "Well, Daisy, I'll tell you, he didn't give you any because he saved you for this purpose, to come out here and help with these retarded children. You love David, and you love all children and so that's why he saved ya to come out here. When I go to chapel I always give you and David a special blessing." He had a mass for my birthday and for Martha's too. Martha passed in 1982, ten months after her daughter died. She was happy because she wanted to die. She missed her daughter and couldn't content herself.

I think the staff out there deserves more money. They work! Work very hard, and those children are dead weight. I couldn't lift them. That's why these girls have to leave because their backs go out. We have a fellah from the State who comes in twice a year to check up on what's doing there. When he came in last year he says, "Mrs. Dawe, I come here twice a year, and you have never spoken to me." I said, "I don't want people to think I'm on the make, looking for a husband." He laughed to kill himself. "Next time I come back, I'm gonna take you out to dinner," he said. I passed it off. Next time he came, "Are we going out to dinner?" "Yes," I said, "I'll go." He brought me home later that day and I changed, and off we went to the Park Plaza. His mother stays in his apartment there in the hotel when she comes to Boston. We had a lovely dinner, all the fixin's, even a glass of wine. His mother was a lovely person. He told her all about David and how he admires what I do. "Nobody will ever take David away from you," he said. "I hope they don't 'cause, if they do, they'll kill me."

You know I think that what the foster grandparents do out there is more important than what the teachers and doctors do sometimes. One day, one of the teachers hollered at two children, and I said, "That's abuse," We have all new notices up about hollering at the children. You know anybody who abuses a child is supposed to be reported. I told her, "I've been brought up with children, and I helped raise three children, and I know what's good and what's bad, and it isn't good to holler at children especially when they're trying to eat. If he doesn't want to eat, don't force him. Let him be." She never hollered again.

Betty, my sister-in-law and her three children — well there's only two now because one died in the war. He was a marine. The other, Richard, is a policeman and Judy, she's very special. She's here every Friday for supper, and she always watches over me. Tommy and I were blessed to have them with us. And Jimmy, my nephew, tells everyone, "Aunt Daisy's part of my family. Why would I leave her home all day Sunday alone? My children want her. They always say bring Aunt Daisy." The family is very good to me. If it's a bad day, they'll call and say, "Do you want to go any place?" I feel sorry when I hear people say, "Oh, my family! We don't get along." I feel bad because we're here such a short while. I know that now at eighty-four. I know that.

Chauncy Moore

Chauncy Moore

Living with my aunt and uncle was like 1867 - very rigid and very strict - but they were loving. Honest to God, you couldn't break wind on Sunday. You had to wait till Monday. They had lived in England where everything was prim and proper.

I was 17 and applying for my first job as a bank teller right here in Boston, not Mississippi, but Boston, Massachusetts, 1936. He said, "But we do have jobs for cleaning, because you people are excellent cleaners." I've never forgotten that.

My childhood was very pleasant. I was born in Jamaica, and I lived with my parents. My father was born in Barbados and met my mother in Jamaica. He was a sea-faring man, deep-sea fishing. He met my mother in 1903, and they were married in 1906. A long relationship. I didn't come along until 1919. I am an only child! Yes, the only child. My father was a Spanish-American war veteran. He was born in 1888, and he died in 1932. My mother was a widow for two years. I don't know what happened. People often ask me, but parents didn't discuss things with children at that time.

I'll tell you, like most men say, "My mother didn't work." Most men say that. "Oh, my wife, didn't work." So she washed and ironed and cleaned and cooked and crocheted and knit and did everything. I don't remember any mothers working outside. Yes, my life was pleasant. I completed high school there at sixteen. I didn't have that many relatives in Jamaica that wanted to take me so they shipped me bag and baggage to Boston. I was sad.

I came here to Aunt Lizzie who was my father's sister. She met her husband when she was in the West Indies. She and her husband had been working for these rich English people who brought them along when they came to Boston. Living with my aunt and uncle was like 1867 — very rigid and very strict — but they were loving. Honest to God, you couldn't break wind on

Sunday. You had to wait till Monday. They had lived in England where everybody was prim and proper, people wearing gloves and hats and stuff like that. When the lady of the house was getting ready to go out, my aunt would have to bathe her, help to dress her, and tie her in - that was a lady-in-waiting in those days. And, my uncle, he was a footman or a coachman. My aunt was a lady-in-waiting when I first came here, and they had sort-of settled into their own home. They had bought a three-story brick home for about $5,000. Well, see, when you work for families like that, you don't spend anything, and, then, they gave her some money, I understood, to help them buy the home. So she ran a boarding house. She took in railroad men. A lot of men who worked on the railroad would come. Room and board for $7.00 a week, two good meals and my aunt, well, she could cook. Oh, she could cook! She made everything from scratch, bread and cake and everything. And I used to have to serve the table, see. I didn't mind it, but if I had minded, I'd still have to do it. I wanted to eat and sleep. So I worked around with Aunt Liz and Uncle Josh for about one year. Then, I decided I wanted to go to college.

I went down to State Street Bank because they were hiring tellers, and the gentleman told me, "Oh, we don't have jobs like that for our colored folks." And this was right here in Boston, not Mississippi, but Boston, Massachusetts. He said, "But we do have jobs for cleaning because you people are excellent cleaners." I've never forgotten that - "Oh, you people are such excellent cleaners." So then I asked him, "Do you have a job as a messenger?" He said, "Well, get in touch with me. Call me back in two or three days." I called him back. I wanted him to keep his word. He told me to come in, and he said, "We can give you that job. This is the first time we've ever hired a colored. I talked it over with my staff, and they said to give you a try." And he told me, "If this doesn't work out, I will never hire another colored person." I was 17, and I took it, and they were nice, talked to me only when they had to. In those days, that was happening to all of us, and we just took it. It was just one of those things that happen. So I stayed there until I got ready to got to college. And he gave me a little bonus. They were very nice. They had a party because I was going away. The thing is that I was so hurt; lot of hurt that I received, and I just kept it right here (pointing to heart). They were going around taking up a collection to get one of the girls a wedding gift, and the supervisor, "Oh, you won't be coming so we won't take anything from you." I guess we just learned to accept. We accept these things because we know that it's true that those things are going to happen.

My Aunt Liz gave me some money; the church that I was attending gave me a nice scholarship, and I went to a school called Kittrel in North Carolina. It was an old Methodist School, founded in 1867 there between Henderson and Raleigh. After the Civil War, a lot of abolitionists and well-meaning whites founded schools for Blacks, like Howard University, Morgan State and Fisk University. A lot of wealthy whites funded these schools; they did this so we couldn't go to their schools. They wouldn't be seen as people denying education.

I'd never been south before. When I got to Washington D.C. . . . at that time all colored people had to go to Washington to get the trains going south because that's where the Jim Crow trains were. We were next to the engine and, sometimes, travelling through small towns in Mississippi, the conductor would tell you to get on the floor because the white children knew which trains we were on, and they would throw bricks. Everybody had to get on the floor, grandmother, dear old soul, everybody. When I went down my first time, a gentleman came through and he told us — this was a Black porter — he said, "Breakfast time," and I thought I could go to the diner. I got washed up and went to the dining room, and the gentleman said, "We don't serve colored people." It was such a weight that dropped down. I looked in the door, and I could see all the help were Black, and the cooks were all Black, and the people at the tables all white. I turned back. We had to stay without food. When we got to the railroad station, they had a little place around the back; come out the station and go around to the back, (I can tell you about back doors) and you get a sandwich, but you couldn't eat it there. You had to stand out in the street and eat it. And even the educated Blacks had to, regardless who you were.

The next time I went there, I took a big box of food. I still take a box now because it's cheaper. You know, the older generation more or less took it. When I went to Alabama to a convention, it was 1940, and we were sitting in this park in Birmingham. These two colored women came through and they said, "Don't sit in this park. There's a colored park a few streets away. You can't sit here because you'll get in trouble." We didn't talk back to them, but we just got up and left. Even in Baltimore, there were signs, "Colored Waiting Room."

I came back to Baltimore one year during the summer because a friend told me to come there and I could get a job as a waiter. When I got the job, the woman said to me, "Now our colored folks don't come in the front door. When you come in, you go down through the alley and go in the side entrance." The cooks were all Black. The waiters were Black, the chamber maids were all Black and all the customers were white. The bellhops were all Black, of course. It was the main hotel there, called the Belvedere. In Washington D.C., I worked there one year at the Mayflower Hotel, and all the time come in the side entrance, and no one paid attention. You couldn't go to the theatres, you couldn't eat down town, you couldn't do anything. So you just took it.

Sometimes it grieves me when I hear young Blacks complaining; they never went through the things their parents and grandparents went through. Never. They never had to struggle, see. They didn't have scholarships for Blacks at that time. They had the CCC Camps (Civilian Conservation Corps), and they had the NRA (National Recovery Act) that offered minimal employment. I'm going back quite a way. When I was in Washington, we went to a place called the Glen Echo. It was a beautiful amusement park. We got off the street car and walked to the gate, and he told us the only way you could get in there was to be a butler to a white child. Now, there were Black people there, but they had white children with them. So joking, we said, we're going to grab a white child and take him with us. But these things happened in

Washington. All the government buildings were segregated; they had white dining rooms and colored dining rooms. Anywhere you went in the south at that time, from Baltimore down, it was segregation.

The first time I missed the school bus, I had to take the Greyhound Bus going from Henderson to Raleigh. When I got on, he just kept moving along. He had barely stopped so I had to run with my suitcase, panting. I almost fainted. He said, "O.K., just a moment, boy!" The bus was crowded. Now, they had a sign, and, in the back of that sign, the colored people sat. But, then, a white man or white woman could come back if he or she wanted to and make us get up and give them a seat. So the bus was crowded, and he said, "Just a moment." All the white women on the bus got off, and he said, "Give me your suitcase, boy." So, I gave him the suitcase, and the men on the bus passed my suitcase all the way down until it got to the colored area. I asked my professor, Dr. Dent, why did the women get off? He said because if you had touched, if you had brushed by one of these women like that (showing a brush of sleeve), you'd been swinging on one of those trees. Can you imagine? So they had to get off so I wouldn't bump into them. That's right, and this is not lies. It's something I experienced.

At that time, not too many people had courage to fight it, but Rosa Parks went through quite a bit. She lost her job and almost lost her life. If she had never started it, we might be still waiting. And Selma and Montgomery, where the people went on strike, they lost their jobs, and so many were killed. We just knew when we went to Washington because the conductor would say, "All colored people, all colored people, go down the front of the trains. Come on, come on, all colored people." And, you see the older folks and the young ones running down the train. So we knew where we were.

We've heard some stories, some people might be ashamed to talk about it, but I'm not because it's reality. It's the truth. That's the reason I educated myself when I was younger. One time, I worked as a butler in a private home here in Boston. I worked for only about six months. I didn't like it because the people were nice, that's right, and they gave me some money to go away, and the lady said, "Oh, why would you want to leave us Chauncy, we're so nice here?" I said, "Yes, but, your son is going to Harvard. Do you say anything about that?" So she smiled and said,"I guess you have me there, Chauncy."

They kept in touch with me, oh, for a long time. Christmas, they always sent me a nice envelope. She liked me, but I was a servant. She liked me as a servant. She told me that her grandparents were abolitionists. But they were quite taken aback when I told them I was going to do better for myself. I said, "Why shouldn't I?" I guess in many instances it was my aunt and uncle. They were encouraging, and I needed that. My parents and my aunt and uncle, my guardians, taught me self-esteem. Whatever goes on, always hold your head up. The day that you see me with a bottle of wine on the sidewalk, sitting down with nothing, take me home, give me a dinner and then lecture to me. But I doubt that would happen.

My education was a religious one. I received a B.A. and an S.T.B., (Bachelor of Sacred Theology) in the same school. I had wanted to go to Duke University, but they didn't take in Blacks. I wanted to do something that might be encouraging for somebody else to follow. Then, I went to Philadelphia and worked at The Church of the Advocate as a social worker. I did all the field work with alcoholics and drug addicts in the community. I needed that outreach because it was a chance for me to learn what was going on and to see a lot. I was a firm believer that everybody is not called to pastor a church. Someone has to work on the outside. I worked with families and really could see what was needed not only in the Black race, but people in general. When I was there, I worked with all colors, whatever, and, doing that kind of work, I felt closer to God. Most of his work was among the people. I think that, sometimes, people that pastor a church and pastor alone lose out a lot. They just see the very goody-goodies who come to the church. They never see that man who is in the alley or lying in the street with a bottle in his hand or the drug addict or the alcoholic or the lady of the evening. Some women have brought their children up that way, see? There were times when I could have had a large church, but, I feel, a man of the cloth . . . how could I live in a mansion when my parishioners are on welfare? I prefer being simple. The Gods I believe in live among the poor.

Many times, the young people I meet today are very slow. You can't get them to move. Many are not interested in advancing themselves, and that's the sad thing. Mr. Douglas over there (pointing to the photo of Frederick Douglas on his wall), learned somehow, taught himself to read and write. Can you imagine if he could have gone to Harvard, what would have happened? If he could have gone to MIT? Now DuBois was more educated than he was, and Munroe Trotter was a great man and his wife, she was quite the woman! And there was Bill Harrison, editor of The Boston Chronicle, right here in the South End. His sisters are still living, but they never married. They were maiden ladies. I'm still of the old school. Maiden ladies!

You know, years ago, when a woman lost her husband, she immediately would become "Widow Brown." My mother wore a long heavy veil over her face with black gloves and a mourning fan, a black fan with crepe around it. They even had mourning stationary; if you sent me a letter with a black border around it, I would know at once that you had a death in the family. But they don't do that today. And, you know, the lady down stairs, (who we met on entering the building) I almost slipped up and said, this is Widow Taylor.

When I was at Peter Bent Brigham a couple of years ago for my appendix quite a few Black doctors and Black nurses. Yes, and, in Beth Israel, there are Black registered nurses — not nurses' aides — professional women. So, a lot of things are beginning to shape up. While I was in Philadelphia, they had a Black Surgeons Convention. I was surprised to know that there were quite a few Black surgeons in the U.S. Quite a few. I went so I could see these things. Even with concert singers, they weren't recognized. Leontine Price, Rolland Hayes had a terrible time. And I'll tell

282

you Marian Anderson, she was another one. She kept her dignity. She didn't allow them to put her down. She made one debut in the fifties, and she sang at the Lincoln Memorial because they wouldn't allow her into opera. And now, Jesse Norman is coming up. I went back stage to see her. A stately woman. She reminded me of Marian Anderson. Well, these are younger women. I think she is about 38. And then, there was Paul Robeson. Such a big person! See, as I said before, that's the reason I can always look up, and that's part of my family. (The walls of his house were fully covered with photos of important Black people intermingled with photos of his own family, all beautifully framed and placed in carefully measured patterns that gave each individual photo the best presentation.) That's my heritage, and it constantly gives me self-pride.

One of the teachers at the Youth Service Center told me that the Black kids and the Puerto Rican kids and the white kids have a chance to see me working in that capacity as a tutor. They don't have that chance too often, that is, to see older Black men with any kind of education. So, she said, it was good for them to see this although they didn't have any Black educators there. The men that worked there, the child care workers, were none of them college men. They were more like strong-arm men. The clean-up men were Black, the professionals were white. The psychiatrists, the social workers, the teachers were all white. They tell me that at the other site for the Department of Youth Services (DYS), all the teachers are white also. That's today, now.

I told the boys out at the Center they needed a lot of help with reading and writing and etymology and stuff like that. So I would tell them, you need self-esteem. "What is that Brother Moore?" "Self-esteem is being proud of yourself out of your heritage." I sort of seep that into them. I don't preach to them, but I give them something to make them feel proud of themselves. You can't run around and get into a lot of trouble and feel that you're going to be recognized because you don't want to be that boy that's a thief or a liar. They claim that when you are eighteen, everything is behind you, but, in a way, it's not. I'm a firm believer. All Blacks are not going to be teachers, doctors, lawyers, preachers, under-takers or whatever. I said carpentry, there's an excellent vocation and all kinds of trades. I'm not going to say that every Black man is going to be a doctor because every white man is not a doctor. So I would tell it as it is. Some of the kids saw the Holocaust on T.V. They didn't know that the Jewish people came through all that. I said, yes and, in many instances, they went through things that we didn't go through. I told them Hitler was terrible and that I was around at that time and I read the papers and we were able to talk about it. "But," I said, "most of the Jewish people that I know have gotten out and made great strides in life. You will very rarely see a Jewish woman or man not doing well for themselves because they were taught self-pride, self-esteem."

Well, it's easier being Jewish than Black 'cause you can change your name to Edith Brook or Edith Brown. I could change my name to Chauncy Stein, but my complexion is still black. Can you imagine, 30 years ago, if we would have hugged each other in Alabama, where you would have been and where I would have been? You know I'm going to tell you this - I was talking to a lady one day, one of the grandparents, and she told me, "Rev. Moore, all the years that I have worked," she said, " I've never been treated so much like a woman until I came in with the foster grandparents." But, you know, we struck it off very well the very first time I was at the office. When I walked out, I said, "You won't forget me," and you said, "No, I'll never forget you," as if to say, "I might forget somebody else but I'll never forget Chancy Moore." Even though with so many slaps in the face, I was always able, I had a certain dignity, and I guess it was self-esteem.

I think my experience as a foster grandparent made me grow, made a better man of me. Yes, a lot of the kids at the Center were very unhappy when I told them I was going to leave. Hopefully, they will send somebody else out there. Beatrice is out there, of course. She has trouble with some of the boys sometimes, but she's good. Those boys at the Center, they could get off sometimes, slam a chair and stuff like that.

I told one young man one time, "Listen young man, you're big and Black, and Moore is big and Black, and we can't have two big, Black people in the same room so go in that room and try to get all the black off you." He says, "Right on Brother Moore." One of the teachers said, if she had said that, it would be war!

I used to tell the kids, I'm not here to play games, I'm not here to talk about you behind your back, I'm here to give you some educational advice. You're going to need to know how to read and how to write. When it comes time for job interviews, if you're not prepared, you're going to suffer. I tried to get through to them.

I want to tell you what I think of the Program because I think it is wonderful. There are a lot of women in there, if it had not been for the program, probably would have just pined away. It gives them something to do. It gives them self-esteem. It makes them say, "Well, I have something to do. Somebody cares for me." When you hire any older woman or man, sixty or over, it gives them the feeling that you care for them. You have concern.

I lived and worked in Philadelphia, in Tennessee, Washington, Baltimore, and I was married in Baltimore and Washington. I was married twenty-three years. My wife died of a heart attack. I only had one son. He's in California. He's in the service, a career man in the army. That makes me feel good. And he has six children. I try to go out every year. I tell him, don't come this way, it gives me a chance to go there. I take a nice long trip. I go on the train, travel by days, take off and sleep at night and take my time getting there. I guess I have this slow pace because of my Victorian training. Yea, I was never what you call a follower. If you were rushing, I'd say, "O.K., I'll see you when I get there." I knew I couldn't rush through life. The streets were here when I came, and they'll be here after I leave, so there isn't a need. You lose when you rush because just like sometimes people coming to pick me up and most of the time, if I have to rush, I'll forget something, and that's the way life is. If you rush through life, you lose a lot, never see the things that are most important, only see the things that are flourishing. I've never driven, never driven in my life. I walk all over. Not too much at night now. I do have common sense.

I have always felt that the good Lord has me here for something. It may be to help that poor boy or poor girl or poor man or woman like I tried to do with the boys at the Center. Maybe as an image, but it's for some reason I'm here. Sometimes I feel I've been here before, and, then, it has made me feel wanted, see? When you told me you were coming, I said, "Wonderful!" I had thoughts when I was younger, wondering what I was going to do. When I was in my thirties, I began to deal with getting older. I said to myself, if the Lord allows me to get older, I guess I better start preparing myself. I better start dealing because there are people who would like me and accept me as an older man and like me only as that, and there are other people who couldn't care less if I were 100. I trained myself so I have no qualms about getting old. In fact, I love it. People have made me like it. Somebody calls me, "Brother Moore, how are you feeling?" "Brother Moore, what's going on?" Every day somebody calls me; "I missed you, wondered where you were." That makes me feel like living. It also makes me feel that someone cares for me, and it doesn't make me feel that I'm in the grave. I moved into it quietly, gracefully, see. I hope, when I am 90 years old, you can come back and interview me again. Then, we'll dance together with a rose between our teeth. I do hope I will be as active as Mr. Johnson was at 90. They say he never took a day off, and the people at his Day Care Center used to call him Grandpa Johnson. Now, he's my inspiration.

At the present time, I've been helping a young group called the African Pentacostal Church. They have meetings on Sundays, and I've sort of been giving them a helping hand. These are all young people. I feel, wherever I am needed, send me, send me, send me. I enjoy that. My own church is Episcopal, but I visit different churches - all one direction, right? I feel more rewarded at the present time. I just told the bishop, "Let me do my own thing." So when I think about death, well, it happens more as you grow older than when you are thirty. To me, it's another stage I have to go through. I do believe there is eternal rest so I don't have qualms about it. I would like to die a very peaceful death, see. I'd like to just sit up and just drop off and leave it at that.

Resources

Families in Peril
    Marian Wright Edelman, 1987, HUP
    President, Children's Defense Fund 122 C Street, N.W
    Wash. D.C. 20001

Child Poverty in America
    CDF's Child, Youth and Family Futures Clearinghouse
    1991- Children's Defense Fund

State of America's Children
    Children's Defense Fund, 1991

Children In Need
    By the Research and Policy Committee of the Committee
    for Economic Development

Growing Old; New Statesman, 29 July, 1966, J.B. Priestley